Part I

God's Revised Will

A Study of the Old and New Covenants

and

Part II

The *"Rest"* of the Story

A study of Hebrews Three and Four

Roy A. Marrs

Focus on Faith Studies

Part 1
God's Revised Will

Section Titles

i

God's Revised Will
Section Titles Continued ....

God's Revised Will
Section Titles Continued ....

Part II
The "Rest" of the Story

Section Titles

The "Rest" of the Story
Section Titles Continued........

---o-O-o---

Part I

God's Revised Will

A Study of the Old and New Covenants

Foreword

Why is it important to study God's will and His revised will, the old and New Covenants? Why should you be interested enough to read a long dissertation on the subject? The biblical discussion of "covenants," "testaments," and "wills" is important primarily because God's covenant with His people identifies the heirs of God and Christ, and because it spells out what God expects of His heirs, and specifies what they are to inherit – or not inherit, as the case may be.

Giving urgency to the discussion are the undercurrents of change among Sabbath keeping people, and misunderstanding the issues involved poses a very real problem for peace in homes and in the church. Many families and congregations are being torn apart over these issues, dividing them into factions and seriously eroding long-standing friendships.

In very fact, the multiplicity of Sabbath keeping denominations is a reflection of the issues involved, as also the controversy of Sabbath keeping versus Sunday keeping. Misunderstanding the role of the covenants and their provisions is a source of great confusion as to what God expects of His people.

If you are vitally interested in the stability of the church, in the doctrinal direction of the church, then you need to get in on the "ground floor" with a biblical understanding of old and New Covenants. This study takes for granted your "need to know" and to thoroughly understand the matter, for breezes of change can quickly become tornadoes of destruction unless they are blowing steadily at a bearable rate in one direction only.

The Church is ill-prepared for what is ahead, because for too long we have ignored this topic, which was carefully and frequently discussed by our forefathers (not that they necessarily all came to the same understanding). Without understanding the subject, we cannot understand how they arrived at some of their doctrinal conclusions, and consequently we may become too easily persuaded to change doctrinal positions, or water-down the seriousness of disobedience to God. You should be keenly interested. This is not a problem that goes away. Like the poor, it is always with us.

Making the situation more difficult to deal with effectively, adult Sabbath School classes are divided into segments, some of which (not only younger adults) prefer to use material that deal with social issues or issues that do not give adequate exposure to the biblical issues which form the foundation of our doctrinal heritage.

While discussion of social issues may more easily excite interest, and do have a rightful place in class discussions, we must have a systematic approach to teaching the biblical foundations of our beliefs.

If we have no programmed goals for the instruction of our youth before they are mature adults, we face a justifiable charge of a serious lack of wisdom, or of intentionally programming our youth to be on a different page with different concerns than the adults.

In such laboratories, generation gaps are born and exacerbated. They do not just exist in secular society, and they are not all spawned by the new generations. The older generations can easily, intentionally or unintentionally, allow improper change by neglect.

If pastors and teachers in their congregations do not confer to seek a consensus of opinion on doctrinal issues, studying to understand the positions taken by the Ministerial Council and the reasons for suggested or adopted change, there is no opportunity for unity within the church, and congregations will be doing what God did not condone long ago – and still doesn't!

"In those days there was no king in Israel, but every man did that which was right in his own eyes" (Judges 17:6).

"Ye shall not do after all the things that we do here this day, every man whatsoever is right in his own eyes" (Deuteronomy 12:8).

"The way of a fool is right in his own eyes: but he that hearkeneth unto counsel is wise" (Proverbs 12:15).

"Where no counsel is, the people fall: but in the multitude of counsellors there is safety" (Proverbs 11:14).

"Without counsel purposes are disappointed: but in the multitude of counsellors they are established" (Proverbs 15:22).

Even Apostle Paul understood the necessity of comparing of spiritual concepts with other Apostles:

"And I went up by revelation, and communicated unto them that gospel which I preach among the Gentiles, but privately to them which were of reputation, lest by any means I should run, or had run, in vain" (Galatians 2:2).

"Holding forth the word of life; that I may rejoice in the day of Christ, that I have not run in vain, neither laboured in vain" (Philippians 2:16). *This series of scriptures is from the KJV.*

We need to work together on these issues, *often* enough to really understand them as presented in the Bible.

---o-**O**-o---

Introduction – The Issues

While this study is prepared with the Church of God, Seventh Day fellowship in mind (with which the author is associated), it covers many facets of biblical thought common to other fellowships, and ought to be of interest to any serious student of the Bible.

For the past few decades a difference of theology has been developing in our fellowship, much of it manifested in discussions of the role of biblical law, and whether law has a role at all in defining our relations with God, Christ, and the church.

Called into question is whether obedience plays any part in either justification or sanctification. This confusion arises in great measure from not understanding why God saw the need for the Old Covenant, then need for a New Covenant, and failure to understand the ways the New is like or unlike the Old.

Answers to these questions even impact such doctrines as eternal security, predestination, the foreknowledge of God, and our calling and election to be a part of His people. While those doctrines are not dealt with in depth in this study, nonetheless without a correct understanding of the covenants, those subjects will be misunderstood, in quite distinct and contradictory ways.

At the least, lack of understanding the differences between the Old and New Covenants aids and abets the confusion that causes us to develop contradictory theological views within the ministry, and hence in the church at large.

Perhaps more to the point, and currently more likely to cause friction in Church of God (Seventh Day) circles, is the fact that failure to understand the roles of the Old and New Covenants will impact our use of the Old Scriptures in formulating doctrinal statements for the denomination.

Our understanding of what constitutes the Old and New Covenants is clouded at times by rubbing shoulders with folk who equate the biblical books of Genesis through Malachi with "the Old Covenant." This is reflected in *calling* those books the "Old Testament," and in calling Matthew through Revelation "the New Testament." Theologically, biblically, "covenant" and "testament" have the same meanings.

Hence, do we read the entire Bible to find the will of God for or lives, or just Matthew through Revelation? Some among us already prefer to ignore the old Scriptures in doctrinal formulation, as though they constitute, are equal to, the Old Covenant.

This subject should have been studied before the *North American Ministerial Council* discussed whether Old Scripture guidelines for support of the ministry are still valid (payment of tithes and offerings);

before discussing whether Old Scripture guidelines for observing the Sabbath are valid; and before discussing such subjects as a required time for observing the Lord's Supper, whether it is still to be called "the Passover," and whether Christians ought to observe the feast days.

It impacts the subject of eating unclean meats as well. We cannot afford to formulate such doctrines without first having a clear understanding of the covenants. What is the basis of Christian faith? The Bible, or only Matthew through Revelation?

If everything from Genesis to Malachi is "Old Covenant" and the Old Covenant has passed away to make room for the New Covenant, then reference to those books in the formulation of doctrine makes no sense whatever: *"By calling this covenant 'new,' he has made the first one obsolete; and what is obsolete and aging **will soon disappear"*** (Hebrews 8:13).

If Genesis through Malachi are "the Old Covenant" which would soon disappear, why are those books still around being studied ardently by Christians of most persuasions? Is it a mistake to search them for an understanding of God's will?

It will be shown in this study that it is one thing to correctly state that the Old Covenant has been replaced by the New, but quite a different thing to state that the Old Scriptures (Genesis through Malachi) have been replaced by the New Scriptures (Matthew through Revelation).   ---o-O-o---

What Are the Specific Issues?

1) What constituted the Old Covenant? A Verbal Agreement Between Israel and God? The Ten Commandments? The Law of Moses? All of these elements and more?

2) Was the Old Covenant a static document or a growing body of law?

3) Did Israel make the old covenant with God before knowing its contents?

4) Are the books of the Bible, Genesis through Malachi, the "Old Covenant," and the Books of the Bible Matthew through Revelation the "New Covenant"?

5) What was the attitude of Jesus and the Apostles toward use of the Old Scriptures, those formulated before John the Baptist, for teaching Faith and Practice?

6) Are the "Gospels," Matthew through John, Old Covenant or New Covenant? Do they teach New Covenant or Old Covenant doctrine? Do they teach both?

7) Was Jesus a "Gospel" Preacher and Teacher, or an Old Covenant Prophet, or both?

8) What part today, if any, does "law" play in God's covenant-making with His people?

9) Is the New Covenant about law, about Christ, or about both law and Christ?

10) Do passages of the new scriptures which affirm the validity of "law," speak of old scriptures law, or new scriptures law?

11) Could God change His covenant with His chosen people, His church, after the Cross? Did He?

12) Was Jesus the "Testator" of both the Old and New Covenants?

13) Was there more than one covenant in operation at the same time? Is there more than one in operation at this time?

14) Is the law God writes on the hearts of His people under the new covenant a continuing law, a changed law, a new law formulated for the New Covenant, a definable law, or a different law for every believer as the Spirit impresses individual hearts?

15. When Paul wrote, *"And so he condemned sin in sinful man, in order that the righteous requirements of the law might be fully met in us, who do not live according to the sinful nature but according to the Spirit,"* what law did Paul have reference to?

16. When Paul wrote, *"Do we, then, nullify the law by this faith? Not at all! Rather, we uphold the law,"* what law did Paul have reference to?

17) What is the role of the Cross in covenant matters?

The study will not always be clearly defined sections on these issues. They so overlap that at times more than one of these issues will
be under consideration.   ---o-O-o---

Role of the Cross in Covenant Matters

As many denominations have traditionally done, we have begun to
question the teachings of Jesus in doctrinal matters because most of
His teaching ministry was pre-cross. This confusion is typical of the
"dispensation" paradigm of such men as C.I. Scofield, who divides believers among Jews and Gentiles, and would admit the teachings of Jesus in the four Gospels as relevant to Jewish Christian behavior, but
not Gentile Christian behavior. This view is sought to be buttressed
with such scriptures as Acts 15:19-21.[1]

The cross is usually recognized as the pivotal point between Old
and New Covenants. Consequently, it is important to understand the
covenants to know whether Jesus Christ ministered as an Old Covenant Prophet, or as a New Covenant Prophet.

Do Matthew through John serve as reliable source material in formulation of Christian doctrines *for all Christians, Jewish Christians, or
no Christians*? Was His ministry an introduction to the Gospel, an exposition of the Gospel, a dying reflection of all God's previous dealings
with man, or all of these things?

In some sense, the ministry of Christ was certainly a period of transition, but if the teaching ministry of Christ is not reliable for Christian
doctrine, then the Gospels (Matthew, Mark, Luke, and John) ought to
be classified as Old Covenant Books, and Jesus should be understood
as an Old Covenant prophet.

---

[1] "It is my judgment, therefore, that we should not make it difficult for the Gentiles
who are turning to God. Instead we should write to them, telling them to abstain
from food polluted by idols, from sexual immorality, from the meat of strangled animals and from blood. For Moses has been preached in every city from the earliest
times and is read in the synagogues on every Sabbath."

In other words, why are the old and new Scriptures divided between Malachi and Matthew, why not between John and the book of Acts? Essentially, the crucifixion took place between the Gospels and the book of Acts.

So as a beginning point, it is necessary to understand what the New Scriptures teach about the Old Scriptures, to observe how the Apostles did or did not make use of them after the death, resurrection and ascension of Jesus.

This study will begin, therefore, by illustrating the New Scriptures' view of the Old Scriptures, so as to understand the usefulness or reliability of the Old Scriptures in the formulation of doctrine and as a source authority for teaching the will of God.

The same approach will then be used to discuss the New Scriptures' view of the law, to determine whether the law of the Old Scriptures is spoken of as having validity, or if Old Scripture law is an archaic understanding of God's will for the behavior of post-crucifixion man.

If the writers of the New Scriptures freely and frequently uphold the Old Scriptures and the law as valid source materials for understanding God's expectations for Christian behavior, then we must not use a few obscure references to invalidate a plethora of evidence to the contrary. It is conceded that some of Paul's statements are difficult.

After a discussion of these questions, the study will then proceed to illustrate various covenants between God and man, compare them, and suggest proper understandings.

This is presented prayerfully and with great concern. It presents a viewpoint that needs to be heard, either because it is biblical, factual, and rational, or otherwise because those who hold this view need to know why the view is incorrect.

---o-O-o---

The New Scriptures' View of the Old Scriptures

A simple approach to learning what the New Scriptures teach about the validity of the Old scriptures is to study each passage in the New where the words "writings" or "scriptures" occur. It will be discovered that each of these passages with one or two exceptions refer to scriptures already written before the birth of Christ – that is, Genesis through Malachi.

Therefore, if the things stated about "scriptures" in the "New Testament" affirm the validity and usefulness of "the scriptures" (Old Testament), generally that would be a validation of the Books of the Bible Genesis through Malachi as appropriate resource materials for understanding the will of God for our lives. Consider the evidence found in the following passages:

"Jesus saith unto them, Did ye never read in the scriptures, The stone which the builders rejected, the same is become the head of the corner: this is the Lord's doing, and it is marvellous in our eyes?" (Matthew 21:42).

"But how then shall the scriptures be fulfilled, that thus it must be?" (Matthew 26:54).

"But all this was done, that the scriptures of the prophets might be fulfilled. Then all the disciples forsook him, and fled" (Matthew 26:56).

"And Jesus answering said unto them, Do ye not therefore err, because ye know not the scriptures, neither the power of God"? (Mark 12:24).

"I was daily with you in the temple teaching, and ye took me not: but the scriptures must be fulfilled" (Mark 14:49).

"And beginning at Moses and all the prophets, he expounded unto them in all the scriptures the things concerning himself" (Luke 24:27).

"And they said one to another, Did not our heart burn within us, while he talked with us by the way, and while he opened to us the scriptures?" (Luke 24:32).

"Then opened he their understanding, that they might understand the scriptures" (Luke 24:45).

"(Ye) Search the scriptures; for in them ye think ye have eternal life: and they are they which testify of me" (John 5:39).

(This series of quotations are from the KJV.)

Regardless whether the above passages represent an Old Covenant or New Covenant perspective of the old Scriptures, the above scriptures indicate clearly the status of the Old Scriptures in the mind of God.

According to Jesus, the old Scriptures *"must be fulfilled,"* they were authoritative, and accurately predicted the coming and ministry of Jesus; therefore they continued to be useful after the cross in persuading listeners that Jesus was the Christ, as seen in the following passages:

"And Paul, as his manner was, went in unto them, and three sabbath days reasoned with them out of the scriptures" (Acts 17:2).

"These were more noble than those in Thessalonica, in that they received the word with all readiness of mind, and searched the scriptures daily, whether those things were so" (Acts 17:11).

"And a certain Jew named Apollos, born at Alexandria, an eloquent man, and mighty in the scriptures, came to Ephesus" (Acts 18:24).

"For he mightily convinced the Jews, and that publicly, showing by the scriptures that Jesus was Christ" (Acts 18:28).

"Which he had promised afore by his prophets in the holy scriptures" (Romans 1:2).

"For whatsoever things were written aforetime were written for our learning, that we through patience and comfort of the scriptures might have hope" (Romans 15:4).

"But now is made manifest, and by the scriptures of the prophets, according to the commandment of the everlasting God, made known to all nations for the obedience of faith" (Romans 16:26).

"For I delivered unto you first of all that which I also received, how that Christ died for our sins according to the scriptures; And that he was buried, and that he rose again the third day according to the scriptures"[2] (1 Corinthians 15:3, 4).

"And that from a child thou hast known the holy scriptures, which are able to make thee wise unto salvation through faith which is in Christ Jesus" (2 Timothy 3:15).

"As also in all his epistles, speaking in them of these things; in which are some things hard to be understood, which they that are unlearned and unstable wrest, as they do also the other scriptures, unto their own destruction"[3] (2 Peter 3:16).

(Scriptures in the above series from the KJV.)

---o-**O**-o---

---

[2] Does this passage refer to the Gospels? Had Paul read the Gospels? Which Old Scripture passage speaks of Christ being raised again the third day? Jonah?

[3] This passage and 1 Cor. 15:3,4 apparently are the only two passages in the New Testament which do or may refer to the writings of the Apostles as "Scriptures."

Conclusions to Be Drawn

1) From those passages referring to "scriptures" in the Gospels it is evident that their validity was important to Jesus. The validity of the Old Scriptures was important in two distinct ways:

a. As a witness to the claim of Jesus that He was the Messiah, the validity of the Old Scriptures was affirmed, and their prophecies verified by their fulfillment during His ministry.

b. Validity of the Old Scriptures was important not only to events of Jesus' ministry which fulfilled prophecy, that validity also related to the importance of fulfilling and complying with the law. Jesus said:

"Do not think that I have come to abolish the Law or the Prophets; I have not come to abolish them but to fulfill them. I tell you the truth, until heaven and earth disappear, not the smallest letter, not the least stroke of a pen, will by any means disappear from the Law until everything is accomplished.

"Anyone who breaks one of the least of these commandments and teaches others to do the same will be called least in the kingdom of heaven, but whoever practices and teaches these commands will be called great in the kingdom of heaven.

"For I tell you that unless your righteousness surpasses that of the Pharisees and the teachers of the law, you will certainly not enter the kingdom of heaven" (Matthew 5:17-20).

The teaching of Jesus about the importance of obedience to the law is clear. But, was He teaching from a *New Covenant* perspective, an *Old Covenant* perspective, or both? One thing is sure, *He was teaching from God's perspective! Does God's perspective ever change?*

Is Jesus' "Sermon on the Mount," from which the passage above is preserved, part of that enduring truth or is it "dispensation" truth? Did Jesus preach the Gospel, or Old Covenant theology? Both?

Some directives from God remain the same from covenant to covenant – Love God with all your heart, mind, might and soul; love your neighbor as yourself. Some truths never change – God is still God; the earth is still His creation; He still has a chosen people.

We must respond in honest heart when we read such passages as Matthew 5:17-20. Notice what Jesus said in particular about the commandments, the importance attached to practicing and teaching *even the least of them.* Then notice the importance attached to fulfillment of both law and prophecy, as shown in the above passages.

Notice also that how well we have observed the commands of God will still be an issue *in the kingdom of God!*

The issue of our observing the commandments now will be an issue then! This is affirmed as well in the Book of Revelation:

"And the dragon was wroth with the woman, and went to make war with the remnant of her seed, which keep the commandments of God, and have the testimony of Jesus Christ" (Revelation 12:17).

"Here is the patience of the saints: here are they that keep the commandments of God, and the faith of Jesus" (Revelation 14:12:).

"Blessed are they that do his commandments, that they may have right to the tree of life, and may enter in through the gates into the city" (Revelation 22:14; series from KJV).

2) It is evident from the following series of texts about "scriptures" that after the resurrection, both Jesus and the Apostles continued to teach from the Old Scriptures:

"They asked each other, 'Were not our hearts burning within us while he talked with us on the road and opened the Scriptures to us?'" (Luke 24:32).

Luke 24:45: *"Then he opened their minds so they could understand the Scriptures."*

"And Paul, as his manner was, went in unto them, and three sabbath days reasoned with them out of the scriptures" (Acts 17:2).

"But as for you, continue in what you have learned and have become convinced of, because you know those from whom you learned it, and how from infancy you have known the holy Scriptures, which are able to make you wise for salvation through faith in Christ Jesus. All Scripture is God-breathed and is useful for teaching, rebuking, correcting and training in righteousness, so that the man of God may be thoroughly equipped for every good work" (2 Timothy 3:14-17).

3) It is important to understand that *fulfilling the law* and *abolishing the law* are not the same thing. Jesus said: Matthew 5:17: *"Do not think that I have come to abolish the Law or the Prophets; I have not come to abolish them but to fulfill them."* Because Jesus makes a distinction between "fulfill" and "abolish," we also must distinguish between them.

Fulfilling the law sometimes simply means complying with its demands, for example: *"Bear ye one another's burdens, and so fulfil the law of Christ"* (Galatians 6:2 KJV).

Sometimes to "fulfill" means to accomplish intended roles or predicted events: *"But how then shall the scriptures be fulfilled, that thus it must be?"* (Matthew 26:54).

4) Not just the *general ideas* of the Old Scriptures were important; God had been very exacting in His inspiration of Moses and the other Prophets. Jesus said: *"I tell you the truth, until heaven and earth disappear, not the smallest letter, not the least stroke of a pen, will by any means disappear from the Law until everything is accomplished"* (Matthew 5:18).

This statement by Jesus is tacit affirmation that when everything is accomplished, (or "fulfilled") something would *disappear from* the law. It is important to notice the wording. It is not that *the law would disappear* but that *something from the law* would disappear. This agrees with the book of Hebrews speaking of a "change" in the law.[4]

---

[4] Hebr. 7:12: "For when there is a change of the priesthood, there must also be a change of the law."

5) The Old Scriptures had a purpose which continued after the cross. Paul wrote: *"For everything that was written in the past was written to teach us, so that through endurance and the encouragement of the Scriptures we might have hope"* (Romans 15:4).

That teaching was not just history lessons. He said to Timothy: *"All Scripture is God-breathed and is useful for teaching, rebuking, correcting and training in righteousness, so that the man of God may be thoroughly equipped for every good work."* This had no reference to what Paul or other apostles were or had been writing.

Since Paul wrote to the Romans after the Cross, after the ascension of Jesus to the Father, after the establishment of the New Covenant, since he wrote that *everything that was written in the past was written to teach him and the Christians to whom he wrote,* the Old Scriptures had *and still have* continuing teaching purposes.

6) Paul wrote to Timothy, *"But as for you, continue in what you have learned and have become convinced of, because you know those from whom you learned it, and how from infancy you have known the holy Scriptures, which are able to make you wise for salvation through faith in Christ Jesus"* (2 Timothy 3:14, 15).

7) For the purposes of this study, the main thing to be observed is the positive affirmation of the Old Scriptures *found throughout the New Scriptures.* Nothing in the New Scriptures suggests the Old *Scriptures* (as in contrast to Old *Covenant*) were destined to expire and become obsolete. They were still referred to as the "holy Scriptures," they were still valid for study, they were still for our learning, they were still able to make people wise unto salvation through Christ.

People who followed the advice to study the Old Scriptures were commended as noble. The very ministry of Christ was validated by the prophetic accuracy of the Old Scriptures, as seen in Jesus repeatedly calling attention to their being fulfilled by the things He was doing, before and after the cross.   ---o-**O**-o---

---

Three Points In Historical Context

a. Timothy was advised by Paul to *continue* in what he *had learned* and become convinced of *as a child*. Is it pertinent to ask, what had Timothy learned as a child from the holy Scriptures?

b. Timothy's learning was to be considered valid because the people who *taught him as a child were trustworthy* – his mother and grandmother.

c. *From infancy Timothy had known the holy Scriptures* – the new Scriptures had not been written yet in Timothy's infancy. *One* part of the *new* scriptures was this very letter to Timothy.

Paul could only have been referring to the Old Scriptures, Genesis through Malachi. These Scriptures written before the birth of Timothy were *able to make Timothy wise for salvation through faith in Christ Jesus, and thoroughly equip the man of God.*

Modern Christians do not believe what Paul said about it!

The New Scriptures View of Old Covenant Law

"What shall we say then? Is the law sin? God forbid. Nay, I had not known sin, but by the law: for I had not known lust, except the law had said, Thou shalt not covet. But sin, taking occasion by the commandment, wrought in me all manner of concupiscence.

"For without the law sin was dead. For I was alive without the law once: but when the commandment came, sin revived, and I died. And the commandment, which was ordained to life, I found to be unto death. For sin, taking occasion by the commandment, deceived me, and by it slew me.

"Wherefore the law is holy, and the commandment holy, and just, and good. Was then that which is good made death unto me? God forbid. But sin, that it might appear sin, working death in me by that which is good; that sin by the commandment might become exceeding sinful.

"For we know that the law is spiritual: but I am carnal, sold under sin. For that which I do I allow not: for what I would, that do I not; but what I hate, that do I. If then I do that which I would not, I consent unto the law that it is good" (Romans 7:7-16 KJV).

Even though the law is holy, the law is just, the law is good, the law is spiritual, the law explains what constitutes sin, yet the law does not save. It was not intended to save, and made no attempt to save.

It is a tutor, or as the King James Version states, "a schoolmaster," and serves the function of leading us to Christ: *"So the law was put in charge to lead us to Christ that we might be justified by faith. Now that faith has come, we are no longer under the supervision of the law"* (Galatians 3:24, 25).

Those who have been led to Christ and have been justified by faith in Him are not under the supervision of the law, but those who have no faith, have not been justified by faith, have not been led to Christ, are still under its supervision. This is the basic understanding one must have of Paul's statement to Timothy:

"But we know that the law is good, if a man use it lawfully; Knowing this, that the law is not made for a righteous man, but for the lawless and disobedient, for the ungodly and for sinners, for unholy and profane, for murderers of fathers and murderers of mothers, for manslayers, For whoremongers, for them that defile themselves with mankind, for menstealers, for liars, for perjured persons, and if there be any other thing that is contrary to sound doctrine; According to the glorious gospel of the blessed God, which was committed to my trust. (1 Timothy 1:8-11, KJV).

The law spoken of in the above passage that defines sin, is *primarily but not exclusively* the Ten Commandments, which constituted the basic law of the Old Covenant. There is no way to lawfully use laws of sacrifice other than as a history of God's approach to atonement with man and worship of God prior to the cross, or in appreciation of the better sacrifice now available to us. It cannot be said that laws of sacrifice have a continuing use, either in leading us to Christ, worshipping God, or in providing reconciliation with God.

First Timothy 1:8-11 is not a statement of "what used to be" before the cross, but the current status of a *lawful use of the law years after the cross.* As an assessment of the current status of the law at the time Paul was writing to Timothy; it gives the same answer regarding the results of our being justified by faith and not by the works of the law that Paul explains to the Christians at Rome.

Paul asks them, *"Do we, then, nullify the law by this faith? Not at all! Rather, we uphold the law"* (Romans 3:31). Why? Because by the law we learn the will of God more fully; by the law we learn sound doctrine; and by the law we are led to Christ, by Whom we find relief from our guilt; *and,* by the law *sin becomes exceeding sinful* – excuses are removed when sin is defined clearly for those not led of the Spirit to understand spiritual things.---o-O-o---

Applied to Covenant Study

We must, therefore, in our study of the New Covenant keep in mind these two general attitudes expressed in the New Scriptures:

1) The attitude of the New Scriptures toward the Old Scriptures as a whole: they are for our learning, able to make us understand salvation.

2) The attitude of the New Scriptures, toward the law found in the Old Scriptures: there is a continuing valid use of the law.

The New Scriptures affirm both the Old Scriptures and the Old Scripture law as valid and intended for our learning, as currently serving God's purposes in teaching morality and sound doctrine. This understanding comes with the necessary recognition that parts of the law did not pertain to daily living, but were intended to be fulfilled and expire with the death of Christ, who is the New Covenant sacrifice, and more.

What, then, of difficult to understand scriptures, which seem to suggest otherwise? One must read them in light of the broad picture painted in the multitude of Scriptures. One must not select isolated, obscure texts out of context to suggest and impose a new covenant theology that is obviously contrary to the plain statements of the authors who wrote both the Old and the New Scriptures.

A correct new covenant theology absolutely must agree with the above illustrated and often repeated affirmation of the Old Scriptures and Old Scripture law. Otherwise, we cannot trust the New Scriptures themselves!   ---o-O-o---

A Short Course in Old Plus New Testament Doctrine
The Oracles of God–What Are They?

Stephen testified to the Sanhedrin:

*"This is that Moses, which said unto the children of Israel, A prophet shall the Lord your God raise up unto you of your breth-ren, like unto me; him shall ye hear. This is he, that was in the church in the wilderness with the angel which spake to him in the mount Sina, and with our fathers: **who received the lively oracles to give unto us:** To whom our fathers would not obey, but thrust him from them, and in their hearts turned back again into Egypt"* Acts 7:37-39).

Paul testified to the church at Rome:

*"What advantage then hath the Jew? or what profit is there of circumcision? Much every way: chiefly, because that **unto them were committed the oracles of God.** For what if some did not be-lieve? shall their unbelief make the faith of God without effect? God forbid: yea, let God be true, but every man a liar; as it is written, That thou mightest be justified in thy sayings, and mightest over-come when thou art judged"* (Romans 3:1-4).

The writer to the Hebrews witnessed:

"And being made perfect, he became the author of eternal salva-tion unto all them that obey him; Called of God an high priest after the order of Melchisedec. Of whom we have many things to say, and hard to be uttered, seeing ye are dull of hearing. For when for

*the time ye ought to be teachers, **ye have need that one teach you again which be the first principles of the oracles of God**; and are become such as have need of milk, and not of strong meat. For every one that useth milk is unskilful in the word of righteousness: for he is a babe. But strong meat belongeth to them that are of full age, even those who by reason of use have their senses exercised to discern both good and evil"* (Hebrews 5:9-14).

Peter admonished:

"As every man hath received the gift, even so minister the same one to another, as good stewards of the manifold grace of God. If any man speak, let him speak as the oracles of God; if any man minister, let him do it as of the ability which God giveth: that God in all things may be glorified through Jesus Christ, to whom be praise and dominion for ever and ever. Amen" (1 Peter 4:10, 11).
(The above scriptures are from the KJV.)

In all these verses, "oracles" refers to the oral instructions given to Israel by the Lord. The writer of Hebrews considered it the very beginning point of Christian knowledge to know "the oracles of God."

The "first principles" of the oracles of God have specific reference to the Ten Commandments. The Ten Commandments were what were spoken first, and therefore "first in importance" as shown by God doing the writing, and His writing them on stone, not just on parchment.

It becomes very significant, therefore, when Peter admonishes that if we speak, it must be in agreement with the "oracles of God," primary of which are the Ten Commandments. How do you speak, Brother, Sister? According to, or against the "oracles" – the spoken word heard from Mount Sinai? Does He Who speaks from Mount Zion speak differently than He Who spoke from Sinai? Indeed, NO!

---o-O-o---

God's New Covenant
Equates with "Last Will and Testament"

One purpose of this study is to understand the biblical use of the words "covenant" and "testament" as they relate to God, His children, and their inheritance. The subject becomes important as a means of understanding what God expects of us in three main respects:

First: What kind of lives does God expect His children to live?
Second: What does God intend His children to inherit?
Third: What results when God's children fail His expectations?

Much more than pleasing a rich uncle is at stake in the matter of qualifying as an heir to the LORD's estate. Our inheritance consists of two main items, eternal life, and the kingdom of God on earth.[5]

This kingdom is spoken of two ways in the New Testament, the kingdom of God and the kingdom of heaven, both meaning the same thing.[6] Disobedient, unrepentant sinners will not inherit the kingdom of God. They cannot be God's heirs.[7]

---

[5] Matthew 19:29: "And everyone who has left houses or brothers or sisters or father or mother or children or fields for my sake will receive a hundred times as much and will inherit eternal life."

[6] These two terms mean the same thing: Luke 6:20 Looking at his disciples, he said: "Blessed are you who are poor, for yours is the kingdom of God. Matthew 5:3 "Blessed are the poor in spirit, for theirs is the kingdom of heaven." Comparing parallel passages in the Gospels reveals the terms to be used interchangeably.

[7] 1 Corinthians 6:9: "Do you not know that the wicked will not inherit the kingdom of God? Do not be deceived: Neither the sexually immoral nor idolaters nor adulterers nor male prostitutes nor homosexual offenders."

Galatians 5:21: "...and envy; drunkenness, orgies, and the like. I warn you, as I did before, that those who live like this will not inherit the kingdom of God."

Revelation 5:9, 10: "And they sang a new song: "You are worthy to take the scroll and to open its seals, because you were slain, and with your blood you purchased men for God from every tribe and language and people and nation. You have made them to be a kingdom and priests to serve our God, and they will reign on the earth."

In this context, a covenant between God and His heirs began to be a common theme in the Bible, beginning with God's covenant with Abraham.[8] The covenant with Abraham specified what God expected of Abraham and his offspring, if they were to be recognized as His children. The covenant with Abraham continues in effect, and by extension, includes all genuine Christians.[9]

---o-O-o---

Different Kinds of Covenants

"Covenants" in the Scriptures do not refer just to *making out wills,* but also to mutual agreements and arrangements for getting along with other individuals. For example, a covenant between Abraham and Abimelech spelled out how they might live in harmony. Abimelech also had such a covenant with Abraham's son Isaac; Jacob made such a covenant with Laban, his father-in-law; and God commanded Israel *not to make* such covenants with surrounding nations.[10]

These "covenants" were not "wills" specifying what anyone's heirs would receive; rather they were working arrangements between individuals and between nations; however, the same Hebrew word (bereeth') referred to each type. "Ber-eeth'" referred to

> Covenants between individuals,
> Covenants between nations, and

---

[8] Note: In this study, the New International Version is intended to be used unless otherwise specified. The word count for "covenant" and "covenants" is based on this translation. The word used for covenant in the Old Scriptures is, universally, the Hebrew word "bereeth," with the basic concept of "a cutting," referring originally to the method of establishing an agreement, a compact, a covenant, such as is pictured between God and Abraham in Genesis 15.

[9] Galatians 3:6-8: "Consider Abraham: "He believed God, and it was credited to him as righteousness." Understand, then, that those who believe are children of Abraham. The Scripture foresaw that God would justify the Gentiles by faith, and announced the gospel in advance to Abraham: "All nations will be blessed through you." So those who have faith are blessed along with Abraham, the man of faith."

[10] Genesis 21:27-32; Genesis 26:28; 31:44;

Covenants between God and His heirs, His "children."

God's covenants with Abraham and his heirs were a combination of the above. In part, they were day-to-day living and working arrangements between God and His children; and in part, they spelled out what their inheritance would be.

God first made out His will telling what His children were to inherit several thousand years ago. It was first made out to Abraham, and because he was faithful until death, that covenant is valid for him and all his "seed."

That covenant was extended to Abraham's son Isaac and his grandson Jacob, then to "Israel," the nation of twelve tribes descendant from the twelve sons of Jacob. It was then extended to believers from all nations who by faith in Christ "take hold" of God's covenant promise to Abraham and his seed (Isaiah 56:1-8; Galatians 3:22-29).

As the "seed" of Abraham, Christ is the primary heir of the promise, and our being "in Christ," a part of His body, we, too are heirs.

Millions of potential heirs have copies of that original will or covenant made with Abraham, and *correctly* expect God's estate to be settled according to its terms, for that covenant was a promise, and it is still in effect.

It has never been replaced, it has never been nullified, and it has always been the connecting link between successive generations of God's people, including Jew and Gentile, including Israel and the Church.

If you feel inclined to challenge the concept that "ber-eeth" (the Hebrew word for covenant) can connote a "will," consider the fact that God's covenant with Abraham, Isaac, Jacob, and the nation of Israel and *with us* – was, is, and always will be primarily concerned with an "inheritance" dependent on our "Father-child" relationship with God.

The abundant use of the terms "heir," "heirs," "inherit," and "inheritance" permeate the old Scriptures and the new. This covenant with Abraham being guaranteed to him and to his seed speak of the same concept, heirs and inheritance.

The covenants with Abraham, Isaac, Jacob, and the children of Israel (as also the new covenant and the church) not only determined who were and are the heirs, but also spell out the obligations and qualifications to be named as heirs.

More than 175 passages[11] speak of the inheritance of God's people, both in reference to the land of Canaan, and in reference to the Christian inheritance.

This is a theme throughout the Old and New Testaments. This supports the concept that both covenants, old and new, were in effect "wills." *See Appendix A, "Heir, Heirs, Inherit, Inheritance."*

They spell out what God leaves His children, all of whom have been bought by the blood of Christ from slavery to sin.[12] Their inheritance is confirmed in His death as the "Testator," or Maker of the will. God's will was made effective by His death (through the death of His Son), by which both covenants have been ratified.

---o-O-o---

God Keeps Record of His Heirs

One theme found in both the old and new scriptures is that God keeps a record of the eligible heirs, that He will and does erase names from the record of heirs:

"Yet now, if thou wilt forgive their sin–; and if not, blot me, I pray thee, out of thy book which thou hast written. And the LORD said unto Moses, Whosoever hath sinned against me, him will I blot out of my book" (Exodus 32:32, 33);

"Then they that feared the LORD spake often one to another: and the LORD hearkened and heard it, and a book of remembrance was

---

[11] See Appendix A.

[12] Hebr. 9:15 For this reason Christ is the mediator of a new covenant, that those who are called may receive the promised eternal inheritance – now that he has died as a ransom to set them free from the sins committed under the first covenant. (NIV)

Hebr. 9:15 And for this cause he is the mediator of the new testament, that by means of death, for the redemption of the transgressions that were under the first testament, they which are called might receive the promise of eternal inheritance. (KJV)

written before him for them that feared the LORD, and that thought upon his name" (Malachi 3:16);

"And I entreat thee also, true yokefellow, help those women which laboured with me in the gospel, with Clement also, and with other my fellowlabourers, whose names are in the book of life" (Philippians 4:3);

"He that overcometh, the same shall be clothed in white raiment; and I will not blot out his name out of the book of life, but I will confess his name before my Father, and before his angels" (Revelation 3:5. The series is KJV).

So when the Bible speaks of a covenant being broken by His children, at risk is the status of remaining an heir; at risk is whether the heir actually inherits; and when the Bible speaks of a new covenant taking the place of a broken covenant, the covenant with Abraham is not the covenant or "will" which expired:

"What I mean is this: The law, introduced 430 years later, does not set aside the covenant previously established by God and thus do away with the promise.

"For if the inheritance depends on the law, then it no longer depends on a promise; but God in his grace gave it to Abraham through a promise."

"If you belong to Christ, then you are Abraham's seed, and heirs according to the promise" (Galatians 3:17, 18, 29).

Part of that "promise" is seen in this repeated prophecy:

*"I will bless those who bless you, and whoever curses you I will curse; and **all peoples on earth will be blessed** through you"* (Genesis 12:3).

*"Abraham will surely become a great and powerful nation, and **all nations on earth will be blessed through him"** (Genesis 18:18).*

*"...and **through your offspring all nations on earth will be blessed**, because you have obeyed me"* (Genesis 22:18).

*"I will make your descendants as numerous as the stars in the sky and will give them all these lands, and **through your offspring all nations on earth will be blessed"** (Genesis 26:4:).*

The covenant with Abraham found in the book of Genesis and often referred to in both the old and new scriptures, *has never been voided, and will never be voided.* That is also true of the law of God, found in the old scriptures: *"Do we then make void the law through faith? God forbid: yea, we establish the law"* (Romans 3:31 KJV). "Do we, then, nullify the law by this faith? Not at all! Rather, we uphold the law" (Romans 3:31 NIV). Changed, yes![13] Nullified, No!

Individuals could have their names deleted from the list of "heirs" but they could not nullify God's covenant of promise to Abraham that he and his seed would inherit the kingdom.

"If you belong to Christ, then you are Abraham's seed, and heirs according to the promise" – this statement alone should put believers on their guard against the claim that the books of the Bible, Genesis through Malachi, constitute the "old covenant," that all of these books and their entire contents were voided with the initiation of a new covenant between God and His people. The covenant with Abraham remains valid; it is not a new promise, but one made to Abraham 430 years before God spoke the law at Sinai.

It must be understood that Christ was the confirmation of the covenant made with Abraham, it *"was confirmed before of God in Christ."* There are many mysteries in the Bible, and this is one of them – how the covenant with Abraham, 430 years before God spoke the law to Israel from Mount Sinai, was confirmed *"in Christ".*[14]

---

[13] Hebr. 7:12   For when there is a change in the priesthood, there is necessarily a change in the law as well. (NRSVA).

[14] It is also a mystery how that "in Christ" appeared in some Greek texts and disappeared in others. See notes on the passage in Nestle, *Novum Testamentum Graece,* Stuttgart, 1949. Is there a relationship to the statement of Christ in John 8:56, "Your father Abraham rejoiced to see my day: and he saw it, and was glad"? Undoubtedly the concept is to be understood in the sense that Christ is the seed of Abraham which guaranteed the fulfillment of the promise to Abraham of a seed to inherit the earth (Gal. 3:16).

"In Christ" is explained in Paul's statement to the Galatians, *"Now to Abraham and his seed were the promises made. He saith not, And to seeds, as of many; but as of one, And to thy seed, which is Christ"* (Galatians 3:16). The greater fulfillment of this promise is found in the Gospel.

It will be seen that in fact, even though God extended Abraham's covenant of promise to the seed of Abraham, a newer covenant was made with the nation of Israel *at Mount Sinai,* and it was this newer covenant with Israel (never called a new covenant in the Bible) that was replaced *with yet another new covenant* based on faith in Christ which is the covenant referred to as the "new covenant" in the old and new Scriptures.

This later "new covenant," inaugurated by the death of Christ, re-placed the covenant made with Israel at Sinai, but it did not replace the covenant made with Abraham. To keep things straight, we must ac-knowledge the new covenant was still with God's people "whom he foreknew."

Promise of a New Covenant

"'The time is coming,' declares the LORD, 'when I will make a new covenant with the house of Israel and with the house of Judah. It will not be like the covenant I made with their forefathers when I took them by the hand to lead them out of Egypt, because they broke my covenant, though I was a husband to them,' declares the LORD.

"This is the covenant I will make with the house of Israel after that time,' declares the LORD. 'I will put my law in their minds and write it on their hearts. I will be their God, and they will be my peo-ple'" (Jeremiah 31:31-33).

God declares in the very promise of the new covenant that the new covenant would be "with the house of Israel and the house of Judah." These recipients are the descendants of the same people who stood at the base of Mount Sinai: *"It will not be like the covenant I made with their forefathers when I took them by the hand to lead them out of Egypt, because they broke my covenant"* (Jeremiah 31:32).

So it must be understood that the covenant with Abraham, Isaac and Jacob was also extended to Israel, Abraham's seed; and that God's covenant with Abraham continued (and continues today) unaffected by the giving of the law as a covenant with Israel at Mount Sinai, ***and*** unaffected by the establishment of a new covenant through Christ with the very same people. This New Covenant, inaugurated by the cross, replaced the covenant made with Israel at Sinai.

The covenant made with Israel at Sinai was *in addition to the covenant* made with Abraham, and these two covenants were concurrently in effect from Mount Sinai to Mount Calvary. It was this additional covenant based on law which Israel broke by disobedience.

The covenant God made with the fathers of Israel at Sinai was God's agreement with the nation of Israel. It was an agreement that He would be their God and they would obey Him and be His people. God's "law" declared orally to Israel from Mount Sinai, with His extended judgments, statutes and ordinances given through Moses to Israel, contained the provisions and contingencies of His "will," both in the sense of what God *desires* and in the sense of provisions for inheritance.

Whether the children of Israel were to be heirs and remain heirs, if they were to obtain their inheritance, depended on their obedience to God's laws and instructions. It was this covenant that Israel broke, and it was this covenant that became "old" and was replaced with a new covenant. This study reveals the details.[15]

It was also Israel's breaking of the covenant made at Sinai and their resultant failure to realize the promised "rest" in the Promised Land to which the third and fourth chapters of Hebrews refer when Hebrew

---

[15] It is to be observed that even the covenant with Abraham also had qualifying provisions, for example circumcision. Any of the seed (offspring) of Abraham who refused or neglected to be circumcised, were cut off from the people of God. Deleting circumcision from the covenant with Abraham did not annul that covenant. So even the covenant with Abraham was amended, *NOT NULLIFIED,* so that Christians as the seed of Abraham are not required to be circumcised to be heirs of the covenant of promise (Acts 15 and related passages.)

and Gentile Christians, as heirs according to the promise, are admonished not to harden our hearts as Israel did "in the day of provocation."

---o-O-o---

Do We Understand What We Read?
With Whom Was the New Covenant Made?

One of the main points of contention in discussing the Ten Commandments, whether they are valid for Christians as a body of instruction, is whether they were written *to Christians* or *only to Israel.* You probably see where this is headed.

In the "preamble" to the Ten Commandments, these words are found: *"I am the LORD your God, who brought you out of Egypt, out of the land of slavery."*

One who thinks the Ten Commandments are not for Christians may point out that the people to whom the Ten Commands are addressed are the ones who had been enslaved in Egypt – Israel, implying it applies only to them.

The question is then asked, "Were you slaves in Egypt?"

We who uphold them as valid for Christians are expected to respond, "Well, no!"

Then a conclusion is suggested, "How, then can you claim they are addressed to you? Are you an Israelite?"

And a Christian is supposed to respond, "Well, I guess not! Why didn't I notice that before?"

But, the very same set of reasonings also apply to the new covenant. Look at the preamble:

*"'The time is coming,' declares the LORD, 'when **I will make a new covenant with the house of Israel and with the house of Judah.** It will not be like the covenant I made with their forefathers when I took them by the hand to lead them out of Egypt, because they broke my covenant, though I was a husband to them,' declares the LORD.*

"'This is the covenant I will make with the house of Israel after that time,' declares the LORD. 'I will put my law in their minds and write it on their hearts. I will be their God, and they will be my people'" (Jeremiah 31:31-33).

Let's point out that the people to whom the new covenant was to be made were those whose forefathers stood at the foot of Mount Sinai, who had been slaves in Egypt, the same people to whom the Ten Commandments were given. So let's have the conversation again!

"Christian, did *your* forefathers make a covenant with God at the foot of Mount Sinai?"

"Well, no!"

"Are you an Israelite?"

"Well, no!"

"With whom did God say He would make a new covenant? Read Jeremiah 31:31-33 again and see!"

"Well, it says with Israel, with the House of Israel and with the House of Judah."

"WELL? Are you 'Israel'? Are you of the House of Israel? Are you of the House of Judah?"

"Well, NO!"

"Then, Gentile Christian Friend, how can you claim the right to participate in a promise that was not made to you, but to Israel?"

Both conversations (they do happen!) are of the same cloth. They are no different than the following conversation:

"Christian Friend! You claim that Jesus was your Messiah, right?"

"Yes, of course!"

"But Jesus said in Matthew 15:24, *'I was sent only to the lost sheep of Israel'!* How can you claim He was sent to you? Are you one of the 'lost sheep' of the house of Israel?"

Using the same argument illustrated before, Christians are supposed to respond, "Well, no! Why didn't I notice that? Jesus wasn't even sent to me!"

"Well! Christian, are you also not aware that the disciples of Jesus were told to go only to the Israelites? Matthew 10:5 says, *"These twelve Jesus sent out with the following instructions: 'Do not go among the Gentiles or enter any town of the Samaritans.'"*

And Christians are supposed to respond, "Why didn't I notice that before!"

What's the problem with these arguments? The problem is the same, they leave out important information – they ignore important facts!

The argument that Jesus and the Apostles were not sent to Gentiles, and therefore the Gospel ministry of Jesus does not pertain to the Gentiles is cut from the same defective bolt of cloth from which the other arguments about the Ten Commandments and Covenant are cut!

Arguing that Jesus and the Apostles were not sent to Gentiles and is therefore not their Savior has just as much validity as the argument that Gentiles are not addressed in the preamble of the Ten Commandments and therefore the Ten Commandments are not for Gentiles.

Arguing that the promise of a new covenant was made to Israel and Judah (even the New Testament affirms that[16]) and therefore doesn't include Gentiles is just as valid as arguing the Ten Commandments do not pertain to Christians.

---

[16] Hebr. 8:7-13: "For if there had been nothing wrong with that first covenant, no place would have been sought for another. But God found fault with the people and said: "The time is coming, declares the Lord, when I will make a new covenant with the house of Israel and with the house of Judah. It will not be like the covenant I made with their forefathers when I took them by the hand to lead them out of Egypt, because they did not remain faithful to my covenant, and I turned away from them, declares the Lord. This is the covenant I will make with the house of Israel after that time, declares the Lord. I will put my laws in their minds and write them on their hearts. I will be their God, and they will be my people. No longer will a man teach his neighbor, or a man his brother, saying, `Know the Lord,' because they will all know me, from the least of them to the greatest. For I will forgive their wickedness and will remember their sins no more." By calling this covenant "new," he has made the first one obsolete; and what is obsolete and aging will soon disappear."

These arguments, if valid, lead to the conclusion that the Gospels are not part of the new covenant, and that Jesus was an Old Testament Prophet. Some virtually teach that, mainly because Jesus supported Sabbath observance and paying tithes.

It could just as well be reasoned, *Jesus and the Apostles were not sent to Gentiles, so the Gospel of the Kingdom is only for Israel!* It not only *could* be reasoned that way, some people *do* reason that way! Imagine what fanciful doctrines could be developed from Jesus saying, *"You Samaritans worship what you do not know; we worship what we do know, for salvation is from the Jews"* (John 4:22).

In fact, there is no validity to the argument that the Ten Commandments were given to Israel and therefore *had* and *have* no validity for Gentile Christians.

John the Baptist admonished the Jews, *"Produce fruit in keeping with repentance. And do not begin to say to yourselves, 'We have Abraham as our father.' For I tell you that out of these stones God can raise up children for Abraham"* (Luke 3:8).

"These stones" refers to Gentile Christians who through Christ become "seed" or descendants of Abraham: *"If you belong to Christ, then you are Abraham's seed, and heirs according to the promise"* (Galatians 3:29). This was a letter to a Gentile Christian congregation.

Paul wrote to the Roman Christians, calling them "wild olive branches" and Israel a tame, or cultivated olive tree, *into which Gentile Christians are grafted.* He said: *"I am talking to you Gentiles. Inasmuch as I am the apostle to the Gentiles, I make much of my ministry"* (Romans 11:14).

Paul illustrates Israel's disobedience and the downfall of some:

"If some of the branches have been broken off, and you, though a wild olive shoot, have been grafted in among the others and now share in the nourishing sap from the olive root, do not boast over those branches. If you do, consider this: You do not support the root, but the root supports you" (verses 17, 18).

"After all, if you were cut out of an olive tree that is wild by nature, and contrary to nature were grafted into a cultivated olive

tree, how much more readily will these, the natural branches, be grafted into their own olive tree!" (verse 24).

Gentile believers are called "wild" olive branches; Jews (Israelites) are called "tame" olive branches. Israel is called a "tame olive tree" *into which we Gentile wild olive branches are grafted!*

It is in the same vein of speech that Paul says to the Christian church of Galatia, *"Peace and mercy to all who follow this rule, even to the Israel of God"* (Galatians 6:16).

So, we Gentiles, as seed of Abraham, as part of the Israel of God through faith in Christ, *"...have been grafted in among the others and now share in the nourishing sap from the olive root,"* and therefore are admonished, *"do not boast over those branches. If you do, consider this: You do not support the root, but the root supports you."*

Therefore, we participate in the new covenant promise, *because we by faith in Christ become part of the seed of Abraham, part of "the Israel of God," by being grafted in.*

We must ask then, "Were the 'forefathers' of the recipients of the new covenant promise (Jeremiah 31:31-33) therefore also *our forefathers?* Indeed they are!

Are the Ten Commandments therefore also addressed to us, or just to the literal seed of Abraham, Isaac, and Jacob? You be the judge as you listen to Paul speak to gentile Romans: *"Do we, then, nullify the law by this faith? Not at all! Rather, we uphold the law"* (Romans 3:31).

Is the law still valid for doctrine? Decide by listening to Paul:

*"But we know that the law is good, if a man use it lawfully; Knowing this, that the law is not made for a righteous man, but for the lawless and disobedient, for the ungodly and for sinners, for unholy and profane, for murderers of fathers and murderers of mothers, for manslayers, For whoremongers, for them that defile themselves with mankind, for mensteaIers, for liars, for perjured persons, **and if there be any other thing that is contrary to sound doctrine;** According to the glorious gospel of the blessed God, which was committed to my trust "* (1 Timothy 1:8-11).

Why? Because the law is holy, just, good, spiritual (Romans 7:12-14). *"So the law was put in charge to lead us to Christ that we might be justified by faith"* (Galatians 3:24).

Let's summarize the logic of the claim that the Ten Commandments were written to Israel and not to Gentiles, therefore they were not written to Christians:

Such arguments deny that we are seed of Abraham and heirs according to the promise; they deny that Gentiles are participants in the new covenant; they deny that the Gospels pertain to Christians; for each of these were written to, addressed to, promised to, preached to Israel.

Such an argument just as logically suggests that since the Messiah was promised to Israel, the promised Messiah does not pertain to us.

Let's be careful lest we completely disassociate ourselves from God by denying any relationship to the Israel of God!

The argument that the Ten Commandments were addressed to Israel and not to Christians, and therefore do not pertain to Christian conduct, is a specious argument without merit. Paul is helpful here: *"For everything that was written in the past was written to teach us, so that through endurance and the encouragement of the Scriptures we might have hope"* (Romans 15:4).

---o-O-o---

God Revised the Sinai "Covenant"

God revised[17] this will, this Sinai covenant with Israel, and those who cling to the provisions of the entire out-dated copy are in for a surprise when God's estate is settled. Similarly, some who claim an inheritance under the terms of His revised will are in for a surprise because they ignore the provisions of His will relating to their behavior.

God's will was revised with new stipulations, and it names a multitude of adopted children as heirs, as well as other benefits for all. As we have seen, He gave notice of His intent to change His will hundreds of years before the actual changes were made (Jeremiah 31:31-33).

God also gave notice of His intent to adopt children from among other nations to be His heirs.[18]

His new will has been recorded and validated in the courts of heaven,[19] but those who consider themselves the legitimate heirs have gotten into squabbles, as heirs commonly do, over the provisions of His will.

At first, the natural heirs protested the inclusion of the adopted sons and daughters, unless they complied with all provisions of the old will (see Acts chapters 10, 11, 15); in particular with the provision of circumcision;[20] and sadly, some of the natural children (Israelites) have been disqualified.[21] They do not agree to God's revised will!

---

[17] Some readers may object to the use of the word "revised"; however the Book of Hebrews declares the New Covenant required a "change" in the law; and the fact that Paul declares the law confirmed by faith, rather than voided, and the fact that Paul says the law continues to have a lawful use, affirm the use of the word "revised."

[18] (Isaiah 56:1-8; Also Acts 15:14: "Simon has described to us how God at first showed his concern by taking from the Gentiles a people for himself.").

[19] Hebrews 9:24 in context. Matthew 5:5: "Blessed are the meek, for they will inherit the earth."

[20] Acts 7:8: "And he gave him the covenant of circumcision: and so Abraham begat Isaac, and circumcised him the eighth day; and Isaac begat Jacob; and Jacob begat the twelve patriarchs." This covenant of circumcision was included as a part of the covenant with Israel in the law of Moses, Leviticus 12:3.

[21] See Romans 11:1-22.

Some challenge the concept that it was a "revised" will. Rather, they conceive that God's law as contained in His "decaying" old covenant was completely abolished, and any elements of law pertaining to the new covenant constitute a new law, the law of Christ.

The Old Scriptures speak of God "magnifying" His law and making it honourable – respectable and obeyable – *an interesting concept to reconcile with the concept of destroying it!*

So, when God promises by making a new covenant to write His law in the hearts of His heirs, they propose it was a new law, not an old law, which God promised to write in their hearts. It is to be noted:

1) Both the Old and New Scriptures speak of a "new covenant."

2) Neither the Old nor the New Scriptures speak of a new law!

3) The New Scriptures speak of a "change" in the law, to allow for a different sacrifice, a different priesthood, etc.

Effectively, claiming that the Ten Commandments are not for Christians breaks God's new will, His New covenant (for themselves). They are not willing to submit themselves to His commandments, His law of righteousness, even though writing His law on their hearts is God's declared purpose of a new covenant.[22]

Part of the declared purpose of the coming of Christ is thus denied:

*"For **what the law was powerless to do** in that it was weakened by the sinful nature, **God did by sending his own Son** in the likeness of sinful man to be a sin offering.*

*"And so he condemned sin in sinful man, **in order that the righteous requirements of the law might be fully met in us,** who do not live according to the sinful nature but according to the Spirit.*

---

[22] Rom. 8:7: ... the sinful mind is hostile to God. It does not submit to God's law, nor can it do so."

Jeremiah 31:33: "But this shall be the covenant that I will make with the house of Israel; After those days, saith the LORD, I will put my law in their inward parts, and write it in their hearts; and will be their God, and they shall be my people."

*"The mind of sinful man is death, but the mind controlled by the Spirit is life and peace; the sinful mind is hostile to God. **It does not submit to God's law, nor can it do so**"* (see Romans 8:3-9).

The purpose of the new covenant is that we may be enabled to submit to and obey the law of God by it being written on our hearts; and the coming of Christ was to do what the law could not do – the law being weakened by our sinful nature.

Notice the wording carefully. Christ did not come to obey the law in place of our obeying the law – He condemned sin in sinful man in order that the righteous requirements of the law might be fully met *in us,* changing our nature so that we are able to submit to the law of God.

But some, remaining carnal in nature, rebel against God writing His law in their hearts. They assume that Christ, by obeying the law perfectly and living a sinless life, relieves them of the need to submit to the law of God.   ---o-**O**-o---

Why the Disagreements?

The provisions of God's will have been made accessible to the public, they are not secret, so why the disputes? The human courts of theological opinion haggle over the "real meaning" of the new will.

We argue whether *"fulfilled"* means "abolished," whether *"end"* means "purpose" or "termination," and whether *"eternal"* means "for a while" or "time without end"; and whether *"if"* means the same thing in English that it meant in Hebrew and Greek. This goes down the road of "It all depends on what the meaning of is, is."

Sometimes those who expect to be heirs don't get along very well, as they seek to disqualify one another and reserve God's estate to themselves. However, *there are* disqualifications which Paul summarized.[23] How the disputes work is shown in a letter to Timothy:

---

[23] See 1 Corinthians 6:9, 10; Galatians 5:19-21.

- 37 -

"As I urged you when I went into Macedonia, stay there in Ephesus so that you may command certain men not to teach false doctrines any longer nor to devote themselves to myths and endless genealogies. These promote controversies rather than God's work — which is by faith.

"The goal of this command is love, which comes from a pure heart and a good conscience and a sincere faith. Some have wandered away from these and turned to meaningless talk. They want to be teachers of the law, but they do not know what they are talking about or what they so confidently affirm" (1 Timothy 1:3-7).

So, arguments and misinterpretations began between the beneficiaries of God's will early in the Christian era – but, weren't we talking about *God's will, His "last will and testament," instead of law?* God's covenant, His old and His new covenants, were both based on law. Consider these texts about the Ten Commandments:

"Moses was there with the LORD forty days and forty nights without eating bread or drinking water. And he wrote on the tablets the words of the covenant – the Ten Commandments" (Exodus 34:28).

"He declared to you his covenant, the Ten Commandments, which he commanded you to follow and then wrote them on two stone tablets" (Deuteronomy 4:13).

"'This is the covenant I will make with the house of Israel after that time,' declares the LORD. 'I will put my law in their minds and write it on their hearts. I will be their God, and they will be my people'" (Jeremiah 31:33).

If the Ten Commandments were important enough to be spoken of as "the words of the covenant – the Ten Commandments," and were called "the law," by what reasoning would we say they were not the law God intended to write on the hearts of His people?

The central concept of God's old and new wills (covenants) is embodied in God's law, His "family rules and regulations" (see Deuteronomy 9:11; Hebrews 9:4; Jeremiah 31:31-33), and the responses of His family to His law.

The central concept of newness in making a "new" covenant is not the change made in law but change in the place of its writing – not on stone but in our hearts. The change declared was not a change in the Ten Commandments, but a change in sacrifice and change in priesthood. *"For when there is a change of the priesthood, there must also be a change of the law"* (Hebrews 7:12).

Even though both the old and the new Scriptures state that the covenant concerns law, some deny that the New Covenant is even about law, stating rather that it is about Jesus Christ.

The truth, as we shall see, is that it is both about law and about Jesus Christ, for it is breaking the law that necessitated the death of Jesus; it is breaking the law that makes every sinner need a Savior. It is Christians losing faith and breaking the law which "crucifies Christ afresh" (see Hebrews 6:4-9). ---o-O-o---

So Why a *New* Will?

The need of a new will (New Covenant) arose from God's heirs disqualifying themselves by breaking the conditions imposed in the first will, the Old Covenant. God said, *"It will not be like the covenant I made with their forefathers when I took them by the hand to lead them out of Egypt because they broke my covenant"* (Jeremiah 31:32). They broke it by lack of faith and disobedience (see Hebrews 3, 4).

According to the Prophet Jeremiah and the Apostle Paul, the primary difference between God's old will and His new will is that under the Old Covenant God wrote His law on stone with His own finger, and Moses wrote further revelations from God with ink in a book; whereas in His New Covenant, *God does all the writing* – He writes His law on the hearts of His people.[24]

---

[24] Jeremiah 31:31-33: "Behold, the days come, saith the LORD, that I will make a new covenant with the house of Israel, and with the house of Judah: Not according to the covenant that I made with their fathers in the day that I took them by the hand to

Circumcision was *typical* of a change in heart, as shown in these passages:

"Circumcise therefore the foreskin of your heart, and be no more stiffnecked" (Deuteronomy 10:16 KJV):

"Circumcise yourselves to the LORD, and take away the foreskins of your heart, ye men of Judah and inhabitants of Jerusalem: lest my fury come forth like fire, and burn that none can quench it, because of the evil of your doings" (Jeremiah 4:4 (KJV).

The command was first given that men were to circumcise their own hearts, but the ability to do it was lacking. Therefore the prophecy of Moses in Deuteronomy 30:6, KJV: **"And the LORD thy God will circumcise thine heart**, *and the heart of thy seed, to love the LORD thy God with all thine heart, and with all thy soul, that thou mayest live."*

Success as a child of God depended on submission to this action of God even in the Old Covenant.

The circumcision God would perform depended on the seed of Abraham being submissive to the Word of God: *"For the word of God is living and active. Sharper than any double-edged sword, it penetrates even to dividing soul and spirit, joints and marrow; it judges the thoughts and attitudes of the heart"* (Hebrews 4:12). This is the means of God's circumcision, hearing and submitting to His living Word.

This "seed" God would circumcise takes into consideration several qualifying statements in the New Scriptures:

"It is not as though God's word had failed. For not all who are descended from Israel are Israel" (Romans 9:6).

---

bring them out of the land of Egypt; which my covenant they brake, although I was an husband unto them, saith the LORD: But this shall be the covenant that I will make with the house of Israel; After those days, saith the LORD, I will put my law in their inward parts, and write it in their hearts; and will be their God, and they shall be my people";

2 Corinthians 3:3: "Forasmuch as ye are manifestly declared to be the epistle of Christ ministered by us, written not with ink, but with the Spirit of the living God; not in tables of stone, but in fleshy tables of the heart."

"I know your afflictions and your poverty --yet you are rich! I know the slander of those who say they are Jews and are not, but are a synagogue of Satan" (Revelation 2:9).

"Abraham is our father," they answered. *"If you were Abraham's children,"* said Jesus, *"then you would do the things Abraham did"* (John 8:39).

"If you belong to Christ, then you are Abraham's seed, and heirs according to the promise" (Galatians 3:29).

These are the ones who qualify as the seed of Israel whose hearts God would circumcise.

This relates to the prophecy of a New Covenant found in Jeremiah 31:31-33, where God determines to make a new covenant, whereby His law would be written on the hearts of His people.

What God wants His children to do and not do, to think and not think, to believe and not believe, is intended to mean a lot more to His children when written on their hearts than when His instructions were written simply on stone and in a book.

God's intention of making a New Covenant with His children is the exact opposite of that commonly taught. It is to "magnify" God's law and make it honorable, not diminish it and make it vanish away!

The common teaching about the New Covenant is that Christ abolished God's law by dying on the cross; whereas the truth is that under the new covenant, law becomes an integral part of our spiritual makeup, no longer an impersonal matter written on stone.

---o-O-o---

The New Covenant Makes God's Law "Obeyable"

Rather than God giving His children a feeling of abhorrence toward His law (as commonly expressed in some Christian circles) it is God's intent to impress it more deeply upon the conscience of His children, and make it a heart felt desire to obey and please God; and as He said through the prophet Isaiah, *"The LORD is well pleased for his right-*

eousness' sake; he will magnify the law, and make it honourable" (Isaiah 42:21, KJV).

We have discussed this earlier, and will return to it again. When a person "honors" a covenant, a contract, a law, first he holds it in esteem; he shows respect for it, does not speak disparagingly of it; second, he obeys it, complies with its stipulations.

The esteem with which people view God's law in great degree indicates whether God has been allowed to write it upon that person's heart. Man's obedience to God's law is an indicator of whether he has turned from a carnal, sinful nature to a spiritual nature, whether he has submitted to God's circumcision of his heart.

In short, it's an important indicator of whether that person has been born again, whether that person is a participator in the New Covenant.

Man, therefore, has no excuse claiming it is impossible to obey God's law, because God took away that excuse by impressing it on our hearts; and further, by supplying the Holy Spirit as our comforter, enabler, and guide, God has made it possible for us to obey His law.

The Lord made the law "honourable" in both respects: "Respectable" and "Obeyable" – Do you doubt it?

"No temptation has seized you except what is common to man. And God is faithful; he will not let you be tempted beyond what you can bear. But when you are tempted, he will also provide a way out so that you can stand up under it" (1 Corinthians 10:13).

To claim, as some do, that it is impossible for man to obey the law of God, is to deny the very Spirit and power of God! It is also to deny one of the very purposes of the coming of Christ and the Holy Spirit:

"For what the law was powerless to do in that it was weakened by the sinful nature, God did by sending his own Son in the likeness of sinful man to be a sin offering. And so he condemned sin in sinful man, in order that the righteous requirements of the law might be

fully met in us, who do not live according to the sinful nature but according to the Spirit" (Romans 8:3, 4).

Note the elements of this passage:

1) What the law was powerless to do, God did!

2) God did what the law was powerless to do by sending His own Son as a sin offering.

3) God condemned sin in sinful man in order that the righteous requirements of the law might be fully met in us.

4) Those in whom the righteous requirements of the law are fully met *do not live according to the sinful nature but according to the spirit.*

The fact those in whom the righteous requirements of the law are fully met *do not live according to the sinful nature but according to the spirit* answers

1) Whether the passage means only that Jesus kept the righteous requirements of the law in our stead (thus we are not required to); or

2) Whether the passage means only that the righteous requirement of the law is that somebody die for sin, and Jesus did that for us.

Those are conclusions some impose on the text, thus releasing the believing sinner from either having to die *or* live righteously!

If those in whom the righteous requirements of the law are fully met *do not live according to the sinful nature but according to the spirit,* then they themselves live a life practicing the righteous requirements of the law!

This change from living according to the sinful nature to living according to the Spirit was the primary purpose of the coming revision of God's covenant with His people. It pertained to the place God's family rules and regulations are to be written – on our hearts – and that place of writing was to correct disobedience and lack of faith.

We say "primary purpose" because when the concept of a New Covenant was first introduced, the statement of its newness was the place it was to be written: *"But this shall be the covenant that I will make with the house of Israel; After those days, saith the LORD, I will* *put **my law in their inward parts, and write it in their hearts;** and will be their God, and they shall be my people"* (Jeremiah 31:33).

---o-O-o---

Changing the Intent and Content

An important question arises: If God does the writing of His will, if He writes it on our hearts, why all the disputes among the heirs? If God does the writing, doesn't He write the same thing on the hearts of His various children? Isn't it *His law* that He writes there?

And if we have something different written on our hearts than what He writes on the hearts of others who name the name of Christ, who did the writing, and *who changed the **intent** and **the content**?* Is it not quite obvious that we, ourselves, have interfered with what God wants to write there? Either that or we have allowed others to interfere.

It is important to notice exactly what the prophecy says – *"this shall be the covenant"* – what shall be the covenant? *"I will put my law in their inward parts, and write it in their hearts; and will be their God, and they shall be my people."*

There are those who say the difference is to be found in that the New Covenant law would be different than the old covenant law. This concept springs from a misunderstanding of Jeremiah 31:32. Speaking of the New Covenant the prophet wrote: *"'It will not be like the covenant I made with their forefathers when I took them by the hand to lead them out of Egypt, because they broke my covenant, though I was a husband to them,' declares the LORD."*

Please note that the statement was not that it will not be "like" or "according to" *the law* of the first covenant. Nothing is said in the prophecy about a different law, or for that matter, even a change in the law.

One might expect that to have been mentioned, for indeed changes in the law were made – many of them. But the law was not the problem. Man's sinful nature remaining sinful when making a covenant with God was the problem.

This was the problem being addressed in correcting the problem of covenant breaking. To change sinful man into spiritual man was God's solution. Stated briefly, it was to write His law on the hearts of His people rather than on stone and in a book:

"Forasmuch as ye are manifestly declared to be the epistle of Christ ministered by us, written not with ink, but with the Spirit of the living God; not in tables of stone, but in fleshly tables of the heart" (2 Cor. 3:3 KJV).   ---o-O-o---

Obey My Voice and I Will Be Your God
And You Shall Be My People

"I will put my law in their minds and write it on their hearts. I will be their God, and they will be my people" (Jeremiah 31:33b).

The last two clauses 1) *I will be their God,* and 2) *they shall be my people* are not new. That was also part of the Old Covenant: *"I will walk among you and be your God, and you will be my people"* (Leviticus 26:12).

Notice also the promise of God to Israel to "walk among" them. This was certainly carried out by the Lord as His Presence went among them through the wilderness experience. He turned His face from them and would not hear their prayers when they rebelled and worshipped others gods, taking up the customs of the heathen (see 2 Chronicles 7:14 and context).

"I will be their God, and they shall be my people" is a recurring theme of the prophets:

"I will take you as my own people, and I will be your God. Then you will know that I am the LORD your God, who brought you out from under the yoke of the Egyptians" (Exodus 6:7).
"I will walk among you and be your God, and you will be my people" (Leviticus 26:12).

"But I gave them this command: 'Obey me, and I will be your God and you will be my people. Walk in all the ways I command you, that it may go well with you.'" (Jeremiah 7:23).

"The terms I commanded your forefathers when I brought them out of Egypt, out of the iron-smelting furnace.' I said, 'Obey me and do everything I command you, and you will be my people, and I will be your God" (Jeremiah 11:4).

"So you will be my people, and I will be your God" (Jeremiah 30:22).

"You will live in the land I gave your forefathers; you will be my people, and I will be your God" (Ezekiel 36:28:).

The relationship, His being their God and their being His people, was dependent on Israel's obedience. But both houses of Israel broke the covenant they made to obey the voice of God, resulting in God's lament: *"Then the LORD said, 'Call him Lo-ammi, for you are not my people, and I am not your God'"* (Hosea 1:9).

Yet, God always offered hope – very next verse:

"Yet the Israelites will be like the sand on the seashore, which cannot be measured or counted. In the place where it was said to them, 'You are not my people,' they will be called `sons of the living God.'

"The people of Judah and the people of Israel will be reunited, and they will appoint one leader and will come up out of the land, for great will be the day of Jezreel" (Hosea 1:10).

Because Israel was disobedient, God gave both houses of Israel a "divorce": *"I gave faithless Israel her certificate of divorce and sent her away because of all her adulteries. Yet I saw that her unfaithful sister Judah had no fear; she also went out and committed adultery"* (Jeremiah 3:8).

This is written for our learning, as a warning that God will also separate us from Himself if we disobey, as Paul wrote about Israel:

"Well; because of unbelief they were broken off, and thou stan-dest by faith. Be not highminded, but fear: For if God spared not the natural branches, take heed lest he also spare not thee. Behold therefore the goodness and severity of God: on them which fell, se-verity; but toward thee, goodness, **if thou continue in his good-ness: otherwise thou also shalt be cut off"** (Rom. 11:20-22 KJV).

Again, the New Covenant's *newness, its being "not according to the old"; or the declaration, "It will not be like"* the old, was not stated to be *a different law,* but a different place of its writing – although changes were made in Old Covenant law to accommodate a new sacrifice, a new priesthood, and new ordinances of divine worship. Other changes in the law will also be noted as the study progresses.

The newness God foretold was to write His law in the hearts of His people, and the result would be, Yahweh would be their God, and they would be His people.

Although *this was the objective of the Old Covenant also,* the objec-tive was not reached because Israel broke the covenant with God. Un-der the new covenant, the objective could be achieved, *"I can do all things through Him who strengthens me"* (Philippians 4:13).

So it must be seen that when we speak of "Old Covenant" and "New Covenant,"[25] the subject will on occasion shift from God's Last

---

[25] "Old Testament" is commonly used to refer to the books of the Bible Genesis through Malachi, and "New Testament" is thought to refer to the books Matthew through Revelation. This concept originated from the concept that all scriptures writ-ten before the birth of Christ were part of the Old Covenant and therefore since the Old Covenant passed away and was replaced by the New Covenant, those scriptures, Genesis through Malachi, are not valid for the Christian era. The concept is not valid, because the New Scriptures validate the Old Scriptures consistently and repeat-edly.

In the Bible, the words "covenant" and "testament" have roughly the same mean-ing, and sometimes exactly equating with what we commonly term "Last Will and Testament," or a statement of what our heirs are to receive. The Covenant God made with Abraham had to do with what he and his offspring would inherit. The covenant made with Israel at Mt. Sinai had to do with the inheritance of the children of God (the children of Israel at that time); and the New Covenant made with the Children of God through the blood of His Son Jesus is also about inheritance. Both the cove-nants, new and old, deal with promises of an inheritance God made to His children.

Will and Testament as a whole to a discussion of the contents of the law God said He would write on the hearts and minds of His people, for His law was called "the covenant."

---o-O-o---

A Review – Kinds of Covenants

There are at least three kinds of covenants spoken of in the Bible. One, an agreement entered into by two or more parties. This sort of covenant may define relationships between God and men (*"I...will be their God, and they shall be my people"*); or between men and men: *"...I will hand over to you the people who live in the land and you will drive them out before you. Do not make a covenant with them or with their gods"* (Exodus 23:31, 32).

Such covenants can serve to specify the working relationships of those making the covenant.

For example, God said to Israel:

"'...if you will not listen to me and carry out all these commands, and if you reject my decrees and abhor my laws and fail to carry out all my commands and so violate my covenant, then I will do this to you: I will bring upon you sudden terror, wasting diseases and fever that will destroy your sight and drain away your life. You will plant seed in vain, because your enemies will eat it" (Leviticus 26:14-16).

Such warnings relate to God's requirements for His people, His children, to be and remain heirs to His kingdom and heirs of eternal life. As in the case of covenants between men, actions which breach the covenant make it void, releasing the other party from carrying out his obligations; and if the relations are resumed, at times it involves remedies or changes in the prior covenant; for instance when God promised a new covenant with Israel and Judah:

"'It will not be like the covenant I made with their forefathers when I took them by the hand to lead them out of Egypt, because they broke my covenant, though I was a husband to them,' declares the LORD " (Jeremiah 31:32).

In other words, if they refused to allow God to write His law on their hearts, they would have no covenant relationship with Him!

Another type of covenant is a will with an unqualified listing of heirs. It depends on who the individuals are; as for example, to inherit the kingdom of God and eternal life, one must be "Abraham's seed": *"If you belong to Christ, then you are Abraham's seed, and heirs according to the promise"* (Galatians 3:29).

If you are Abraham's seed, *you will* inherit what is promised to his heirs. However, the definition of "Abraham's seed" is a spiritual definition, and not a physical definition.[26]

It is this latter kind of will or covenant that is referred to in Galatians 3:17, where Paul says, *"What I mean is this: The law, introduced 430 years later, does not set aside the covenant previously estab-*

---

[26] John 8:31-47: To the Jews who had believed him, Jesus said, "If you hold to my teaching, you are really my disciples. Then you will know the truth, and the truth will you free." They answered him, "We are Abraham's descendants and have never been slaves of anyone. How can you say that we shall be set free?" Jesus replied, "I tell you the truth, everyone who sins is a slave to sin. Now a slave has no permanent place in the family, but a son belongs to it forever. So if the Son sets you free, you will be free indeed. I know you are Abraham's descendants. Yet you are ready to kill me, because you have no room for my word. I am telling you what I have seen in the Father's presence, and you do what you have heard from your father." "Abraham is our father," they answered. "If you were Abraham's children," said Jesus, "then you would do the things Abraham did. As it is, you are determined to kill me, a man who has told you the truth that I heard from God. Abraham did not do such things. You are doing the things your own father does." We are not illegitimate children," they protested. "The only Father we have is God himself."

"Jesus said to them, "If God were your Father, you would love me, for I came from God and now am here. I have not come on my own; but he sent me. Why is my language not clear to you? Because you are unable to hear what I say. You belong to your father, the devil, and you want to carry out your father's desire. He was a murderer from the beginning, not holding to the truth, for there is no truth in him. When he lies, he speaks his native language, for he is a liar and the father of lies. Yet because I tell the truth, you do not believe me! Can any of you prove me guilty of sin? If I am telling the truth, why don't you believe me? He who belongs to God hears what God says. The reason you do not hear is that you do not belong to God."

lished by God and thus do away with the promise." This covenant with Abraham depended rather on God's acknowledgment that we qualify as Abraham's seed.[27]

The same sort of covenant was made with David, and is called "the sure mercies of David," a promise that He would always have seed to sit on his throne.

It also is spoken of in the writings of Jeremiah:

"'The days are coming,' declares the LORD, 'when I will fulfill the gracious promise I made to the house of Israel and to the house of Judah. 'In those days and at that time I will make a righteous Branch sprout from David's line; he will do what is just and right in the land. In those days Judah will be saved and Jerusalem will live in safety.

"This is the name by which it will be called: The LORD Our Righteousness. For this is what the LORD says: 'David will never fail to have a man to sit on the throne of the house of Israel, nor will the priests, who are Levites, ever fail to have a man to stand before me continually to offer burnt offerings, to burn grain offerings and to present sacrifices'" (Jeremiah 33:14-18).

This prophecy refers both to the priesthood and the kingship, both of which are fulfilled in one Person, the Lord Jesus Christ:

*"Tell him this is what the LORD Almighty says: 'Here is the man whose name is the Branch, and he will branch out from his place and build the temple of the LORD. It is he who will build the temple of the LORD, and **he will be clothed with majesty and will sit and rule on his throne. And he will be a priest on his throne.** And there will be harmony between the two'"* (Zechariah 6:12, 13).

---

[27] John 8:39: "Abraham is our father," they answered. If you were Abraham's children," said Jesus, "then you would do the things Abraham did.." This may well refer to the statement of Genesis 26:5:

"...Abraham obeyed me and kept my requirements, my commands, my decrees and my laws." God says, in His declaration of a coming New Covenant, that the seed of Abraham failed to do that.

This prophecy is fulfilled in Christ, and it was a covenant with David that could not be broken, just like the covenant with Abraham. It was not a revocable covenant, not a breakable covenant, because it involved the very plan of salvation.

The following passage is quite revealing of this covenant based on a promise of God, and not dependent on performance:

"The word of the LORD came to Jeremiah: This is what the LORD says: 'If you can break my covenant with the day and my covenant with the night, so that day and night no longer come at their appointed time, then my covenant with David my servant – and my covenant with the Levites who are priests ministering before me – can be broken and David will no longer have a descendant to reign on his throne.

"I will make the descendants of David my servant and the Levites who minister before me as countless as the stars of the sky and as measureless as the sand on the seashore.' The word of the LORD came to Jeremiah: 'Have you not noticed that these people are saying, 'The LORD has rejected the two kingdoms he chose'? So they despise my people and no longer regard them as a nation.

"This is what the LORD says: 'If I have not established my covenant with day and night and the fixed laws of heaven and earth, then I will reject the descendants of Jacob and David my servant and will not choose one of his sons to rule over the descendants of Abraham, Isaac and Jacob. For I will restore their fortunes and have compassion on them'" (Jeremiah 33:19-26).

Why stated in such absolutes? Because the guarantee to both houses of Israel, the guarantee to David, the guarantee to the Levites, the guarantee to Abraham are all referring to the salvation ministry of Christ. Jesus was the focus of fulfillment of these promises.

Jesus is "David the King"; Jesus is the High Priest; Jesus is the "seed of Abraham" through whom all Israel *who are Israel* are saved: *"It is not as though God's word had failed. For not all who are descended from Israel are Israel"* (Romans 9:6).

Basically, the promise is secure to Abraham, that he would always have "children," or heirs; and the promise that he and his seed would inherit the earth cannot be nullified by any individual or group of individuals breaking covenant with God. It *was* and *is* an unqualified guarantee to Abraham, just as are the "sure mercies of David."

However, Abraham's *seed* (other than Jesus) did not collectively and do not individually have a guarantee that they will *remain* his seed. Note again what John admonished those coming to his baptism:

"Bring forth therefore fruits meet for repentance: And think not to say within yourselves, We have Abraham to our father: for I say unto you, that God is able of these stones to raise up children unto Abraham. And now also the axe is laid unto the root of the trees: therefore every tree which bringeth not forth good fruit is hewn down, and cast into the fire" (Matthew 3:8-10 KJV).

Was John "preparing the way of the Lord (Jesus Christ), teaching like Jesus taught and like Paul taught, or was John just reiterating an Old Covenant philosophy that God actually held His children accountable for their disobedience?

Jesus: *"He cuts off every branch in me that bears no fruit, while every branch that does bear fruit he prunes so that it will be even more fruitful* (John 15:2).

Paul: *"You will say then, 'Branches were broken off so that I could be grafted in.' Granted. But they were broken off because of unbelief, and you stand by faith. Do not be arrogant, but be afraid. For if God did not spare the natural branches, he will not spare you either"* (Romans 11:19-21).

Parts of God's Covenant: It is important to note these two aspects of God's covenant with Abraham. First, the covenant between God and Abraham was not conditional. God based His promise to Abraham on His personal knowledge of Abraham:

"And the LORD said, Shall I hide from Abraham that thing which I do; Seeing that Abraham shall surely become a great and mighty nation, and all the nations of the earth shall be blessed in him?

"For I know him, that he will command his children and his household after him, and they shall keep the way of the LORD, to do justice and judgment; that the LORD may bring upon Abraham that which he hath spoken of him" (Genesis 18:17-19, KJV).

What God knew about Abraham (above) was the important factor in God making an unconditional covenant with him. Israel breaking God's covenant through disobedience and loss of faith did not and could not nullify God's covenant with Abraham that he, Abraham, and his off-spring, his "seed," would inherit the promised land (a promise later transferred to inheriting the earth as the Kingdom of God).

It is just as true that God knows all of us and what we will do; but it is not true of all of us that *we* will command *our children* and their households after them to keep the way of the Lord, resulting in their doing justice and judgment.

Some who name the name of Christ break covenant with God just as Israel did. Paul states this clearly in Romans 11, where he gives the "Olive Tree" analogy. Citing the example of those of Israel who broke covenant with God, Paul warns us:

"You will say then, 'Branches were broken off so that I could be grafted in.' Granted. But they were broken off because of unbelief, and you stand by faith. Do not be arrogant, but be afraid. For if God did not spare the natural branches, he will not spare you ei-ther.

"Consider therefore the kindness and sternness of God: stern-ness to those who fell, but kindness to you, provided that you con-tinue in his kindness. Otherwise, you also will be cut off" (Romans 11:19-22).

Please be patient with the repetition of certain passages. Because people do not know how to reconcile their theology with the above and other passages, they tend to store them in a file named

"Talk over with Paul After the Resurrection!"

We need to reconcile our theology to these passages before then!

God's covenant with Abraham could not be nullified by the disobedience of some of the descendants of Abraham, as referred to in Genesis 17:7: *"I will establish my covenant as an everlasting covenant between me and you and your descendants after you for the generations to come, **to be your God and the God of your descendants after you**";* as also shown in 2 Kings 13:23: *"But the LORD was gracious to them and had compassion and showed concern for them because of his covenant with Abraham, Isaac and Jacob. To this day he has been unwilling to destroy them or banish them from his presence."*

---o-**O**-o---

The Preliminary Covenant With Israel
An "Open Ended" Covenant

Notice in detail the establishment of this covenant with Israel, as Moses led them out of Egypt and they came to the foot of Mount Sinai. First came the agreement between God and Israel to establish their relationship:

*"Then Moses went up to God, and the LORD called to him from the mountain and said, 'This is what you are to say to the house of Jacob and what you are to tell the people of Israel: 'You yourselves have seen what I did to Egypt, and how I carried you on eagles' wings and brought you to myself. **Now if you obey me fully and keep my covenant, then out of all nations you will be my treasured possession.***

"'Although the whole earth is mine, you will be for me a kingdom of priests and a holy nation.' These are the words you are to speak to the Israelites.' So Moses went back and summoned the elders of

the people and set before them all the words the LORD had com-
manded him to speak.

"The people all responded together, "We will do everything the
LORD has said." So Moses brought their answer back to the LORD"
(Exodus 19:3-8).

This sort of event is an integral part of God establishing a relationship with mankind, of our becoming a child of God, that we agree He
will be our God, we will be His people and obey Him. Note verse five
in the passage: *"Now if you obey me fully and keep my covenant, then*
out of all nations you will be my treasured possession."

This was not like the covenant with Abraham, in which there were
no "ifs," no conditions, as in the agreement between God and Israel.

This initial agreement at the foot of Mount Sinai constituted a covenant between God and Israel, and it was consummated before God
spoke the Ten Commandments audibly to the entire congregation of
Israel.

After making the agreement to serve God and obey Him, God began
revealing to them what they were to obey, which begins with a statement of how Israel was to love Him and show Him respect, being de-
voted only to Him:

"I am the LORD your God, who brought you out of Egypt, out of
the land of slavery. You shall have no other gods before me. You
shall not make for yourself an idol in the form of anything in heaven
above or on the earth beneath or in the waters below. You shall not
bow down to them or worship them;

"... for I, the LORD your God, am a jealous God, punishing the
children for the sin of the fathers to the third and fourth generation
of those who hate me, but showing love to a thousand generations
of those who love me and keep my commandments. You shall not
misuse the name of the LORD your God, for the LORD will not hold
anyone guiltless who misuses his name" (Exodus 20:2-7).

God had introduced Himself to Moses when giving Moses instructions to lead Israel out of Egypt, as He told Moses: *"Say to the Israelites, 'The LORD, the God of your fathers – the God of Abraham, the God of Isaac and the God of Jacob – has sent me to you'"* (See Exodus 3:15).

Again God introduces Himself speaking directly to the entire congregation of Israel, *"I am the LORD your God, who brought you out of Egypt, out of the land of slavery."*

They knew about Him! He was the God Who had poured out all the plagues on Egypt and had spared all Israel; He was the God who pushed back the waters of the "Mighty Red Sea" and let them go over on dry land; He was the God Who let the waters pour back upon the pursuing Egyptian army.

Immediately before this "preamble" to the Ten Commandments, through the mediation of Moses they had just agreed with Yahweh their God, to be His people and obey Him, and now they were beginning to hear directly from God what it was they were to obey.

They continued to hear what they were to obey for the next forty years as their God accompanied them in their desert wanderings, while God spoke to Moses and they received additional instructions.

In a very real sense, it was an open ended covenant. Even the prophets added, clarified, or modified as God instructed them.[28]

---o-**O**-o---

---

[28] "If you keep your feet from breaking the Sabbath and from doing as you please on my holy day, if you call the Sabbath a delight and the LORD 's holy day honorable, and if you honor it by not going your own way and not doing as you please or speaking idle words, then you will find your joy in the LORD, and I will cause you to ride on the heights of the land and to feast on the inheritance of your father Jacob." The mouth of the LORD has spoken." No such clarification of how God wished His people to observe the Sabbath was written in the previous laws or prophets, although those principles could be deduced by a careful study of previous commands to "hallow" the seventh day.

The Basic Covenant – Ten Commands

But here at Sinai, as Israel listened to the Voice from the Mountain, a *basic list* of things to obey was spoken directly to them. What they heard was a basic covenant with God, the Ten Commandments, which on occasion were spoken of as "the covenant."

But it was not enough for Israel just to hear the Ten Commandments by the voice of God; lest they forget, they were written down:

"Then the LORD said to Moses, "Write down these words, for in accordance with these words I have made a covenant with you and with Israel." Moses was there with the LORD forty days and forty nights without eating bread or drinking water. And he (God) wrote on the tablets the words of the covenant – the Ten Commandments" (Exodus 34:27, 28).

Later, Moses reminded Israel of their agreement with God:

"Then the LORD spoke to you out of the fire. You heard the sound of words but saw no form; there was only a voice. He declared to you his covenant, the Ten Commandments, which he commanded you to follow and then wrote them on two stone tablets" (Deuteronomy 4:12, 13).

It is important that we note and acknowledge that the Ten Commandments were the primary part of God's covenant with Israel. This becomes important as one recognizes the basis of the New Covenant, which was primarily that God would write His law on the hearts of His people.

There could be no denying the importance of the Ten Commandments in the New Covenant, were all believers to acknowledge this basic fact! It is these Ten Commands that God refers to primarily as "His" law in the promise of a new covenant.

Notice again how it works as Paul instructed the Romans:

"Therefore, there is now no condemnation for those who are in Christ Jesus, because through Christ Jesus the law of the Spirit of life set me free from the law of sin and death.

"For what the law was powerless to do in that it was weakened by the sinful nature, God did by sending his own Son in the likeness of sinful man to be a sin offering.

"And so he condemned sin in sinful man, in order that the right-eous requirements of the law might be fully met in us, **who do not live according to the sinful nature but according to the Spirit"** (Romans 8:1-4).

This law to be fully met in us is *basically* the Ten Commandments; it is what God called "my law" in prophesying the coming of a New Covenant: "I will put my law in their minds and write it on their hearts." *Just as it is God's basic covenant, it is God's basic law.*

One must not hurry on without digesting what is said in this section of the study, in particular the correlation between the above passage and God's declaration of a New Covenant by which He would write His law on the hearts of His people.

Look at the passage. The law which was powerless to set us free from sin and death, is the law which defines sin. It is basically the same Ten Commandment law called "the covenant," although God's "law" encompasses every *moral* precept set forth in the teachings of Moses (see 1 Timothy 1:3-11).

Why acknowledge the Ten Commandments were the basic law called the "covenant"? So that we not miss the point of God sending His Son, which bears repeating: *"And so he condemned sin in sinful man,* ***in order that the righteous requirements of the law might be fully met in us, who do not live according to the sinful nature but according to the Spirit."***

The sinful nature lives contrary to the righteous requirements of the law! The righteous requirements of the law are not met in those who do live according to the sinful nature!

- 58 -

"Not living according to the sinful nature but according to the spirit" is not some nebulous concept like a cloud that floats about the sky, changing shape, changing form, changing substance as it is driven about by "every wind of doctrine," looking like a man's hand to one, like a man's face to another, or completely without form to another!

God's law is an understandable set of concepts clearly stated by the Lord! Paul stated, *"We know that the law is spiritual; but I am unspiritual, sold as a slave to sin"* (Romans 7:14). How do we know the law is spiritual if we do not know its contents?

If the law is spiritual, living according to the instructions of the law is "living according to the Spirit"! One cannot honestly say otherwise, because one cannot live according to the law without having the Spirit of Christ.

When we are unspiritual, the law is powerless to guide us by its spiritual nature. But when we are no longer *unspiritual,* having become *spiritual* through faith in Christ and the Spirit of Christ, then we as spiritual individuals are capable of submitting to and obeying the law.

*"You, however, are controlled not by the sinful nature but by the Spirit, **if** the Spirit of God lives in you. And **if** anyone does not have the Spirit of Christ, he does not belong to Christ"* (Romans 8:9).

What *the law* was powerless to do, *God did!* With what intended results? *"That the righteous requirements of the law might be fully met in us,"* resulting in our not living according to the sinful nature but according to the Spirit.

Although the righteous requirement of a death sentence for *disobeying the law* is "fully met" by the atoning blood of Christ, the righteous requirements of the law being fulfilled *in us* comprehends, ***includes*** our living in agreement with, our submitting to, the law. The composite result is that *"we do not live according to the sinful nature but according to the Spirit."*

This is the fuller statement of the promise of the New Covenant that God would write His law in our hearts. Writing His law on our hearts and in our minds in general is called being "born again."

This is the same basic problem dealt with in clearing our feelings of guilt for sin. The offerings of the Old Covenant could not do that, because under the Old Covenant there was *no operation of the Holy Spirit in the process of making sacrifices* to write the law on men's hearts, nor give confidence of forgiveness. Making animal sacrifices did not change hearts nor ease consciences.

Under the New Covenant, *there is* a Holy Spirit operation to write God's law on our hearts, and consequently our consciences are cleared of the feeling of guilt: *"This is an illustration for the present time, indicating that the gifts and sacrifices being offered were not able to clear the conscience of the worshiper"* (Hebrews 9:9).

The gift (salvation through faith) and the sacrifice (the death of Jesus Christ for our sins) and the filling of the Holy Spirit *are able* to clear the conscience of the worshiper!

The difference is like trashing information on a computer disk, which means the space on the disk can be written over. However, the information is basically still there – this is Old Covenant. Under the Old covenant, the guilt was still there, the person still felt guilty.

But, if you "re-format" your computer hard drive, the information is no longer there, and reference to it cannot discover its former presence – this is New Covenant. Under the New Covenant, the guilt is not still there, and our consciences are wiped free of guilt. If you have not experienced this freedom of conscience, you are missing a wonderful aspect of the work of the Holy Spirit under the New Covenant:

"Let us draw near to God with a sincere heart in full assurance of faith, having our hearts sprinkled to cleanse us from a guilty conscience and having our bodies washed with pure water" (Hebrews 10:22).

It is worth repeating that "law" has validity in the discussion of God's last will and testament because both God's original written will at Sinai and His rewritten will are based on law. Hear it again:

"'The time is coming,' declares the LORD, 'when I will make a New Covenant with the house of Israel and with the house of Judah. It will not be like the covenant I made with their forefathers when I took them by the hand to lead them out of Egypt, because they broke my covenant, though I was a husband to them,' declares the LORD.

"'This is the covenant I will make with the house of Israel after that time,' declares the LORD. 'I will put my law in their minds and write it on their hearts. I will be their God, and they will be my people'" (Jeremiah 31:31-33)

The concept that both the old and New Covenants were (are) based on law rankles those who champion the idea that Christians are freed from observing the law. To be freed from the condemnation of the law is a completely different thing than being freed from observing the law. As children of God, as spiritual children of God, it is intended that we submit to the law of God (Romans 8:4, 7).

God writes His law in the hearts of His people for the purpose of their paying attention to it! Breaking the law is still sin – it is still true that *"Whosoever committeth sin transgresseth also the law: for sin is the transgression of the law"* (1 John 3:4, KJV). *"Therefore by the deeds of the law there shall no flesh be justified in his sight: for by the law is the knowledge of sin"* (Romans 3:20, KJV). The law was not intended for justification.   ---o-O-o---

No Change Without Cause

A last will and testament will not likely be changed without cause, and the reason God gave for changing His covenant with Israel was simply, *"It will not be like the covenant I made with their forefathers ... because they broke my covenant."* This is not a strange concept to parents who rewrite their wills because of rebellious, disrespectful children!

The cause for change was Israel breaking God's agreement with them. He did not criticize His own law as being part of the problem, as though He had expected too much of His children. Rather, He said He would write His law on their hearts *and in their minds!*

Today people make what they call "living wills," or "living trusts," and in a sense that is the kind of will God made with His people, Israel.

His old covenant was a "living will," able to be altered before the Will Maker died, but not after. There is however a difference in God's covenant, in that "heirs" can be added or removed after the death of the Will Maker.

Heirs were (and are) to be His people and believe in Him; they were and are to love Him with all their being, love their neighbors as themselves, and obey Him.

Israel, God's natural heirs, His "firstborn,"[29] broke their covenant with Him by not living up to the covenant's provisions. They were not obedient and lost faith (see Hebrews chapters 3, 4); without which they were disqualified as heirs,[30] as the covenant said they would be.

So what was the purpose of the New Covenant, God's revised will? It was to remedy the problems with the Old Covenant, the problems of disobedience and lack of faith – these were the elements by which God's children broke the Old Covenant.

---

[29] Exodus 4:22, 23: "Then say to Pharaoh, 'This is what the LORD says: Israel is my firstborn son, and I told you, "Let my son go, so he may worship me." But you refused to let him go; so I will kill your firstborn son. '"

[30] Jeremiah 11:1-4: "This is the word that came to Jeremiah from the LORD: "Listen to the terms of this covenant and tell them to the people of Judah and to those who live in Jerusalem. Tell them that this is what the LORD, the God of Israel, says: 'Cursed is the man who does not obey the terms of this covenant – the terms I commanded your forefathers when I brought them out of Egypt, out of the iron-smelting furnace.' I said, 'Obey me and do everything I command you, and you will be my people, and I will be your God."

God's method to remedy both problems is simple, and simply explained: *"I will put my law in their minds and write it on their hearts. I will be their God, and they will be my people."*[31]

If understood fully, we recognize that the difference in the place the New Covenant is written is the remedy for both aspects of weakness in the Old Covenant.

Lack of faith and lack of obedience both stemmed from the law not being written in the hearts and minds of God's children; and *even with the New Covenant provision of the law being written in our hearts, we are warned not to make the same mistakes Israel made:*

> *"Let us, therefore, make every effort to enter that rest, so that no one will fall by following their example of disobedience. For **the word of God is living and active.** Sharper than any double-edged sword, it penetrates even to dividing soul and spirit, joints and marrow; it judges the thoughts and attitudes of the heart.*
>
> *"Nothing in all creation is hidden from God's sight. Everything is uncovered and laid bare before the eyes of him to whom we must give account"* (Hebrews 4:11-13).

It is instructive to notice that "the word of God is living and active" – remember "lively oracles"? God Himself, takes note of our obedience or disobedience. He does not ignore the behavior of His children as some men do! But notice also what the "word of God" does – it judges the thoughts and attitudes *of the heart.*

Written within the heart, God's "lively oracles," His law, conflicts with sinful thoughts and attitudes of the heart, making a dissonance, making discord, until the spiritual nature can no longer tolerate the presence of sinful thoughts and attitudes.

One thing for sure, when the Word of God judges the thoughts and attitudes of the heart, His Word will detect whether His law is written

---

[31] In fact, but the practical manifestation of God writing His laws in the hearts and minds of His people encompasses the indwelling of the Holy Spirit, by which the children of God are enabled to believe and behave.

there! And, if it is not, that individual is not a participant in the new covenant!   ---o-O-o---

Worth Repeating

According to the prophecy in Jeremiah 31, one big difference between God's old "will" or covenant and His new or revised covenant, is the place God's law is written, in the hearts and minds of His people instead of on stone and in a book. That is confirmed in Paul's writing to the Corinthians:

"You show that you are a letter from Christ, the result of our ministry, written not with ink but with the Spirit of the living God, not on tablets of stone but on tablets of human hearts. " (2 Corinthians 3:3).

"Not with ink" is a reference to the law of Moses written in the Book of the Law, and "not on tablets of stone" is a reference to the stone tables on which the Ten Commandments were written.

Paul testifies in this observation about the Church at Corinth that the New Covenant was working! This is a question we Christians need to keep in mind about our own relations with God – *can others observe that God has written His law in our hearts and minds?* If not, we have a problem – a very serious problem!

Why? *"Do you not know that the wicked will not inherit the kingdom of God? Do not be deceived: Neither the sexually immoral nor idolaters nor adulterers nor male prostitutes nor homosexual offenders nor thieves nor the greedy nor drunkards nor slanderers nor swindlers will inherit the kingdom of God.*

"And that is what some of you were. But you were washed, you were sanctified, you were justified in the name of the Lord Jesus Christ and by the Spirit of our God" (1 Corinthians 6:9).

---o-O-o---

To a Thousand Generations

These considerations are important, because some teach that since the Ten Commandments are identified as "the covenant" of the old scriptures; and since the New Covenant would not be like the old, therefore the Ten Commandments are not like the New Covenant.

The challenge is simple, and the answer is simple, when one recognizes how the new was not to be like the old – written on hearts and in minds, not on stone and paper; a witness within us, not against us.[32]

Consider also the evidence in God's prelude to the Ten Commandments. After introducing Himself to Israel, God said:

"You shall not make for yourself an idol in the form of anything in heaven above or on the earth beneath or in the waters below. You shall not bow down to them or worship them; for I, the LORD your God, am a jealous God, punishing the children for the sin of the fathers to the third and fourth generation of those who hate me, but showing love to a thousand generations of those who love me and keep my commandments" (Exodus 20:4-6 KJV).

Do you see the intended contrast between punishment of the wicked and reward of the righteous? Compare receiving "three generations" of punishment with "a thousand generations" of reward! But there is more!

Shall we take these words of God as careless exaggeration? Can we make them meaningless as some kind of ancient "poetry" or a borrowed expression from neighboring nations without real meaning?

Perhaps it means only half as much time, like three days and three nights mean only one day and two nights. Will that help cut it down to about 2,000 years or less so as to expire at 33 A.D.?

---

[32] Deuteronomy 31:26: "Take this Book of the Law and place it beside the ark of the covenant of the LORD your God. There it will remain as a witness against you."

The question, *"Would commandment keeping still be important after a thousand generations, or not?"* is answered here!

When God spoke those words, *did He have any reference to the commandments which were just ready to be spoken?* Or was God just saying, "Whatever I am still commanding by then, I'll bless people for obeying"?

And would that be somewhat like the saying of Jesus to the Scribes and Pharisees, *"Thus you nullify the word of God by your tradition that you have handed down. And you do many things like that"* (Mark 7:13)? Probably more like the latter!

What does the Bible mean by a "generation"? Some concept of how time passes in the mind of God (in relation to this matter) is seen in Matthew 1:17: "Thus there were fourteen generations in all from Abraham to David, fourteen from David to the exile to Babylon, and fourteen from the exile to the Christ."

Now, we're not just speaking of "generations" from the time on Mt. Sinai when God gave the commandments, where God spoke of blessing to a thousand generations, we're adding 430 years back past that to Abraham; and from Abraham to Christ were only three sets of 14 generations, or 42 generations.

So how are we to understand these words from the very mouth of God that He would show love to a thousand generations of those who "love Me and keep My Commandments"?

Where did we get to by our own time – how many generations have come and gone since God spoke those words on Mt. Sinai? One chronology gives Abraham's time about 2,000 years before the birth of Christ. If that chronology is anywhere near correct, that was assigning about 50 years per generation.

But let's suppose men started generating earlier, and dying a lot earlier, and cut generations down to time levels of modern reckoning, like "Boomers," "Busters," "X-ers," and "Millennials" – four generations in a time period of about 60 years or less. Let's use that as a liberal concept, and ask, "How many generations from Christ till now?" 2,000 divided by 15 (to be very liberal in generations passed) gives us a little over 132 generations from the cross of Christ till a few years yet in our future. Forty-two generations Abraham to Christ, one for the birth of Christ till His death, makes 133 from Christ's birth till now – that only makes 175 generations.

Even at just 15 years to a generation a thousand generations would be 15,000 years. Cut it in half, like the three days and three nights, which traditionally really means one day and two nights – one still has 7,367 years too much time left to cut the Ten Commandments off by 33 A.D!

Shall we believe God will show a thousand generations of mercy to those who love Him and keep His commandments, or nullify the promises of God by our tradition of re-explaining everything the Bible says as not really meaning what it says, but some sociologically impenetrable meaning of wise men past?

Brethren, I think we've a few generations left to make a "thousand generations," which is how long God said in the preamble of the Ten Commandments that He would be showing mercy to those who love and obey Him!

It is not an accident that God leaves a "witness" here and there in His word and in dealing with His people. This declaration, this "spoken word," is a part of the "Oracles of God" about which Peter admonished that if we speak, we speak in agreement with, according to, those oracles.

But wait, perhaps there is a way out! Choose a different translation!

NASB: "... but showing lovingkindness to thousands, to those who love Me and keep My commandments" (Exodus 20:6).

NIV: "... but showing love to a thousand [generations] of those who love me and keep my commandments" (Exodus 20:6).

With this one, you may point out that "generations" is a supplied word, and only a thousand people will love God and keep His commands! Good going, NIV!

NRSV: "... but showing steadfast love to the thousandth generation of those who love me and keep my commandments" (Exodus 20:6). Perhaps this one should read "to the thousandth [of a] generation" that love and obey God!

RSV: "... but showing steadfast love to thousands of those who love me and keep my commandments" (Exodus 20:6).

Perhaps the Septuagint Greek will help:

Brenton: καὶ ποιῶν ἔλεος εἰς χιλιάδας τοῖς ἀγαπῶσίν με καὶ τοῖς φυλάσσουσιν τὰ προστάγματά μου. — "and bestowing mercy on them that love me to thousands of them, and on them that keep my commandments."

Now we're getting somewhere! You can take your choice, either be among the thousands who love God (a select few, just "thousands of those who love God") or an unlimited number of those who keep God's commandments *in addition to* the thousands who love Him!

Let's try another translation, called "God's Word" – billed as "today's translation that says what it means"! This translation, by the way, dislikes the word "sabbath" so much that it universally replaces "sabbath" with "the day of worship" or "a day of worship."

It reads: "... but I show mercy to thousands of generations of those who love me and obey my commandments." Not just a thousand generations, but "thousands of generations"!

The translators probably didn't think anyone would believe the commandments could be kept, so why not exaggerate a little – either way, nobody will believe or do it anyhow!

A more likely correct translation: How do modern Hebrew scholars translate the passage for modern Hebrews?

"I the LORD your God am an impassioned God, visiting the guilt of the parents upon the children, upon the third and upon the fourth generations of those who reject Me, but showing kindness to the thousandth generation of those who love Me and keep My commandments" (Exodus 20:5b-6 *Tanakh - The Holy Scriptures*, Jewish publication Society, 1988).

The construction seems to fit the concept that the third and fourth generations will suffer for the sins of the fathers of those generations. But, how does it go for those whose children love and obey God? The thousandth generation of those who love and obey God will still be enjoying God's blessing for their loving obedience.

Why, then, does this author choose the rendering, "to a thousandth generation" as preferable? Because it seems clearly to be in contrast to the "third and fourth generation" punishment, evil consequences of sins of the fathers plaguing offspring to the "third and fourth," [ordinal numbers]; contrasted with blessings of God's love and mercy to the thousandth generation [also an ordinal concept in contrast to third and fourth] of those who love God and keep His commandments.

Why do the translators struggle so much with this verse? Is the problem a theological one, that the commandments were not supposed to last so many generations, but only about 34 generations from Sinai till the cross?

The problems multiply! Why would God say "to a thousand generations" or even just to "thousands of them" that love Him <u>and keep His commands</u>, *if as modern Evangelicals claim, no person could or can obey God's law?*

Perhaps the larger problem is the concept embedded in the minds and hearts of many students of the Bible, that the Ten Commandments were the "Old Covenant" that passed away with the cross – which was only 43 generations after Abraham: *"Thus there were fourteen generations in all from Abraham to David, fourteen from David to the exile to Babylon, and fourteen from the exile to the Christ"* (Matthew 1:17). This averages out to about 50 years per generation.

God leaves bits of evidence against us once in a while. For example, the Book of the Law at the side of the ark of the covenant was a witness against Israel: *"Take this Book of the Law and place it beside the ark of the covenant of the LORD your God. There it will remain as a witness against you"* (Deuteronomy 31:26).

As a witness against Israel, the Book of the Law was a reminder of what God required of them as His people, a reminder that they were without excuse since it had been spoken to them by Yahweh Himself, and read to them by Moses. It was also a reminder of what would happen were they to break His covenant. They would not just cease to be His heirs, they would be punished severely.

And, as we have just seen, God has left another witness *inside His Ten Commandments, His "oracles,"* His audibly spoken words. As shown above, embedded within the Ten Commandments is this comment God made about His covenant people, that He would show love to a thousandth generation of those who love Him and keep His commandments."

At least 15,000 years of blessing those who love God *and keep His commandments* goes well past our day into the future from the time of the Exodus and Israel hearing God speak the Ten Commandments.

This author is not advocating a literal fulfillment of the "thousandth generation" concept, then that's all! Rather, an indefinite long time, considerably past the cross, a simple statement that God would always bless loving obedience to His law.

There is something rather lasting in the concept! It is worth consideration when one argues that the New Covenant was not according to the Old Covenant by virtue of abolishing the Ten Commandments! His comment is also an admonition and witness against those who claim they are not able to obey the Ten Commandments, and that *no man has ever been able to.*

Man says nobody has been able to obey the law. In contrast to what man says, *God* said He would show love to a thousandth generation of those who *do love him* and *do keep His commandments* – *at the very least, to thousands who love God and keep His commandments!*

Paul had it right! *"Let God be true, and every man a liar. As it is written: 'So that you may be proved right when you speak and prevail when you judge'"* (Romans 3:4).

No doubt anticipating the false notion that even Christians filled with the Holy Spirit cannot obey Him, God says through Paul:

"No temptation has seized you except what is common to man. And God is faithful; he will not let you be tempted beyond what you

can bear. But when you are tempted, he will also provide a way out so that you can stand up under it" (1 Corinthians 10:13).

Is it just a coincidence that the same theme of love based obedience is reiterated in the words of Jesus? He said, *"If you love me, you will obey what I command"* (John 14:15). And some claimants to His estate essentially respond, "Sorry, Lord! Nobody *has ever* been able to do that!"

Which is equivalent to "Nobody *loves* you *that much!"* And sadly, that is true, so far as perfect love and perfect obedience are concerned. Why? Because if we loved God perfectly, if we loved Him with all our heart, mind, soul and strength, we would have no love for sin and the things of the world, and would have no strength left for sin if we loved God with all our might! God makes it possible to love perfectly, see 1 Corinthians 10:13, above. If we sin, it is a lack of love on our part.

Does God expect perfect obedience of His children? Even though He demands it, makes it possible, He is aware that even His children will be disobedient on occasion, and He provides a remedy. It is two part:

1) Discipline, redeeming correction, and

2) *"My dear children, I write this to you so that you will not sin. But if anybody does sin, we have one who speaks to the Father in our defense – Jesus Christ, the Righteous One"* (1 John 2:1).

"If we confess our sins, he is faithful and just and will forgive us our sins and purify us from all unrighteousness" (1 John 1:9).

Christian, the way of escape, a "way" on which we can stand up under temptation, has been provided. The problem is we just do not seek the way, or if aware of it, do not choose the "way out"!

Admittedly, as Jesus observed, not the majority, but a minority of people obtain, then retain, a status as heirs of God and joint heirs with Christ;[33] however, *there was never a time, never a generation, when God had no faithful heirs – there would be a thousand generations of those who loved God and kept His commandments."* You can bank on it!

---

[33] Matthew 7:13: "Enter through the narrow gate. For wide is the gate and broad is the road that leads to destruction, and many enter through it."

This places God squarely on the opposite side of the modern contention that it is impossible and always has been impossible to keep the law, referring specifically to the Ten Commandments. Some who claim to be His children teach that. But what did God say? That He would show love to *a thousandth generation of those who love Him and keep His commandments* (Exodus 20:4-6).

If it is acceptable for those who oppose God in this matter to repeat over and over that man cannot obey God, it is more acceptable to repeat over and over what God said about it! One may have no difficulty surmising Whose Word man will tire of hearing first – *we men love to hear ourselves talk!*

Paul's response is this: *"What if some did not have faith? Will their lack of faith nullify God's faithfulness? Not at all! Let God be true, and every man a liar. As it is written: 'So that you may be proved right when you speak and prevail when you judge'"* (Romans 3:3,4). God was not unreasonable when He expected Israel (and us) to obey His commandments!   ---o-O-o---

Not Valid Until the Will-Maker Dies

Perhaps you had not thought of "covenants" as "wills" and you need verification that this discussion is on the right track. One confirming concept is that what God promises His children is an *inheritance*. This theme of inheritance is constant throughout both the old and new Scriptures, and God's "wills" (old and new) spell out what the inheritance is to be.

The Bible speaks of the children of God "inheriting" the earth. It speaks of His people inheriting the kingdom of God, and inheriting eternal life (see Matthew 5:5; 19:29; 1 Corinthians 6:9); it speaks of God's people as heirs, as being "joint heirs" with Christ (see Romans 8:17; Galatians 3:29; Ephesians 3:6; Titus 3:7; Hebrews 6:17; Hebrews 11:9).

So being heirs as defined and qualified in God's "Last Will and Testament" is not foreign to the meaning of the text. This *sounds* reasonable, but is it faithful to the biblical usage? The Bible becomes very specific in equating "covenant" with a "will" – a will like men make when they specify the inheritance of their own children:

"For this reason Christ is the mediator of a New Covenant, that those who are called may receive the promised eternal inheritance – now that he has died as a ransom to set them free from the sins committed under the first covenant.

"In the case of a will, it is necessary to prove the death of the one who made it, because a will is in force only when somebody has died; it never takes effect while the one who made it is living. *This is why even the first covenant was not put into effect without blood.*

"When Moses had proclaimed every commandment of the law to all the people, he took the blood of calves, together with water, scarlet wool and branches of hyssop, and sprinkled the scroll and all the people. He said, 'This is the blood of the covenant, which God has commanded you to keep.'

"In the same way, he sprinkled with the blood both the tabernacle and everything used in its ceremonies. In fact, the law requires that nearly everything be cleansed with blood, and without the shedding of blood there is no forgiveness" (Hebrews 9:15-22).

Take particular note of two clauses:

1) *"This is why even the first covenant was not put into effect without blood."* *What* is why? The first covenant required a death because it was a will, and a will does not take effect without a death. There can be no dispute the writer means the first covenant was a will. And then:

2) *"In the case of a will, it is necessary to prove the death of the one who made it, because a will is in force only when **somebody** has died; it never takes effect while the one who made it is living."*

NEVER? *REALLY?* Really! The *One Who made it* must die? Even in the case of the first covenant? Yes! It was not made by bulls and goats, it was made by Yahweh, God of Israel! In other words, Yahweh must

- 73 -

die for it to take effect. The blood of bulls and goats cannot take away sin, but the death of Jesus Christ did!

Is Jesus called "Yahweh"? Yes!

*"See, I am sending an angel ahead of you to guard you along the way and to bring you to the place I have prepared. Pay attention to him and listen to what he says. Do not rebel against him; he will not forgive your rebellion, **since my Name is in him**"* Exodus 23:20, 21).

*"They all ate the same spiritual food, and drank the same spiritual drink; for **they drank from the spiritual rock that accompanied them, and that rock was Christ**"* (1 Corinthians 10:4).

"For this reason Christ is the mediator of a new covenant, that those who are called may receive the promised eternal inheritance – now that he has died as a ransom to set them free from the sins committed under the first covenant" (Hebrews 9:15).

Can a will be changed, once having taken effect by the death of the one who made it? Let us not speculate, since Paul gives the answer: *"Brothers, let me take an example from everyday life. Just as no one can set aside or add to a human covenant that has been duly established, so it is in this case"* (Galatians 3:15).

To adequately consider the implications of the statement, one must answer these questions:

1) Who made the Old Covenant that has faded away? It was not made by the animals, the bulls, calves, goats, sheep, doves and pigeons that died! It was made by God!

2) Does the statement about death of the maker of the will apply to both the first (the old) covenant and the last (the new) covenant? Yes, it does!

3) What are the implications of the fact *the One Who made the first covenant* (God) did not die, but rather, calves, sheep, goats, etc. died?

The Bible explains – read it again: *"For this reason Christ is the mediator of a New Covenant, that those who are called may receive the promised eternal inheritance – now that he has died as a ransom to set them free from the sins committed under the first covenant"* (Hebrews 9:15).

It is important that we understand and believe what is being said, otherwise we will never grasp the fullness of the Covenants and the role they play. For example, why was it necessary for Christ to die as a ransom to set people free from the sins committed under the first covenant, if under the first covenant they had been covered by the blood of animals?

To understand, one must accept the biblical statement, *"...it is impossible for the blood of bulls and goats to take away sins"* (Hebrews 10:4); and accept the statement in the Bible, *"In fact, the law requires that nearly everything be cleansed with blood, and without the shedding of blood there is no forgiveness."*

Particular attention must be given this seldom dealt with statement: *"In the case of a will, **it is necessary to prove the death of the one who made it**, because a will is in force only when **somebody** has died; **it never takes effect while the one who made it is living"*** (Hebrews 9:16, 17).

If the blood of bulls and goats cannot take away sin, then the sins committed under the first covenant were not taken away until the death of Christ, the One Who made it, as declared in Hebrews 9:15.

So, who has to die to put God's will into effect for His heirs? Not bulls, heifers, calves, goats, sheep, doves – they did not make the will, God did!

This is direct affirmation that Christ was the one dealing with Moses and the elders of Israel on Mt. Sinai. He acted in His Father's stead, using His Father's name, and this explains the occasions when the Bible speaks of the "LORD" (Yahweh) being seen by Moses and the elders of Israel, when Jesus says no one has ever seen the Father.

The will also had to be written while the Will-Maker (Christ) was living for His death to ratify it! This truth has profound doctrinal implications, for the will cannot be changed after the death of the "Testator" (King James Version) "one who made it" (NIV):

"Brothers, let me take an example from every day life. Just as no one can set aside or add to a human covenant that has been duly established, so it is in this case" (Galatians 3:15).

"This case" refers to our covenant with God through Christ as "seed" of Abraham. It is our currently valid covenant with God, the New Covenant.

Was the New Covenant "duly established" by the death and blood of Christ? Indeed it was, and hence *there were no changes made in the covenant after the death of Christ – all changes made were ratified by His death and therefore made before He died!*

"Brothers, let me take an example from every day life. Just as no one can set aside or add to a human covenant that has been duly established, so it is in this case" (Galatians 3:15). Did the cross "duly establish" the new covenant? Indeed yes!

The cross also duly established the promises to those who were faithful under the Old Covenant. Christ, the Will Maker, not having died yet is why the Old Covenant could be changed, rewritten, modified, so long as the Maker of the Will had not died. The Old Covenant was changed every time a new provision was added in God's laws given through Moses.   ---o-O-o---

Cause for Great Assurance

Understanding Paul's statement gives certainty and permanence to the New Covenant, *"Brothers, let me take an example from every day life. Just as no one can set aside or add to a human covenant that has been duly established, so it is in this case"* (Galatians 3:15).

This is a guarantee by the death of our Savior that the New Covenant will not be changed, either by God or man. God, by choice, will not change the provisions of the New Covenant sealed by the death of His Son. God will not, and man cannot change God's law which forms an integral part of that now unchangeable covenant.

Galatians 3:15 lays the question to rest whether any changes in the law made by Christ before the cross were part of the New Covenant, and whether changes after the cross have any validity. Only changes made prior to the cross or occasioned by the cross have validity.

Hear it again: *"Brothers, let me take an example from every day life. Just as **no one can set aside or add to a human covenant that has been duly established, so it is in this case"** (Galatians 3:15). The New Covenant was "duly established" by the death of the Testator, Jesus.

The covenant doctrines this truth impacts are those taught by Jesus in His ministry – *they are thereby affirmed;* and any perceived covenant doctrinal changes – or changes in the law – effected after the death and resurrection of Christ, such as the observance of Sunday instead of the Sabbath, *are thereby null and void and exposed as false doctrines of men!*

Why? Because the terms of the covenant had to be stated before His death! Read again the print in bold immediately above – we *must* integrate it into our theology! This has particular reference to terms of the covenant, which relate to law and matters of atonement and justification, not just revelation of kingdom truths, such as explaining the resurrection and end time revelations. *Additional truth* was revealed after His death, but the covenant was not changed after His death.

---o-O-o---

Terms of the Old Covenant Changed Before the Cross?

If we do not understand that the Old Covenant was an "open-ended" covenant which God was free to change at His pleasure, we will not arrive at the truth in covenant matters. First, let's consider the proposition that it was an open-ended covenant, one that God could add to or delete from at will.

So long as the person making a will has not died, he can change his will as he chooses. God chose to follow the same reasoning. Since Jesus Christ had not died before the cross, the covenant could be changed at God's pleasure. He changed it many times by adding rules and regulations or modifying ones previously given, sometimes on the basis of Israel's disobedience.

Consider Israel's response to the terms of God's covenant with them: *"The people all responded together, 'We will do everything the LORD has said.' So Moses brought their answer back to the LORD"* (Exodus 19:8).

At the time of this response, neither the Ten Commandments nor the Book of the Law had been given or written. Then followed the giving of the Ten Commandments aloud to all of Israel. This frightened the congregation, who plead with Moses that he listen to God and tell them later what God said. They feared they would die if they heard the voice of God.

Moses complied, God allowed the request, then spoke the basics of the "Book of the Law" to Moses. This is recorded in Exodus 20b through 23.

Then, *"When Moses went and told the people all the LORD's words and laws, they responded with one voice, 'Everything the LORD has said we will do.' Moses then wrote down everything the LORD had said"* (Exodus 24:3-4a).

To the point of the first two verbal agreements to obey God and be His people, no blood had been shed to ratify the covenant, but then note what happened:

"He (Moses) got up early the next morning and built an altar at the foot of the mountain and set up twelve stone pillars representing the twelve tribes of Israel.

"Then he sent young Israelite men, and they offered burnt offerings and sacrificed young bulls as fellowship offerings to the LORD. Moses took half of the blood and put it in bowls, and the other half he sprinkled on the altar.

"Then he took the Book of the Covenant and read it to the people. They responded, "We will do everything the LORD has said; we will obey."

"Moses then took the blood, sprinkled it on the people and said, "This is the blood of the covenant that the LORD has made with you in accordance with all these words" (Exodus 24:4-8).

Three times Israel agreed to obey everything God commanded: Once before even hearing it; another time before it was written in a book when Moses reported it orally to Israel; then after Moses wrote it in the book he came back and read it to Israel. They agreed again after hearing it all, to obey everything they were commanded.

Sometimes we overlook important clues, as shown before. Notice this statement: *"When Moses had proclaimed every commandment of the law to all the people, he took the blood of calves, together with water, scarlet wool and branches of hyssop, and sprinkled the scroll and all the people"* (Hebrews 9:19).

This event is recorded in Exodus 24:1-8, where it is recorded, "When Moses went and told the people *all the LORD's words and laws,* they responded with one voice, 'Everything the LORD has said we will do.'"

Circumcision is declared to be a part of the law of Moses in John 7:23; but, nothing was said about circumcision in the 19th through 24th chapters of Exodus, and circumcision was not practiced for the next 40 years![34] The Old Covenant was ratified without mention of the rite.

There was nothing about "clean and unclean" animals anywhere from Abraham through the book of Exodus; yet the book of Hebrews and Exodus 24 both affirm that when the book was sprinkled to confirm the covenant, Moses had already "proclaimed every commandment of the law to all the people."

So it was true that Moses had "proclaimed every commandment of the law to all the people" by the time of sprinkling Israel and the book with the blood of the Old Covenant in Exodus 24. What was referred to in the statement included *all that was in the law by then.*

---

[34] Josh. 5:4   Now this is why he did so: All those who came out of Egypt --all the men of military age --died in the desert on the way after leaving Egypt.
Josh. 5:5, 7: "All the people that came out *(i.e., from Egypt)* had been circumcised, but all the people born in the desert during the journey from Egypt had not." "So he raised up their sons in their place, and these were the ones Joshua circumcised. They were still uncircumcised because they had not been circumcised on the way."

But Moses warns Israel in Deuteronomy 28:58, 59, *"If you do not carefully follow all the words of this law, which are written in this book, and do not revere this glorious and awesome name – the LORD your God – the LORD will send fearful plagues on you and your descendants, harsh and prolonged disasters, and severe and lingering illnesses."*

By then, at the end of the 40 years, the law of circumcision, the law of circumcision on the eighth day, and the laws of clean and unclean had been added to the book of the law and became not only a part of the old covenant, but a part of the law of Moses. This is clear evidence of the "open ended" nature of Old Covenant law.

So Let's Review:

Israel made a verbal covenant with God to obey Him and be His people before hearing any of what they were to obey except Passover and Sabbath observance and related rules:

> *"Now if you obey me fully and keep my covenant, then out of all nations you will be my treasured possession. Although the whole earth is mine, you will be for me a kingdom of priests and a holy nation. These are the words you are to speak to the Israelites."*
>
> *"So Moses went back and summoned the elders of the people and set before them all the words the LORD had commanded him to speak. The people all responded together, "We will do everything the LORD has said." So Moses brought their answer back to the LORD"* (Exodus 19:5-8).

They agreed to obey God and be His people before they heard God speak the Ten Commandments. Before they were written they heard additional commandments from God through Moses. They agreed to obey everything God had commanded to that point *before any of it was written.* These additional ordinances, with the Ten, became the first contents of the book of the covenant

The covenant was all written in the Book of the Covenant before Moses went up into the Mount to receive the tables of stone on which were written the Ten Commandments.

You should notice that the book of the covenant was initiated with blood at the same time the Ten Commandments were initiated with blood, for they were all in the Book of the Covenant together, and all were read to the congregation by Moses *before the ten were written on stone!*

The sacrifices were made to ratify the covenant, and half the blood of the animals was used for sprinkling the altar on which they were sacrificed and on the people themselves.

The Ten and the other commands of Exodus 20b through Exodus 23 were all agreed to at the same time again, *after* Moses read them all from the Book of the Covenant. All were verbally agreed to, then initiated with blood at the same time.

These were the initial ingredients of the covenant of God with Israel, as written in Exodus 20-23, the contents of the "Book of the Law," including the Ten Commandments.

These were the beginning commands which Israel covenanted verbally to obey – first when they had not yet heard the commands they were to obey, then when Moses relayed them from the Lord they agreed again, and after they were written and read from the book, they again agreed, then it was sealed with the blood of sacrificed animals.

The Book of the Law, the Book of the Covenant, came into existence after God spoke the Ten Commandments to all the congregation of Israel, but before the Ten were written by the Lord on tables of stone.

So before the covenant was initiated with blood, Israel had agreed three times to obey what God commanded, once before knowing what they were to obey, and twice after knowing; it was first recited to them by Moses, then read to them by Moses, then ratified with blood.

This verbal, then written, covenant that they would obey all that God commanded was made with Israel. Then the covenant was sealed with blood, even before the tablets of stone were fashioned to be written on, before the Ten Commandments were written on stone.

This covenant was worded in such a way that everything God commanded later through Moses and the prophets was automatically included in the law.

This is one of the reasons our "forefathers" in the Church of God (Seventh Day) called attention to the distinctions between the Ten Commandments and the Book of the Law, even though the Ten were written in the Book of the Law before they were written on stone.

The Ten were spoken aloud to all Israel, none of the rest were. *Even after* the covenant was ratified with blood, the Ten were written on tables of stone, while the rest were only written in the book. To suggest God had no particular reason for this distinction would not seem rational.

So, even though the Ten Commandments are called the covenant, even though the Tables of Stone are called the tables of the covenant, the covenant existed in a book before it was initiated with blood; and the book had two and a half chapters of additional words, more than the Ten Commandments, when the Covenant was initiated with the blood of animals.

After this, Moses and the seventy elders of Israel had their encounter with God on the lower parts of the Mount, seeing Him and not suffering from it (Exodus 24:9-11).

Then Moses and Aaron were called further up the Mount, and finally Moses was alone with God for forty days and nights, to receive the stone tablets containing the Ten Commands: *"The LORD said to Moses, 'Come up to me on the mountain and stay here, and I will give you the tablets of stone, with the law and commands I have written for their instruction' "* (Exodus 24:12).

Moses went up into the mount after writing the Book and reading it to Israel, after initiating the covenant by sacrificing and sprinkling the blood on Israel.

Having sealed the covenant with blood, Moses spent forty days in the mount receiving instructions for the tabernacle construction, the priesthood and mode of making sacrifices; God also told Moses to give special instructions to Israel about observing the Sabbath and the Sabbath's significance; then God wrote the Ten Commandments on two stone tablets and sent Moses back down the Mount.

After the rebellion of the people, the making and worshipping of the golden calf, and after Moses broke the tables of the covenant, God had

Moses make another set of stone tablets, called him back into the mountain.

Please note the statement of God below in bold type. It affirms that God was *in process* of making a covenant. When God called Moses, this conversation took place:

"Moses bowed to the ground at once and worshipped. 'O Lord, if I have found favor in your eyes," he said, "then let the Lord go with us. Although this is a stiff-necked people, forgive our wickedness and our sin, and take us as your inheritance.'

"Then the LORD said: 'I am making a covenant with you. *Before all your people I will do wonders never before done in any nation in all the world. The people you live among will see how awesome is the work that I, the LORD, will do for you. Obey what I command you today'"* (Exodus 34:8-11).

---o-**O**-o---

The Covenant Was a "Work in Progress"

This was after Israel made the verbal covenant to obey and be God's people (Exodus 19), after Israel heard God speak the Ten Commandments (Exodus 20), after giving the first set of extra instructions, which, with the Ten Commandments, were written in the original copy of the Book of the Law (Exodus 20b-23); it was after the seventy elders of Israel saw God, after Moses read the Book of the Law to all Israel and the covenant was agreed to verbally by Israel again and initiated with blood (Exodus 24).

Then, after the first forty-day trip of Moses up into the Mount, at the beginning of the second forty-day trip up the mountain, God said He was "making a covenant" with Moses and Israel. During that trip, God wrote on the replacement set of stone tablets, and greatly amplified the instructions for the Book of the Law.

We skip now to the end of the 40 years' wandering in the desert. The writing had continued as the law continued to unfold. This was recorded at the end of Moses' leadership and life: *"So Moses wrote* down this law and gave it to the priests, the sons of Levi, who carried the ark of the covenant of the LORD, and to all the elders of Israel" (Deuteronomy 31:9).

Making the covenant was a process which continued throughout the life and leadership of Moses, and surprisingly, "making a covenant" did not end with the life of Moses. As the leadership of Joshua began, God spoke to Joshua preparing him and Israel for crossing the Jordan into the Promised Land.

God said in part, *"Do not let this Book of the Law depart from your mouth; meditate on it day and night, so that you may be careful to do everything written in it. Then you will be prosperous and successful"* (Joshua 1:8).

Then just before Joshua died, he recounted the history of God calling Abraham, Israel's slavery in Egypt, their deliverance and covenant-making under Moses' leadership, and this noteworthy passage is written:

"Then the people answered, 'Far be it from us to forsake the LORD to serve other gods! It was the LORD our God himself who brought us and our fathers up out of Egypt, from that land of slavery, and performed those great signs before our eyes. He protected us on our entire journey and among all the nations through which we traveled. And the LORD drove out before us all the nations, including the Amorites, who lived in the land. We too will serve the LORD, because he is our God.'

"Joshua said to the people, 'You are not able to serve the LORD. He is a holy God; he is a jealous God. He will not forgive your rebellion and your sins. If you forsake the LORD and serve foreign gods, he will turn and bring disaster on you and make an end of you, after he has been good to you.'

"But the people said to Joshua, 'No! We will serve the LORD.'

"Then Joshua said, "You are witnesses against yourselves that you have chosen to serve the LORD."

"Yes, we are witnesses," they replied.

"Now then," said Joshua, "throw away the foreign gods that are among you and yield your hearts to the LORD, the God of Israel.

"And the people said to Joshua, 'We will serve the LORD our God and obey him.'

"On that day Joshua made a covenant for the people, and there at Shechem he drew up for them decrees and laws. And Joshua recorded these things in the Book of the Law of God" (Joshua 24:16-26).

In fact, this covenant-making between God and Israel continued as the prophets received messages from God for Israel and their messages altered the covenant either by addition or deletion.

Addition: See God's promises regarding faithful tithe-paying in Malachi 3.

Deletion: See Ezekiel 18:2: *"What do you people mean by quoting this proverb about the land of Israel: "'The fathers eat sour grapes, and the children's teeth are set on edge'?";* and Jeremiah 31:29: *"In those days people will no longer say, 'The fathers have eaten sour grapes, and the children's teeth are set on edge.'"*

These sayings had reference to the children of "God haters" bearing the iniquity of their fathers unto the third and fourth generation.

Additions to and deletions from the Book of the Law are even found in the ministry of Christ. Obviously the statement of Christ that not a jot or tittle would pass from the law till all was fulfilled indicated that even before the cross many of God's instructions had already been fulfilled.

This is one reason the word of God is described as *"...living and active. Sharper than any double-edged sword, it penetrates even to dividing soul and spirit, joints and marrow; it judges the thoughts and attitudes of the heart"* (Hebrews 4:12).

---o-O-o---

Possible Because the Covenant-Maker
Had not Died!

Why make the point that the Covenant God made with Israel was a living, pulsating, growing matter? Simply to show that until the death of Christ on the cross God exercised His freedom to change His instructions, His covenant, with Israel – after all, *He is God!*

The covenant maker had not died, and until He died, He was perfectly free according to His own adopted "rules" to change the terms of His will – and He frequently did so, in response to Israel's need of further instructions or correction.

But when the Will-Maker (Jesus) died, no further changes in the Covenant between God and His people would be made. As pointed out earlier, God, like men, even made a new will when the old did not adequately serve His purposes, and when His heirs had broken the terms of His first covenant. To redeem His heirs and establish His kingdom despite the sins of His people, He deleted many of the terms of the Old Covenant, but incorporated His laws of righteousness in the new:

1) *"In the case of a will, it is necessary to prove the death of the one who made it, because a will is in force only when somebody has died; it never takes effect while the one who made it is living"* (Hebrews 9:16, 17).

2) *"Brothers, let me take an example from everyday life. Just as no one can set aside or add to a human covenant that has been duly established, so it is in this case"* (Galatians 3:15).

3) *"For the priesthood being changed, there is made of necessity a change also of the law"* (Hebrews 7:12). For a more complete picture of the changes, read Hebrews 7-10.

4) *"For what the law was powerless to do in that it was weakened by the sinful nature, God did by sending his own Son in the likeness of sinful man to be a sin offering. And so he condemned sin in sinful man, in order that the righteous requirements of the law might be fully met in*

us, who do not live according to the sinful nature but according to the Spirit" (Romans 8:3, 4).   ---o-O-o---

The Covenant at Sinai – Also a "Will"?

Only one word is used in the New Testament Greek to refer to "covenant," "testament," or "will." That word is **"διαθήκη"** (dia-thay'kay) as in Hebrews 9:16, 17: "ὅπου γὰρ **διαθήκη**, θάνατον ἀνάγκη φέρεσθαι τοῦ διαθεμένου. **διαθήκη** γὰρ ἐπὶ νεκροῖς βεβαία, ἐπεὶ μήποτε ἰσχύει ὅτε ζῇ ὁ διαθέμενος."

The above in English: *"In the case of a will, it is necessary to prove the death of the one who made it, because a will is in force only when somebody has died; it never takes effect while the one who made it is living"* (Hebrews 9:16, 17).

This is true of the New Covenant. Is it true also of the covenant made with Israel at Sinai? Is it correct to say that the Old Covenant was a "will"? Who made the first "covenant," the first "will"? According to the Bible, it was God.

If the covenant with Abraham, Isaac, Jacob and the Children of Israel was a "will," stipulating what the Children of God must do to be His heirs (the covenant was that), then according to Hebrews 9:16, 17, ***God must die*** in order that it might take effect.

One can see a complete rejection of this thesis on the basis of that last statement, but hear the thesis out.

There is a relationship here between God's covenant with Abraham, and Abraham's willingness to sacrifice his only son (of the covenant) Isaac,[35] and God's willingness to sacrifice His only begotten Son, Jesus, not only "as good as dead," but actually dead. Their sons (Isaac and Jesus) were the seed through whom the covenant was consummated.

Does the fact that God, the Father, has never died, prove that the first covenant was not a "will," not a *"διαθήκη"*? Or, does it prove

---

[35] Hebr. 11:12 KJV: "Therefore sprang there even of one, and him as good as dead, so many as the stars of the sky in multitude, and as the sand which is by the sea shore innumerable."

that the first covenant also was arranged by Jesus, and the first covenant was ratified by the death of Jesus, just as the New Covenant, the "new will," was ratified by His death?

If the One who made it did not die to ratify it, one might conclude that it was not a will, just a working contract.

But if Christ is spoken of as God (and He is), and

If Christ was the Rock in the Wilderness with Israel as Paul teaches in 1 Corinthians 10:4 (and he was), and

If Jesus Christ was then the One Who made out that first will, and

If He was the One Who died to validate it, then

The plan all falls into place, making it reasonable that *"... for this cause he is the mediator of the new testament, that by means of death, for the redemption of the transgressions that were under the first testament, they which are called might receive the promise of eternal inheritance. For where a testament is, there must also of necessity be the death of the testator "* (Hebrews 9:15 KJV).

If you study the passage carefully, it becomes clear that Jesus became the "testator" or mediator of both the old and the new covenants.

The blood of the first covenant was the blood of sacrificial animals only temporarily. Their blood could not take away sin – and their sins were not taken away until Christ, Who *"...died as a ransom to set them free from the sins committed under the first covenant."* So in reality, even the first covenant was not *fulfilled* until the death of Jesus Christ on the cross! This is the clear meaning of Hebrews 9:15, 16.

Consider the passage again:

"The blood of goats and bulls and the ashes of a heifer sprinkled on those who are ceremonially unclean sanctify them so that they are outwardly clean. How much more, then, will the blood of Christ, who through the eternal Spirit offered himself unblemished to God, cleanse our consciences from acts that lead to death, so that we may serve the living God!

"For this reason Christ is the mediator of a new covenant, that those who are called may receive the promised eternal inheritance – now that he has died as a ransom to set them free from the sins

committed under the first covenant" (Hebrews 9:13 – 15). *"... because it is impossible for the blood of bulls and goats to take away sins"* (Hebrews 10:4).

Again, how can it be that Jesus died as a ransom to set free those who died under the first covenant? That implies He was also the One who made the first covenant, if His death ratified the aims and purposes of that covenant, to set God's called out ones free from sin and assure them an inheritance!

Whereas the New International Version uses the words *"was not put into effect"* (about initiating the first covenant), the NASB *(New American Standard Version)* uses the words, "Therefore even the first covenant *was not inaugurated* without blood" (Hebrews 9:18). "Put into effect" and "inaugurated" speak of the beginning, the initiation, of the first covenant system.

There is a difference between *initiating* or *inaugurating* a system and consummating the purposes of that system. The wills of men are "initiated" or "inaugurated" when men write and validate them. Their provisions are carried out only on the death of the one who made the will.

The Old Covenant sacrifices for sin initiated, began, or started the process of atonement, payment for sin, but they could never complete the process. Completion of atonement depended on the death of the One who made the Covenant, so that the heirs could be certified as righteous and qualified to receive the inheritance.

Remember: *"In the case of a will, it is necessary to prove the death of the one who made it, because a will is in force only when somebody has died; it never takes effect while the one who made it is living."* (Repetition of this passage is intentional. It is seldom dwelt upon in our theological statements.)

The necessary understanding then is this: the Old Covenant was not *in force* until the death on the cross of the One Who made it, Jesus Christ! Please hold in abeyance your possible inclination to reject this explanation, until giving this study a fair hearing.

To affirm that Christ was, indeed a part of the old covenant process, consider that no man has ever seen God, the Father of Jesus,[36] but the seventy elders of Israel and Moses did see "God" Who gave the covenant to Israel; Christ was there in the wilderness with Israel, Paul said so.[37]

This agrees with the statement of Deuteronomy 23:14: *"For the LORD your God moves about in your camp to protect you and to deliver your enemies to you. Your camp must be holy, so that he will not see among you anything indecent and turn away from you."*

Review the above understanding with these scriptures:

1) *"... it is impossible for the blood of bulls and goats to take away sins"* (Hebrews 10:4).

2) *"This is an illustration for the present time, indicating that the gifts and sacrifices being offered were not able to clear the conscience of the worshiper"* (Hebrews 9:9).

One must connect several concepts, that God's Revised Will, His New Covenant, is activated *individually* by God writing His laws in the hearts and minds of His people. This is the process of the new birth.

The results are seen in the effects of the indwelling Holy Spirit in the lives of His people – an obedient God-loving, human loving people of faith, as Paul testified the Corinthians were (2 Corinthians 3:3).

God's covenant, His promises of an inheritance for His people, is made effective, put into force, by the death of the One Who made the covenant; therefore we can lay claim to our inheritance, as John indicated: *"I write these things to you who believe in the name of the Son of God so that you may know that you have eternal life"* (1 John 5:13).

It already belongs to us because the Maker of the Covenant, Jesus Christ, has already died.

---

[36] John 1:18: "No one has ever seen God, but God the One and Only, who is at the Father's side, has made him known.

1 John 4:12: "No one has ever seen God; but if we love one another, God lives in us and his love is made complete in us."

[37] 1 Cor. 10:3, 4: "They all ate the same spiritual food and drank the same spiritual drink; for they drank from the spiritual rock that accompanied them, and that rock was Christ."

The New Covenant and the Old both have already been made effective by the death of Christ, and therefore the Scriptures admonish, *"Let us draw near to God with a sincere heart in full assurance of faith, having our hearts sprinkled to cleanse us from a guilty conscience and having our bodies washed with pure water"* (Hebrews 10:22). We can lay valid and full claim to our inheritance because the Maker of the will specifying our inheritance has already died!

Listen again to the reason for assurance:

"Now it is God who makes both us and you stand firm in Christ. He anointed us, set his seal of ownership on us, and put his Spirit in our hearts as a deposit, guaranteeing what is to come" (2 Corinthians 1:21, 22). Paul affirmed this twice in this letter to the Corinthian church:

"Now it is God who has made us for this very purpose and has given us the Spirit as a deposit, guaranteeing what is to come" (2 Corinthians 5:5).

This is the flowering of the promise of a New Covenant, the writing of God's law in our hearts. Writing God's law in our hearts is a "Holy Spirit" operation; His Spirit in our hearts is a deposit, guaranteeing what is to come.

This is the inescapable conclusion of the Covenant passages of the Book of Hebrews, and that knowledge bears on the identity of the One Who made the first covenant, and the identity of the One who made the second covenant. They both were ratified by the death of their Maker, Jesus Christ.

Again the question: Who made the first covenant with Abraham, Isaac, Jacob, and Israel? The following passages are related to a common truth, that it was the Son of God:

1) John 8:56: *"Your father Abraham rejoiced at the thought of seeing my day; **he saw it and was glad.**"*

2) 1 Corinthians 10:1-4: *"For I do not want you to be ignorant of the fact, brothers, that our forefathers were all under the cloud and that they all passed through the sea. They were all baptized into Moses in the cloud and in the sea. They all ate the same spiritual food and drank*

the same spiritual drink; for they drank from the spiritual rock that accompanied them, and that rock was Christ."

Still skeptical about the role of Christ? Look again at the statement:

*"Nor did he enter heaven to offer himself again and again, the way the high priest enters the Most Holy Place every year **with blood that is not his own**. Then Christ would have had to suffer many times since the creation of the world."*

Why ***"since the creation of the world"*** if Christ were not involved in the covenant making process from the start?

Why does it not say, "Then Christ would have to suffer many more times until the end of the age"? Because "till the end of the age" is covered in the statement, *"Nor did he enter heaven to offer himself again and again."*

The focus turns from His death back to creation in saying "Then Christ would have had to suffer many times *since the creation of the world."* This time-span also indicates clearly that sacrifices were being made for sin prior to Moses.

> *"It was necessary, then, for the copies of the heavenly things to be purified with these sacrifices, but the heavenly things themselves with better sacrifices than these. For Christ did not enter a man-made sanctuary that was only a copy of the true one; he entered heaven itself, now to appear for us in God's presence.*
>
> *"Nor did he enter heaven to offer himself again and again, the way the high priest enters the Most Holy Place every year with blood that is not his own. Then Christ would have had to suffer **many times since the creation of the world**. But now he has appeared once for all at the end of the ages to do away with sin by the sacrifice of himself.*
>
> *"Just as man is destined to die once, and after that to face judgment, so Christ was sacrificed once to take away the sins of many people; and he will appear a second time, not to bear sin, but to bring salvation to those who are waiting for him"* (Hebrews 9:16-28).

Indeed, this one-time offering was the plan from the beginning: *"And all that dwell upon the earth shall worship him, whose names are not written in the book of life of **the Lamb slain from the foundation of the world"*** (Revelation 13:8 KJV).

Why is it true that Christ would have had to suffer many times *since the creation of the world?* Because the Son of God was the covenant maker with Abraham, Isaac, Jacob, Israel, and all the strangers who took hold of the covenant of God before the cross.

---o-O-o---

Christ Enthroned Between the Cherubim

"O LORD Almighty, God of Israel, enthroned between the cherubim, you alone are God over all the kingdoms of the earth. You have made heaven and earth" (Isaiah 37:16).

Six other verses speak of the God of Israel being "enthroned between the cherubim."[38] This is not speaking of a throne in heaven, but the cherubim above the ark of the covenant. While giving Moses instructions regarding building furniture for the Tabernacle, God said:

"Place the cover on top of the ark and put in the ark the Testimony, which I will give you. There, above the cover between the two cherubim that are over the ark of the Testimony, I will meet with you and give you all my commands for the Israelites" (Exodus 25:21. 22).

"The LORD would speak to Moses face to face, as a man speaks with his friend. Then Moses would return to the camp, but his young aide Joshua son of Nun did not leave the tent" (Exodus 33:11).

"When Moses entered the Tent of Meeting to speak with the LORD, he heard the voice speaking to him from between the two

---

[38] 1Sam. 4:4; 2 Sam. 6:2; 2 Kgs. 19:15; 1 Chr. 13:6; Ps. 80:1; Ps. 99:1.

cherubim above the atonement cover on the ark of the Testimony. And he spoke with him" (Numbers 7:89).

"With him I speak face to face, clearly and not in riddles; he sees the form of the LORD..." (Numbers 12:8a).

More than once Moses "sees the form of the LORD." It is the usual occurrence. He, Aaron, Nadab, and Abi-hu, and seventy of the elders of Israel *"... saw the God of Israel: and there was under his feet as it were a paved work of a sapphire stone, and as it were the body of heaven in his clearness"* (Exodus 24:9b, 10 KJV);

And yet, speaking of the Father, the new Scriptures say: *"No man hath seen God at any time; the only begotten Son, which is in the bosom of the Father, he hath declared him"* (John 1:18). John repeats this truth in his first epistle: *"No man hath seen God..."* (1 John 4:12a).

Who, then, was this Person called Yahweh God, Who was seen on Mount Sinai by the leaders of Israel, who then after the tabernacle was made, sat on the mercy seat above the ark of the testimony and spoke face to face with Moses giving instructions for Israel?

Who was He, Whose form was seen and Whose voice was heard by Moses from between the cherubim whose wings stretched over the mercy seat above the ark?

It was God's "Presence," His son, who manifested the Father to His people: *"The LORD replied, 'My Presence will go with you, and I will give you rest'"* (Exodus 33:14). *"They were all baptized into Moses in the cloud and in the sea. They all ate the same spiritual food and drank the same spiritual drink; for they drank from the spiritual rock that accompanied them, and that rock was Christ"* (Romans 10:2-4).

Does it bother you for this to be said, since the one enthroned between the cherubim is called "almighty God"? (Isaiah 37:16)? Then review Isaiah's prophecy of Christ, *"For unto us a child is born, unto us a son is given: and the government shall be upon his shoulder: and his name shall be called Wonderful, Counsellor, The mighty God, **The everlasting Father,** The Prince of Peace"* (Isaiah 9:6).

It was from this place between the cherubim, on the mercy seat that formed the earthly throne of God, that Moses continued to receive instructions for Israel. This is why David, Hezekiah, and Isaiah spoke of the *"God of Israel, enthroned between the cherubim."*

It is written: *"... Hezekiah prayed to the LORD: "O LORD, God of Israel, enthroned between the cherubim, you alone are God over all the kingdoms of the earth.* **You have made heaven and earth"** (2 Kings 19:15).

It is instructive to compare that prayer with Hebrews 1:1, 2: *"In the past God spoke to our forefathers through the prophets at many times and in various ways, but in these last days he has spoken to us by his Son, whom he appointed heir of all things, and* **through whom he made the universe."**

These verses give clarity to the statement of the LORD, *"I will put my dwelling place among you, and I will not abhor you. I will walk among you and be your God, and you will be my people. I am the LORD your God, who brought you out of Egypt so that you would no longer be slaves to the Egyptians; I broke the bars of your yoke and enabled you to walk with heads held high"* (Leviticus 26:11-14).

How literally was this intended to be taken?

"As part of your equipment have something to dig with, and when you relieve yourself, dig a hole and cover up your excrement. For the LORD your God moves about in your camp to protect you and to deliver your enemies to you. Your camp must be holy, so that he will not see among you anything indecent and turn away from you" (Deuteronomy 23:13, 14).

These truths are being pointed out to indicate Who it was who made the Old Covenant with Abraham and Israel, and why it was He, Jesus Christ, Who was the One to die sealing forever the status of the faithful heirs of Abraham who died under the Old Covenant:

"In the case of a will, it is necessary to prove the death of the one who made it, because a will is in force only when somebody has died; it never takes effect while the one who made it is living" (Hebrews 9:16, 17).   ---o-O-o---

A Succession of Wills

God's very first will named His good friend, Abraham as His heir: *"And the scripture was fulfilled that says, 'Abraham believed God, and it was credited to him as righteousness,' and he was called God's friend"* (James 2:23).

This will (covenant) was not made with Abraham on the basis of written law, but on the basis of promise: *"For if the inheritance be of the law, it is no more of promise: but God gave it to Abraham by promise"* (Galatians 3:18).

God's covenant with Abraham is eternally secure, for God made it as an unconditional promise on the basis that He knew Abraham would remain faithful. Abraham was guaranteed by the LORD God that he, Abraham, would always have a faithful seed, as reflected in the statement of John the Baptist:

"Produce fruit in keeping with repentance. And do not begin to say to yourselves, 'We have Abraham as our father.' For I tell you that out of these stones God can raise up children for Abraham" (Luke 3:8) – and God did raise up seed "out of these stones" – we Gentile Christians are those stones. Abraham's seed are Jewish and Gentile faithful believers.

Abraham will have a place in the Kingdom of God, but sadly, some of his offspring will not. *"There will be weeping there, and gnashing of teeth, when you see Abraham, Isaac and Jacob and all the prophets in the kingdom of God, but you yourselves thrown out"* (Luke 13:28).

The Jews understood the permanence of God's covenant with Abraham, and therefore took comfort as though that permanence automatically included them, not taking into account that they had corporately and individually broken covenant with God. Abraham did not.

The old and New Covenants both plainly demand that the *heirs* of Abraham give faithful obedience to God as a condition of remaining heirs to eternal life and the kingdom of God. The covenant with Abraham cannot be nullified by law breaking; *Abraham will have a faithful seed*, and the New Covenant cannot be nullified by law breaking; but individuals can individually disqualify themselves as his heirs by law breaking!

Just as the disobedience of Israel 430 years after the covenant with Abraham could not break God's covenant with Abraham, neither can our disobedience terminate the New Covenant put into force by the blood of Jesus. The New Covenant is validated for eternity, it will never be voided or replaced, *simply and unequivocally because the Covenant Maker, Jesus Christ, has died,* sealing the validity of the covenant for eternity.

The covenant with Abraham's offspring, the nation of Israel, was broken by Israel, and this necessitated the making of a New Covenant with the people of God. God said of the New Covenant: *"It will not be like the covenant I made with their forefathers when I took them by the hand to lead them out of Egypt, because they broke my covenant, though I was a husband to them, declares the* LORD.*"*

This assured permanence of the new covenant is another important difference between the old and New Covenants. Under the old, the people of God could break the covenant and thereby necessitate a New covenant.

That cannot happen to the New Covenant, because it is immutable and unchangeable, like God's covenant with Abraham, for it indeed is the means of fulfilling the covenant with Abraham: *"And if ye be Christ's, then are ye Abraham's seed, and heirs according to the promise"* (Galatians 3:29 KJV).

We as individuals can be broken off from the New Covenant (Romans 11:21, 22), but the New Covenant stands eternally for the faithful people of God, since it was ratified by the death of the One who made it, Jesus Christ.

Reminder of what we've been presenting:

Legitimate heirs under both covenants are still covered under the promise to Abraham: *"If you belong to Christ, then you are Abraham's seed, and heirs according to the promise"* (Galatians 3:29). The faithful under the Old Covenant belong to Christ, were bought by His blood, just as surely as we belong to Him who come to Him under the New.

The next "will" after the one with Abraham is called the Old Covenant; it was made with the literal descendants of Abraham, the Israelites, as they stood at the foot of *Mount Sinai.* Having made the agreement with God to obey Him and He would be their God, they then heard God speak the Ten Commandments.

The next will after that of Sinai was His newly revised will, the New Covenant, which was ratified on *Mount Zion,* called "Mount Calvary" (see Galatians 4).

Although this covenant was made with Israel, as shown earlier, it does not mean that the Covenant made with Israel did not pertain to others who wished to "join themselves to the Lord" (see Isaiah 56).

What we are discussing, of course, is what Christians speak of as "the Old Covenant," and the "New Covenant." Covenants, Testaments, Wills – in the Bible these words have the same meaning, and are used to refer to the same thing.

These three words – covenants, testaments, and wills – have to do with inheritance, stipulating what a person receives from their parents when their parents die. God is the Parent, our Father; we are His children, His heirs *if we belong to Christ.*

Is it wrong to think of Christ as our "Parent," our "Father," One Who may die and leave His inheritance to us through His will? Perhaps we need again to listen to the prophet Isaiah:

"For unto us a child is born, unto us a son is given: and the government shall be upon his shoulder: and his name shall be called Wonderful, Counsellor, The mighty God, **The everlasting Father,** *The Prince of Peace"* (Isaiah 9:6).

"Therefore the Lord himself shall give you a sign; Behold, a virgin shall conceive, and bear a son, and shall call his name Immanuel" (Isaiah 7:14).

"Behold, a virgin shall be with child, and shall bring forth a son, and they shall call his name Emmanuel, which being interpreted is, God with us" (Matthew 1:23).

As human covenants or wills sometimes have stipulations which qualify or disqualify potential heirs, God's Old Covenant had, *and* His

New Covenant *has* such qualifying or disqualifying stipulations. These provisions are constituent parts of His covenant with His people.

So, are "wills" and "covenant" the same thing? Students of the Bible don't always think of God's covenants in the same way one thinks of a will. One of the reasons, they think of wills as something that have no validity (in the sense of something heirs can take advantage of) until the parents or will makers die.

That doesn't seem to fit in the case of the Old Covenant, since people think of God as immortal – and He is – so how can it be that we who expect to be heirs must wait until the death of the parent (thinking of God, the Father) in order to be validated as heirs and receive the inheritance? Did Jesus play the role of Father? How quickly we can forget the words of the prophets! "... *his name shall be called Wonderful, Counsellor, The mighty God,* ***The everlasting Father.***"

The answer, as shown earlier, lies in recognition of the role of Christ as the One who spoke with Moses, on behalf of His Father, and thus qualified to be the Covenant Maker who died to validate both the old and New Covenants.

Do some of God's heirs still break covenant with God?

Unfortunately, yes!

"Anyone who rejected the law of Moses died without mercy on the testimony of two or three witnesses. How much more severely do you think a man deserves to be punished who has trampled the Son of God under foot, who has treated as an unholy thing the blood of the covenant that sanctified him, and who has insulted the Spirit of grace? For we know him who said, "It is mine to avenge; I will repay," and again, "The Lord will judge his people." It is a dreadful thing to fall into the hands of the living God" (Hebrews 10:28-31).   **---o-O-o---**

Can the New Covenant Be changed
After the Cross?

This "trampling the Son of God underfoot" and "insulting the Spirit of Grace"[39] bring up these interesting questions. When converted people turn like a dog to its vomit and like a sow to her wallowing in the mire,[40] what happens to the covenant?

Is it possible that the New Covenant could be nullified by the faithless disobedience of the children of God, as the Old Covenant was broken by Israel – known as the people of God, under the Old Covenant?

The answer is "NO!" Why? Because covenants, even God's covenant (by His own choice!) cannot be changed after the person dies who has made it!

Could the terms of the covenant be changed after the cross? The answer is a straightforward "NO!" Same reason as above. Wholesale disobedience in any age subsequent to the cross cannot and will not nullify or change the New Covenant.

Could (would) God make *another New Covenant because of our disobedience?* Again, "NO!" It is sealed for eternity by the death of the "Will-Maker."

---

[39] Zech. 12:10: "And I will pour out on the house of David and the inhabitants of Jerusalem a spirit of grace and supplication. They will look on me, the one they have pierced, and they will mourn for him as one mourns for an only child, and grieve bitterly for him as one grieves for a firstborn son."

Heb. 10:29: "How much more severely do you think a man deserves to be punished who has trampled the Son of God under foot, who has treated as an unholy thing the blood of the covenant that sanctified him, and who has insulted the Spirit of grace?"

[40] 2 Pet. 2:20-22: "For if after they have escaped the pollutions of the world through the knowledge of the Lord and Saviour Jesus Christ, they are again entangled therein, and overcome, the latter end is worse with them than the beginning. For it had been better for them not to have known the way of righteousness, than, after they have known it, to turn from the holy commandment delivered unto them. But it is happened unto them according to the true proverb, The dog is turned to his own vomit again; and the sow that was washed to her wallowing in the mire."

Further, Hebrews 10:16-18 reads: *"'This is the covenant I will make with them after that time, says the Lord. I will put my laws in their hearts, and I will write them on their minds.' Then he adds: 'Their sins and lawless acts I will remember no more.' And where these have been forgiven, there is no longer any sacrifice for sin."*

Do the new scriptures, called the "New Testament," reveal *the last and final covenant?* The answer is a joyful "YES! This is it!" A covenant can't get any better than the New one ratified by the blood of Christ!

It is the prerogative of *living parents* to change their wills. Even God had changed His will, many times – every time a new commandment was given before Christ's death.[41] But living parents *cannot* change their wills after they die, and God *will not* change His will after the death of His Son.

Do these "rules" apply to God, and the inheritance He promises His children? Yes, *by His own choice, they do.* Like living human parents, God could change the provisions of His will anytime He wished, *until His Son died on the cross.*

Thereafter, the New Covenant, God's *"Last* Will and Testament," could never be changed. When a person making a will dies, the will is "set in concrete" so to speak, and cannot be changed. Just human reasoning? Consider that the canon of the Bible has not been added to by any prophet since the writings of the Apostles. Many have tried, but they fall under the condemnation of adding to the Word of God.

Consider again the covenant made with Abraham and his seed. Paul said about the New Covenant: *"Brothers, let me take an example from every day life. Just as no one can set aside or add to a human covenant that has been duly established, so it is in this case"* (Galatians 3:15).[42]

---

[41] The many times of changing are reflected in the instructions given Moses by the One who spoke to him from the mercy seat between the cherubim: *"Place the cover on top of the ark and put in the ark the Testimony, which I will give you. There, above the cover between the two cherubim that are over the ark of the Testimony, I will meet with you and give you all my commands for the Israelites"* (Exodus 25:21. 22). This continuation of giving commands was after the sealing of the covenant by the blood of old covenant sacrifices.

[42] Please do not become weary in reading this passage repeatedly. It bears mightily on Covenant Theology.

"And this I say, that the covenant, that was confirmed before of God in Christ, the law, which was four hundred and thirty years after, cannot disannul, that it should make the promise of none effect" (Galatians 3:17 KJV). Be sure to note that the covenant which God made with Abraham four hundred years before the Ten Commandments were written on stone, *was confirmed before of God **in Christ.***"

This affirms the role of Christ in the covenant making at the time it was made with Abraham in at least two ways:

1) Christ is identified as "the seed" of Abraham. It was "confirmed before of God in Christ, in that *"The promises were spoken to Abraham and to his seed. The Scripture does not say 'and to seeds,' meaning many people, but 'and to your seed,' meaning one person, who is Christ"* (Galatians 3:16).

2) It was confirmed *before* of God in Christ in that it was already in the plan of God that Jesus would put the covenant into effect by His death: *"All inhabitants of the earth will worship the beast – all whose names have not been written in the book of life belonging to the Lamb that was slain from the creation of the world "* (Revelation 13:8).

That is, it was in God's plan as the world began for His Son Jesus to make the covenant with His people effective by His sacrificial death.

There is much to be learned from these verses. A covenant that has been duly established – that is, established *by the death of the covenant maker* – cannot be changed after the covenant maker's death: *"Just as no one can set aside or add to a human covenant that has been duly established, **so it is in this case."*** The New Covenant was established at the cross by the death of Christ, and the promises of the Old Covenant were also confirmed in His death! (See Hebrews 3, 4.)

Can men change it after the death of Christ? In no wise – contrary to the belief of those church prelates who think God gave them that power, and that they take His place here upon earth, thinking to have the power to change the very laws of God!

Would God, did God, change His will after the death of the Covenant Maker? In no wise! *Are we listening? "Just as no one can set aside or add to a human covenant that has been duly established, so it is in this case."* Has God's New Covenant been duly established? Indeed it has, by the death of the Covenant Maker, Jesus Christ.

Consequently, those covenant provisions which were revealed after the cross were already initiated before the cross, and do not, cannot, conflict with the teachings of Jesus, Who, by His teachings and life was spelling out the qualifying elements of the covenant He would put into force by His death!

Hopefully, you have not gone to sleep, for the points being made here are essential to our understanding!

Whatever was to be included in the New Covenant, God's revised will, had to be stipulated in His will *before the cross,* before the death of the Testator (Jesus, the Son of God). The Bible clearly says it cannot be nullified or added to after the death of Christ (Galatians 3:15).

We must acknowledge and rest in the assurance that those revelations to Paul in the deserts of Arabia[43] did not add new provisions to

---

[43] See Galatians 1:12: "I did not receive it from any man, nor was I taught it; rather, I received it by revelation from Jesus Christ"; and Galatians 1:6-24: "I am astonished that you are so quickly deserting the one who called you by the grace of Christ and are turning to a different gospel – which is really no gospel at all. Evidently some people are throwing you into confusion and are trying to pervert the gospel of Christ. But even if we or an angel from heaven should preach a gospel other than the one we preached to you, let him be eternally condemned! As we have already said, so now I say again: If anybody is preaching to you a gospel other than what you accepted, let him be eternally condemned! Am I now trying to win the approval of men, or of God? Or am I trying to please men? If I were still trying to please men, I would not be a servant of Christ. I want you to know, brothers, that the gospel I preached is not something that man made up. I did not receive it from any man, nor was I taught it; rather, I received it by revelation from Jesus Christ. For you have heard of my previous way of life in Judaism, how intensely I persecuted the church of God and tried to destroy it. I was advancing in Judaism beyond many Jews of my own age and was extremely zealous for the traditions of my fathers. But when God, who set me apart from birth and called me by his grace, was pleased to reveal his Son in me so that I might preach him among the Gentiles, I did not consult any man, nor did I go up to Jerusalem to see those who were apostles before I was, but I went immediately into Arabia and later returned to Damascus. Then after three years, I went up to Jerusalem to get acquainted with Peter and stayed with him fifteen days. I saw none of the other apostles – only James, the Lord's brother. I assure you before God that what I am writing you is no lie. Later I went to Syria and Cilicia. I was personally unknown to the churches of Judea that are in Christ. They only heard the report: "The man who formerly persecuted us is now preaching the faith he once tried to destroy." And they praised God because of me."

the Last Will and Testament of God, previously ratified by the death of the Testator on the cross! Why?

Let's hear it again: *"Brothers, let me take an example from every day life. Just as no one can set aside or add to a human covenant that has been duly established, so it is in this case"* (Galatians 3:15).

This statement was made by that same Paul who learned his "New Covenant Theology" in the desert of Arabia. "Duly established" refers to the sealing of the covenant, the will, by the death of the Will Maker.

Please do not grow weary in the repetition of this truth, for it is vital to sound doctrine! Take into consideration that you probably haven't even memorized it yet, and to memorize a verse you would repeat it more times than we have here! At least remain familiar with it!

This evidence confirms that Jesus was indeed preaching the provisions of the New Covenant as He went about preaching the Gospel of the Kingdom. There was not a "new" or different gospel revealed after His death on the cross. Keep in mind these two principles:

1) *"In the case of a will, it is necessary to prove the death of the one who made it, because a will is in force only when somebody has died; it never takes effect* while the one who made it is living" (Hebrews 9:16, 17).

2) *"Brothers, let me take an example from every day life. Just as no one can set aside or add to a human covenant that has been duly established, so it is in this case"* (Galatians 3:15).

The terms of the New Covenant that was "duly established" by the death of Christ on the cross were of necessity already determined *before* His death in order to be established *by* His death.

If the terms must be established before His death, and cannot be changed after His death, then what do we do with the teachings of Jesus prior to His death? Jesus said: *"Heaven and earth will pass away, but my words will never pass away"* (Matthew 24:35). Mark and Luke affirm the same words of Jesus (Mark 13:31; Luke 21:33).

Can we then dismiss His teachings as "pre-cross, Old Covenant" and therefore at least *suspect* if He says *"Heaven and earth will pass away, but my words will never pass away"*?

Perhaps we can interpret Him to mean "a permanent record of what He said," not a permanent expression of His will! Do we really think Jesus would come preaching the gospel of the kingdom *then fail to teach kingdom truths?*

Parts of the New Covenant are revealed in the old Scriptures:

"He (Jesus) said to them, 'This is what I told you while I was still with you: Everything must be fulfilled that is written about me in the Law of Moses, the Prophets and the Psalms.'

"Then he opened their minds so they could understand the Scriptures. He told them, 'This is what is written: The Christ will suffer and rise from the dead on the third day, and repentance and forgiveness of sins will be preached in his name to all nations, beginning at Jerusalem. You are witnesses of these things'" (Luke 24:44-48).

"This is what is written" does not refer to what was yet to be written! Confirmation of the New Covenant through the death of Christ had been revealed in the Old Scriptures, and this was proclaimed by Him *before and after His death.*

It has already been shown that God's law would continue as a part of that New Covenant, as prophesied by Jeremiah and confirmed in the book of Hebrews. Was this New Covenant revealed before the cross? Indeed it was!

So, back to the question: *Can God's New Covenant be revised? Could it be revised after the death of the one Who made the covenant?* Both questions are answered by the Bible, "No, they cannot!"

These truths are of more than casual importance, and should be kept in mind as one studies the portion of the Bible dealing with doctrines as explained before and after the cross.

One should expect to find *confirmation* in the books of Acts, in Paul's epistles, in those of Peter, James, Jude and John, of the teachings of Christ during His ministry (found in the Gospels), *not contradictions or changes* in His teachings!

And, indeed, that confirmation is found in those books, as shown in the previous sections of this study on the New Scriptures affirming the Old Scriptures, and the New Scriptures affirming the law of the Old Scriptures.

This is in keeping with the simple statement of God to Jeremiah, *"I will put my law in their minds and write it on their hearts."* He says nothing about a "new law" to replace the old law.

The law of the new covenant is no more a new law because of the changes in the law, than the law of Moses was a new law every time it was amended by the Lord.

Neither did changes in and additions to the law given regularly to Moses from between the cherubim constitute a new covenant! The discussion of law in Paul's writings is not about new law, they are discussions of the same covenant law God spoke on Sinai to Israel.

This understanding is also in keeping with the command of Jesus: *"Therefore go and make disciples of all nations, baptizing them in the name of the Father and of the Son and of the Holy Spirit, and **teaching them to obey everything I have commanded you**. And surely I am with you always, to the very end of the age"* (Matthew 28:19, 20).

The Apostles could not change what had been taught by Jesus and comply with those instructions. Consider the qualifications the Apostles used to replace Judas:

> *"Therefore it is necessary to choose one of the men who have been with us the whole time the Lord Jesus went in and out among us, beginning from John's baptism to the time when Jesus was taken up from us. For one of these must become a witness with us of his resurrection"* (Acts 1:21, 22).

Why a person who had been "with us" (with the Apostles) "beginning from John's baptism to the time when Jesus was taken up from us"? If it were *only to witness of the resurrection of Jesus,* any of more than 500 people would qualify![44]

---

[44] 1 Corinthians 15:3-8: "For what I received I passed on to you as of first importance: that Christ died for our sins according to the Scriptures, that he was buried,

Clearly it had to do with their experiences with Christ during His ministry, and their understanding of what it was He wished them to teach and do.

Jesus, as His final charge, said to them: "Therefore go and make disciples of all nations...and *teaching them to obey everything **I have commanded you**"* (See Matthew 28:19, 20). This is what Jesus *did say.*

It is appropriate to point out that Jesus *did not say,* "Teaching them to obey everything *I am going to command"* or *"everything I will later reveal to you."*

Whatever was later revealed to them was in confirmation of what He had already taught. The death of Christ on the cross *sealed the terms of the covenant, and those terms could not be, and were not changed after His death, according to the book of Hebrews and according to Paul, explaining things to the Galatians and Corinthians!*

---o-O-o---

So Who Are the Valid Heirs?

Many children wonder what's in the will of their parents, what their inheritance will be when their parents die; some even daydream about being named in the will of some "rich uncle" or grandparent. Some parents reveal ahead of death the basics of their wills, and then children wonder whether anything will be left when their parents die – will the children, some rest home, or the government, get their parents' life savings?

Children even wonder whether they have been good enough to deserve a greater than equal share, or have they been too distant and disrespectful, and will they be lucky to receive anything? Will they consequently receive a diminished share, perhaps just a dollar to let a pro-

---

that he was raised on the third day according to the Scriptures, and that he appeared to Peter, and then to the Twelve. After that, he appeared to more than five hundred of the brothers at the same time, most of whom are still living, though some have fallen asleep. Then he appeared to James, then to all the apostles, and last of all he appeared to me also, as to one abnormally born."

bate judge know they intentionally were not given a significant portion?[45] And we, as children of God, have many of the same doubts and fears if we haven't been consistently faithful to God our Father.

Children get into arguments over their promised inheritance, and sad to say, children of God do the same thing. We argue about our Father's will, who is included, and whether each of us deserve our portion of the inheritance.

Some resent "adopted" siblings (Gentiles, adopted into the household of faith). Heirs even argue over who gets to be executor of the will! So do different denominations! Each thinks it should be in charge of the kingdom! Well, if we're worried about "What's in it for us?" we can rest assured, there is plenty and to spare!

What about God's "will"? Does it stipulate who may be His heirs? Does it stipulate who is ineligible to inherit under the terms of His will? Does it provide for adopted sons and daughters? Indeed, it does each of these things.

Psalm 37:9 is a very brief statement of God's will: *"For evildoers shall be cut off: but those that wait upon the LORD, they shall inherit the earth."* This is about as short a summary of the Last Will and Testament of God as could be imagined!

God began with Abraham, promising Canaan as an inheritance to him and his offspring: *"By faith Abraham, when he was called to go out into a place which he should after receive for an inheritance, obeyed; and he went out, not knowing whither he went"* (Hebrews 11:8).

---

[45] The wicked do indeed receive their "dollar" to show they have not been overlooked:

Matthew 6:2: "So when you give to the needy, do not announce it with trumpets, as the hypocrites do in the synagogues and on the streets, to be honored by men. I tell you the truth, they have received their reward in full."

Matthew 6:5" "And when you pray, do not be like the hypocrites, for they love to pray standing in the synagogues and on the street corners to be seen by men. I tell you the truth, they have received their reward in full."

Matthew 6:16: ""When you fast, do not look somber as the hypocrites do, for they disfigure their faces to show men they are fasting. I tell you the truth, they have received their reward in full."

That being what they wanted, that is what they received, but unfortunately, it was reward–inheritance–in full!

Just as the covenant with Abraham cannot be changed by the disobedience of some of His heirs, neither could it be changed by the heirs themselves. So it is with the New Covenant confirmed by the death of the Covenant Maker, Jesus Christ. God made out His will, and revised it many times, but it cannot be revised again, for it has been sealed by the death of Him who made the will.

---o-**O**-o---

Peculiarity of God's Will

Now, a very peculiar truth makes God's "Last Will and Testament" quite a different matter than usually happens with a human-made will. Abraham died long before the inheritance could become his possession to enjoy, and long before the "Testator" died – that is, God the Will Maker; who made out the will with Abraham as His heir.

The heir (Abraham) died before the Will Maker, God, had Himself died (through His Son, Jesus); but Abraham will enjoy the inheritance nonetheless: *"There will be weeping there, and gnashing of teeth, when you see Abraham, Isaac and Jacob and all the prophets in the kingdom of God, but you yourselves thrown out"* (Luke 13:28).

As a human being, if you die before your human parents die, you have no hope of inheriting according to their will, but faithful children of God who died before the Covenant Maker died will yet receive their inheritance! The resurrection of the saints is the key facilitator of this promise to Abraham, and to all those who have died "in the Lord."

Impossible for God to die? Unless we acknowledge the role of Christ in dealing with Abraham and with Israel in the wilderness and at Mount Sinai, we will never fully understand these matters.

Jesus acted in His Father's stead in covenant matters, including not only dying in our own stead for our sins that we might be forgiven, but also dying in His Father's stead to validate His Father's "Last Will and Testament."

Why? *"... because a will is in force only when somebody has died; it never takes effect while the one who made it is living."* God, the Father, having never taken on human form, could not die.

If it *was* Christ Who was "God" speaking to and making the covenant with Abraham, if it *was* Christ Who was God speaking with Israel on Mount Sinai making the covenant with Israel, if it was Christ Who was God speaking to Moses, sitting between the cherubim over the ark of the covenant, then it makes logical sense to speak of the "Testator," the One making the will, having to die in order to validate God's will, His covenant with His people.

Unless we readily affirm that it is appropriate to assign that role to Christ, the Son of God, we have insurmountable theological problems. That Christ was with Israel in the wilderness is affirmed most positively by Paul in 1 Corinthians 10:4: *"...for they drank from the spiritual rock that accompanied them, and that rock was Christ."*

So, when Hebrews 9:16, 17 states: *"In the case of a will, it is necessary to prove the death of the one who made it, because a will is in force only when somebody has died; it never takes effect while the one who made it is living,"* we can understand that God's covenant, both with Abraham and Israel, both Old and New Covenants, were validated by the death of the Testator, that is, Jesus Christ the Son of God.

Since the Covenant Maker has already died, we can now lay claim to the inheritance! John said, *"I write these things to you who believe in the name of the Son of God so that you may know that you have eternal life"* (1 John 5:13).   ---o-O-o---

Doubts

To state it inadequately, some do not like to speak of Jesus as "God," nor to contemplate the concept that it was the Son of God who made the Old Covenant with Abraham and Israel; but without that concept, it leaves us with neither the old nor the New Covenant "in force." But both were validated by the death of Christ on the cross (see the whole of Hebrews chapter nine).

"But if it is preached that Christ has been raised from the dead, how can some of you say that there is no resurrection of the dead? If there is no resurrection of the dead, then not even Christ has been raised.

" And if Christ has not been raised, our preaching is useless and so is your faith. More than that, we are then found to be false witnesses about God, for we have testified about God that he raised Christ from the dead.

"But he did not raise him if in fact the dead are not raised. For if the dead are not raised, then Christ has not been raised either. And if Christ has not been raised, your faith is futile; you are still in your sins. Then those also who have fallen asleep in Christ are lost. If only for this life we have hope in Christ, we are to be pitied more than all men" (1 Corinthians 15:12-19).

This agrees with the teachings of Hebrews 11:39, 40, about Abraham and all other faithful folk who died after Abraham: *"These were all commended for their faith, yet none of them received what had been promised. God had planned something better for us so that only **together with us would they be made perfect.**"* Again, this is contingent on being born again and the resurrection, and they both are contingent on the death *and resurrection* of the Testator, Jesus Christ.

Now that the "Testator," the Maker of the will, has died on the cross and has put into force the terms of the will, the testament, the covenant, those terms are "locked in place," and await only the arrival of "probate day," when all of the heirs have been identified, resurrected from the dead or transformed at the time of resurrection, to be brought before the Judge to receive their inheritance:

"For we must all appear before the judgment seat of Christ; that every one may receive the things done in his body, according to that he hath done, whether it be good or bad" (2 Corinthians 5:10, KJV).

Two things make God's will very different – they are:

1) The heirs who have died both before and after the cross will yet be "made perfect" – that is, resurrected from the dead, that they may yet receive the inheritance; and

2) The Testator, or Maker of the will, God, through the death of His Son Jesus, validated the will by His own Son's death, Who then was resurrected.

This portion of the subject, the resurrection of both *the Maker of the will* and *the heirs named in the will* (covenant) will not be pursued further here, but it is the vitalizing element which makes the covenant, the Last Will and Testament of God, meaningful to all of us who die before the return of our Lord and the resurrection of His saints.

---o-O-o---

Abraham's Children and the Disinherited

This inheritance was promised to Abraham and his offspring, *including all his adopted children:*

"He (God) predestined us to be adopted as his sons through Jesus Christ, in accordance with his pleasure and will" (Ephesians 1:5).

"If you belong to Christ, then you are Abraham's seed, and heirs according to the promise" (Galatians 3:29).

The concept is very simple, so why complicate the subject with a detailed study? Mainly because the heirs early on began quarreling over who shares in the inheritance and whether they have to obey their Father to remain an heir. God, our Father, requires us, His children, to abide by His standards, as John the Baptist explained to the Jews, and as Paul explained to the Corinthian and Galatian Gentile churches.

Unless we get straight what behavior God expects, we do not know whether we are or are not His children!

The Disinherited

"I will smite them with the pestilence, and disinherit them, and will make of thee a greater nation and mightier than they" (Numbers 14:12, KJV).

"Therefore say I unto you, The kingdom of God shall be taken from you, and given to a nation bringing forth the fruits thereof" (Matthew 21:43, KJV).

"If some of the branches have been broken off, and you, though a wild olive shoot, have been grafted in among the others and now share in the nourishing sap from the olive root, do not boast over those branches. If you do, consider this: You do not support the root, but the root supports you.

"You will say then, "Branches were broken off so that I could be grafted in." Granted. But they were broken off because of unbelief, and you stand by faith. Do not be arrogant, but be afraid. For if God did not spare the natural branches, he will not spare you either. Consider therefore the kindness and sternness of God: sternness to those who fell, but kindness to you, provided that you continue in his kindness. Otherwise, you also will be cut off " (Romans 11:17-22).

Losing one's inheritance isn't always anticipated. By ignoring what our parents expect of us, we can be unhappily surprised on probate day! All our arguments over eternal security will mean nothing. It will be of no avail on that day to bemoan the fact our name has been removed from the list of heirs, the book of life.[46] All previous arguments over the stipulations of the will, will have no bearing whatever.

Being *reasonably wrong,* making our "case" sound logical by digging out irrelevant meanings of Greek and Hebrew words will mean nothing

---

[46] Philippians 4:3 And I entreat thee also, true yokefellow, help those women which laboured with me in the gospel, with Clement also, and with other my fellowlabourers, whose names are in the book of life.
Revelation 3:5 He that overcometh, the same shall be clothed in white raiment; and I will not blot out his name out of the book of life, but I will confess his name before my Father, and before his angels (KJV).

at all on "probate day" (judgment day)! *"'Come now, let us reason to-gether,' says the LORD"* doesn't refer to persuading God on judgment day how reasonable it was that we were wrong!

On that day, God, our Father, will be Probate Judge, and our Advocate, Jesus Christ the righteous, will need no witnesses to prove His case, because both Judge and Advocate will know all the facts and all the pertinent law, as well as the contents of the Father's Last Will and Testament – after all, they wrote the book of pertinent law, and they made out the Will! There will be no jury of our peers, for *the facts will not be in dispute!*   ---o-O-o---

Squabbles Among the Heirs, Disagreeable Results

"I say this to shame you. Is it possible that there is nobody among you wise enough to judge a dispute between believers? But instead, one brother goes to law against another – and this in front of unbelievers!

"The very fact that you have lawsuits among you means you have been completely defeated already. Why not rather be wronged? Why not rather be cheated? Instead, you yourselves cheat and do wrong, and you do this to your brothers.

"Do you not know that the wicked will not inherit the kingdom of God? Do not be deceived: Neither the sexually immoral nor idolaters nor adulterers nor male prostitutes nor homosexual offenders nor thieves nor the greedy nor drunkards nor slanderers nor swindlers will inherit the kingdom of God. And that is what some of you were. But you were washed, you were sanctified, you were justified in the name of the Lord Jesus Christ and by the Spirit of our God" (1 Corinthians 6:5-11).

"As I urged you when I went into Macedonia, stay there in Ephesus so that you may command certain men not to teach false doctrines any longer nor to devote themselves to myths and endless genealogies. These promote controversies rather than God's work – which is by faith. The goal of this command is love, which comes

from a pure heart and a good conscience and a sincere faith. Some have wandered away from these and turned to meaningless talk. They want to be teachers of the law, but they do not know what they are talking about or what they so confidently affirm" (1 Timothy 1:3-7).

"The acts of the sinful nature are obvious: sexual immorality, impurity and debauchery; idolatry and witchcraft; hatred, discord, jealousy, fits of rage, selfish ambition, dissensions, factions and envy; drunkenness, orgies, and the like. I warn you, as I did before, that those who live like this will not inherit the kingdom of God" (Galatians 5:19-21).

It is essential that we heirs get along with one another!

Perhaps we overlook some of the factors which disinherit and cause some in the Lord's registry of the saved to be "blotted out."[47] Please note these "acts of a sinful nature" included among those for which a person will be disinherited: *discord, dissensions, factions* – about

---

[47] Psalm 69:28 May they be blotted out of the book of life and not be listed with the righteous.

Phil. 4:3 Yes, and I ask you, loyal yokefellow, help these women who have contended at my side in the cause of the gospel, along with Clement and the rest of my fellow workers, whose names are in the book of life.

Revelation 3:5 He who overcomes will, like them, be dressed in white. I will never blot out his name from the book of life, but will acknowledge his name before my Father and his angels.

Revelation 13:8 All inhabitants of the earth will worship the beast –all whose names have not been written in the book of life belonging to the Lamb that was slain from the creation of the world.

Revelation 17:8 The beast, which you saw, once was, now is not, and will come up out of the Abyss and go to his destruction. The inhabitants of the earth whose names have not been written in the book of life from the creation of the world will be astonished when they see the beast, because he once was, now is not, and yet will come.

Revelation 20:12 And I saw the dead, great and small, standing before the throne, and books were opened. Another book was opened, which is the book of life. The dead were judged according to what they had done as recorded in the books.

Revelation 20:15 If anyone's name was not found written in the book of life, he was thrown into the lake of fire.

Revelation 21:27 Nothing impure will ever enter it, nor will anyone who does what is shameful or deceitful, but only those whose names are written in the Lamb's book of life.

which it is stated, "*those who live like this will not inherit the kingdom of God.*"

"Christianity" does not take this seriously enough. Modern ecumenicity is not the answer, for Paul said, "Warn a divisive person once, and then warn him a second time. After that, have nothing to do with him." Or as stated in the KJV: "*A man that is an heretic after the first and second admonition reject*" (Titus 3:10).

The subject was doctrinal discussions, arguments about our lineage (i.e., "We have Abraham to our Father! We've got it made!")

And then sexual immorality: "*Do you not know that the wicked will not inherit the kingdom of God? Do not be deceived: Neither the sexually immoral nor idolaters nor adulterers nor male prostitutes nor homosexual offenders*" (1 Corinthians 6:9).

Among the disinherited are the drunkards and homosexual offenders. Have you heard, "But God made me that way! *It's God's fault if being homosexual is wrong!*"

Or, "*I'm a drunkard because of this gene I inherited! I'm homosexual because God gave me a homosexual gene!*" It's reminiscent of "God, I sinned on account of this woman you made for me!"

Genetic disposition to sin, any kind of sin, will not be an arguable defense! Look at Galatians 5:19-21 above! So Jesus says of that day:

"*Behold, I am coming soon! My reward is with me, and I will give to everyone according to what he has done. I am the Alpha and the Omega, the First and the Last, the Beginning and the End.*

"*Blessed are those who wash their robes, that they may have the right to the tree of life and may go through the gates into the city. Outside are the dogs, those who practice magic arts, the sexually immoral, the murderers, the idolaters and everyone who loves and practices falsehood*" (Revelation 22:12-15).

For religious falsehood? *Especially religious falsehood!*

These are among the disinherited who already have their reward, the praise of men and the material rewards, the fleshly gratification gained through their evil deeds. They have no further benefits coming!

So what about those who lived faithfully under the Old Covenant, the ones who died before the making of the New Covenant? They are not disinherited, because:

"For this reason Christ is the mediator of a New Covenant, that those who are called may receive the promised eternal inheritance – now that he has died as a ransom to set them free from the sins committed under the first covenant" (Hebrews 9:15).

Consider again this statement made by Jesus: *"There will be weeping there, and gnashing of teeth, when you see Abraham, Isaac and Jacob and all the prophets in the kingdom of God, but you yourselves thrown out"* (Luke 13:28).

These men, Abraham, Isaac, Jacob and *"all the prophets,"* died under the Old Covenant, but their place in the kingdom is secure because of the death of Christ, just as is our own place because of His death.

"Praise be to the God and Father of our Lord Jesus Christ! In his great mercy he has given us new birth into a living hope through the resurrection of Jesus Christ from the dead, and into an inheritance that can never perish, spoil or fade – kept in heaven for you, who through faith are shielded by God's power until the coming of the salvation that is ready to be revealed in the last time.

"In this you greatly rejoice, though now for a little while you may have had to suffer grief in all kinds of trials" (1 Peter 1:3-5).

That is the general picture. It is time for a closer look at details.

---o-O-o---

God Making Covenant
With Abraham and His Offspring

One of the great events in covenant making, and one which both the Old and New Scriptures use as a reference point for the beginning of inheritance covenant making, is found in Genesis 15:

"After this, the word of the LORD came to Abram in a vision: "Do not be afraid, Abram. I am your shield, your very great reward."

"But Abram said, 'O Sovereign LORD, what can you give me since I remain childless and the one who will inherit my estate is Eliezer of Damascus?' And Abram said, 'You have given me no children; so a servant in my household will be my heir.'

"Then the word of the LORD came to him: 'This man will not be your heir, but a son coming from your own body will be your heir.' He took him outside and said, 'Look up at the heavens and count the stars – if indeed you can count them.' Then he said to him, 'So shall your offspring be.'

"Abram believed the LORD, and he credited it to him as righteousness.

"He also said to him, 'I am the LORD, who brought you out of Ur of the Chaldeans to give you this land to take possession of it.'

"But Abram said, 'O Sovereign LORD, how can I know that I will gain possession of it?'

"So the LORD said to him, 'Bring me a heifer, a goat and a ram, each three years old, along with a dove and a young pigeon.'

"Abram brought all these to him, cut them in two and arranged the halves opposite each other; the birds, however, he did not cut in half. Then birds of prey came down on the carcasses, but Abram drove them away.

"As the sun was setting, Abram fell into a deep sleep, and a thick and dreadful darkness came over him. Then the LORD said to him,

'Know for certain that your descendants will be strangers in a country not their own, and they will be enslaved and mistreated four hundred years. But I will punish the nation they serve as slaves, and afterward they will come out with great possessions.

"You, however, will go to your fathers in peace and be buried at a good old age. In the fourth generation your descendants will come back here, for the sin of the Amorites has not yet reached its full measure.'

"When the sun had set and darkness had fallen, a smoking fire-pot with a blazing torch appeared and passed between the pieces. On that day the LORD made a covenant with Abram and said, 'To your descendants I give this land, from the river of Egypt to the great river, the Euphrates – the land of the Kenites, Kenizzites, Kadmonites, Hittites, Perizzites, Rephaites, Amorites, Canaanites, Girgashites and Jebusites.'

This picture of covenant making gave rise to the very Hebrew word for "covenant," a Hebrew word which means "a cutting," in the process of establishing the covenant. It has the significance of a willingness to die in order to validate and put into force the agreement made between the covenant makers.

How seriously did God intend the significance of this ceremony with Abraham? Very seriously! He gave His life, through His Son Jesus, to put the Old Covenant, as well as the new, into effect.

While God carried through with His portion of the covenant in having His own Son die to validate the covenant, God allowed Abraham to spare Isaac, when God commanded Abraham to sacrifice Isaac to prove his willingness to do as much.

At God's command, Abraham took His son Isaac to the very same mountain where God later sacrificed His Son Jesus in order to validate both His covenant with Abraham and with Abraham's seed. God spared Isaac because of Abraham's faith that God could provide a seed in Isaac's place, and Abraham's complete willingness to obey.

God proved His faithfulness in actually sacrificing His own Son, Jesus. Abraham's willingness to sacrifice Isaac was a type of God's willingness to sacrifice His own Son.

This is how seriously God took His covenant with Abraham, and how seriously Abraham took the covenant as well. Both were willing to sacrifice their sons that Abraham's seed may inherit the earth, which "seed" the New Scriptures identify as Christ, Himself![48]

We fathom with difficulty the depth of symbolism here. The Bible, speaking of Isaac, said: *"And so from this one man, and he as good as dead, came descendants as numerous as the stars in the sky and as countless as the sand on the seashore"* (Hebrews 11:12). That was a first century A.D. assessment of Abraham's seed. Consider, in comparison, how great a multitude have now accrued to Abraham as his "seed" through the death of Christ, whom Isaac typified!

The covenant described above between God and Abraham established the promised inheritance, which came to be understood as a general promise to the "seed" of Abraham *to inherit the entire earth:*

"If you belong to Christ, then you are Abraham's seed, and heirs according to the promise (Galatians 3:29).

"Blessed are the meek, for they will inherit the earth" (Matthew 5:5).

"This mystery is that through the gospel the Gentiles are heirs together with Israel, members together of one body, and sharers together in the promise in Christ Jesus" (Ephesians 3:6).

"Therefore, there is now no condemnation for those who are in Christ Jesus, because through Christ Jesus the law of the Spirit of life set me free from the law of sin and death.

"For what the law was powerless to do in that it was weakened by the sinful nature, God did by sending his own Son in the likeness of sinful man to be a sin offering. And so he condemned sin in sinful man, in order that the righteous requirements of the law might be

---

[48] Galatians 3:16: "Now to Abraham and his seed were the promises made. He saith not, And to seeds, as of many; but as of one, And to thy seed, which is Christ."

fully met in us, who do not live according to the sinful nature but according to the Spirit.

"Those who live according to the sinful nature have their minds set on what that nature desires; but those who live in accordance with the Spirit have their minds set on what the Spirit desires. The mind of sinful man is death, but the mind controlled by the Spirit is life and peace; the sinful mind is hostile to God. It does not submit to God's law, nor can it do so. Those controlled by the sinful nature cannot please God" (Romans 8:1-8).

The sinful mind does not submit to God's law, but those who live in accordance with the Spirit do submit to God's law. Jesus *condemned sin in sinful man, in order that the righteous requirements of the law might be fully met in us, who do not live according to the sinful nature but according to the Spirit.*

We must recognize that this is the essence of the New Covenant promise through the prophet Jeremiah, that God would write His laws in the hearts of His people, and through this means God would secure to Himself a believing, obedient people, to whom He would be "God." Writing His law in our hearts is part of the process of re-birth, the change from a carnal nature to a spiritual nature.

---o-O-o---

Not Only the Ten Commandments Are Called "the Covenant"

The Ten Commandments: "...he wrote on the tablets the words of the covenant – the Ten Commandments" (Exodus 34:28).

Circumcision: "Then he gave Abraham the covenant of circumcision" (Acts 7:8).

The Sabbath: "The Israelites are to observe the Sabbath, celebrating it for the generations to come as a lasting covenant" (Exodus 31:16).

The book of the covenant: "Then he took *the Book of the Covenant* and read it to the people" (Exodus 24:7).

It was this "book of the covenant" that was to be at or in the side of the ark of the covenant:

"Take this Book of the Law and *place it beside the ark* of the covenant of the LORD your God. There it will remain as a witness against you" (Deuteronomy 31:26 NIV).

"Take this Book of the Law, and *put it in the side of the ark* of the covenant of the LORD your God, that it may be there for a witness against thee" (Deuteronomy 31:26, KJV).

---o-**O**-o---

Kings of Israel to Keep a Copy at Hand

"When you enter the land the LORD your God is giving you and have taken possession of it and settled in it, and you say, 'Let us set a king over us like all the nations around us,' be sure to appoint over you the king the LORD your God chooses. He must be from among your own brothers. Do not place a foreigner over you, one who is not a brother Israelite."

"When he takes the throne of his kingdom, he is to write for himself on a scroll a copy of this law, taken from that of the priests, who are Levites. It is to be with him, and he is to read it all the days of his life so that he may learn to revere the LORD his God and follow carefully all the words of this law and these decrees and not consider himself better than his brothers and turn from the law to the right or to the left. Then he and his descendants will reign a long time over his kingdom in Israel" (Deuteronomy 17:14, 15, 18-20).

"He is to write for himself on a scroll a copy of this law"! Can you imagine a president or king having to begin his term of office by writing out his own copy of God's law, and to keep it at hand as a guide in his executive decisions? Having done that, a national leader would have little excuse to be ignorant of what the Lord requires!

While it is true that there were curses in the book of the covenant, there were also blessings: *"Do not let this Book of the Law depart from your mouth; meditate on it day and night, so that you may be careful to do everything written in it. Then you will be prosperous and successful"* (Joshua 1:8).

The same is true of the writings of the Prophets, for example:

"So I will come near to you for judgment. I will be quick to testify against sorcerers, adulterers and perjurers, against those who defraud laborers of their wages, who oppress the widows and the fatherless, and deprive aliens of justice, but do not fear me," says the LORD Almighty.

"I the LORD do not change. So you, O descendants of Jacob, are not destroyed. Ever since the time of your forefathers you have turned away from my decrees and have not kept them. Return to me, and I will return to you," says the LORD Almighty.

"But you ask, 'How are we to return?'

*"Will a man rob God? Yet you rob me. But you ask, 'How do we rob you?' In tithes and offerings. **You are under a curse** – the whole nation of you – because you are robbing me. Bring the whole tithe into the storehouse, that there may be food in my house.*

"Test me in this,' says the LORD Almighty, 'and see if I will not throw open the floodgates of heaven and pour out so much blessing that you will not have room enough for it. I will prevent pests from devouring your crops, and the vines in your fields will not cast their fruit,' says the LORD Almighty.

"'Then all the nations will call you blessed, for yours will be a delightful land,' says the LORD Almighty" (Malachi 3:5-12).

---o-**O**-o---

Covenant Similarities and Differences

Not everything about the old will, the Old Covenant, was to differ from the new! In fact, they contain many similarities!

It is worthwhile to note the similarity of the wording of the Old Covenant, and the wording promised for the New Covenant:

Presence Similarities

Old Covenant: *"I will walk among you and be your God, and you will be my people"* (Leviticus 26:12). *"Be strong and courageous. Do not be afraid or terrified because of them, for the LORD your God goes with you; he will never leave you nor forsake you"* (Deuteronomy 31:6).

New Covenant: *"This is the covenant I will make with the house of Israel. I will put my law in their minds and write it on their hearts. I will be their God, and they will be my people"* (Jeremiah 31:33). *"And surely I am with you always, to the very end of the age"* (Matthew 28:20).

Promise Similarities:

Old Covenant: *"Now if you obey me fully and keep my covenant, then out of all nations you will be my treasured possession. Although the whole earth is mine, you will be for me a kingdom of priests and a holy nation.' These are the words you are to speak to the Israelites"* (Exodus 19:5, 6).

New Covenant: *"...from Jesus Christ, who is the faithful witness, the firstborn from the dead, and the ruler of the kings of the earth. To him who loves us and has freed us from our sins by his blood, and has made us to be a kingdom and priests to serve his God and Father – to him be glory and power for ever and ever!"* (Revelation 1:5, 6).

Sin Definition Similarities:

Old Covenant: Exodus 20:1-17:

"And God spoke all these words: I am the LORD your God, who brought you out of Egypt, out of the land of slavery. You shall have no other gods before me.

"You shall not make for yourself an idol in the form of anything in heaven above or on the earth beneath or in the waters below. You shall not bow down to them or worship them; for I, the LORD your God, am a jealous God, punishing the children for the sin of the fathers to the third and fourth generation of those who hate me,

but showing love to a thousand generations of those who love me and keep my commandments.

"You shall not misuse the name of the LORD your God, for the LORD will not hold anyone guiltless who misuses his name.

"Remember the Sabbath day by keeping it holy. Six days you shall labor and do all your work, but the seventh day is a Sabbath to the LORD your God. On it you shall not do any work, neither you, nor your son or daughter, nor your manservant or maidservant, nor your animals, nor the alien within your gates. For in six days the LORD made the heavens and the earth, the sea, and all that is in them, but he rested on the seventh day. Therefore the LORD blessed the Sabbath day and made it holy.

"Honor your father and your mother, so that you may live long in the land the LORD your God is giving you.

"You shall not murder.

"You shall not commit adultery.

"You shall not steal.

"You shall not give false testimony against your neighbor.

"You shall not covet your neighbor's house. You shall not covet your neighbor's wife, or his manservant or maidservant, his ox or donkey, or anything that belongs to your neighbor."

New Covenant: *"Everyone who sins breaks the law; in fact, sin is lawlessness"* (1 John 3:4). This statement does not specify what is in "the law" but it defines the basic concept that sin is lawlessness, or lawbreaking.

But in the following statements Paul gets quite specific as to what the law condemns, kinds of actions that are "lawlessness," and reference to most of the sins listed can be found in the Old Covenant law:

"The acts of the sinful nature are obvious: sexual immorality, impurity and debauchery; idolatry and witchcraft; hatred, discord, jealousy, fits of rage, selfish ambition, dissensions, factions and envy; drunkenness, orgies, and the like. I warn you, as I did before, that those who live like this will not inherit the kingdom of God" (Galatians 5:19-21*)*.

- 125 -

"We know that the law is good if one uses it properly. We also know that law is made not for the righteous but for lawbreakers and rebels, the ungodly and sinful, the unholy and irreligious; for those who kill their fathers or mothers, for murderers, for adulterers and perverts, for slave traders and liars and perjurers – and for whatever else is contrary to the sound doctrine" (1 Timothy 1:9, 10).

"Do you not know that the wicked will not inherit the kingdom of God? Do not be deceived: Neither the sexually immoral nor idolaters nor adulterers nor male prostitutes nor homosexual offenders nor thieves nor the greedy nor drunkards nor slanderers nor swindlers will inherit the kingdom of God" (1 Corinthians 6:9, 10).

In fact, one of the more easily recognized similarities between the old and New Covenants is the common reference to God's law, and both covenants affirm the goodness and rightness of God's law. Moses, about to finish his leadership of Israel, said to them:

"Behold, I have taught you statutes and judgments, even as the LORD my God commanded me, that ye should do so in the land whither ye go to possess it. Keep therefore and do them; for this is your wisdom and your understanding in the sight of the nations, which shall hear all these statutes, and say, Surely this great nation is a wise and understanding people.

"For what nation is there so great, who hath God so nigh unto them, as the LORD our God is in all things that we call upon him for? And what nation is there so great, that hath statutes and judgments so righteous as all this law, which I set before you this day?

"Only take heed to thyself, and keep thy soul diligently, lest thou forget the things which thine eyes have seen, and lest they depart from thy heart all the days of thy life: but teach them thy sons, and thy sons' sons; Specially the day that thou stoodest before the LORD thy God in Horeb, when the LORD said unto me, Gather me the people together, and I will make them hear my words, that they may learn to fear me all the days that they shall live upon the earth, and that they may teach their children" (Deuteronomy 4:5-10 KJV).

Notice the problem Moses anticipated, that God's laws would depart *from the hearts* of His people. That problem is specifically addressed in God's promise of a New Covenant, that He would *write His law in their hearts*.

And, notice the praise of the law other nations would give: *"...what nation is there so great, that hath statutes and judgments so righteous as all this law?"*

Why would those other nations recognize that the statutes and judgments of the law were righteous? Paul explains it:

> *"All who sin apart from the law will also perish apart from the law, and all who sin under the law will be judged by the law. For it is not those who hear the law who are righteous in God's sight, but it is those who obey the law who will be declared righteous.*
>
> *"Indeed, when Gentiles, who do not have the law, do by nature things required by the law, they are a law for themselves, even though they do not have the law, since they show that the requirements of the law are written on their hearts, their consciences also bearing witness, and their thoughts now accusing, now even defending them."* (Romans 2:12-15)

When those nations who observed the statutes and judgments of God's law in operation in Israel, *they knew by nature* that those statutes and judgments were righteous!

What we see in these evaluations of the law, both from an old and new Scriptures standpoint, is that the problem causing the need of a New Covenant was not the law: *"Is the law, therefore, opposed to the promises of God? Absolutely not! For if a law had been given that could impart life, then righteousness would certainly have come by the law"* (Galatians 3:21).

If law could impart life, the law God gave Israel would have done the job. Therefore, what was needed was not a new law! A new law could not impart life any more than the old law imparted life!

Had It Not Been for Sin ...

Had it not been for sin, there would have been no need for law![49]
Had it not been for sin, there would have been no need for a Savior;
had it not been for sin, there would have been no need of forgiveness and salvation; had it not been for sin, there would have been
no death penalty; had it not been for sin, there would have been no
need for sacrifices or priests to offer the sacrifices; had it not been
for sin, there would have been no penalties for sin, ranging from
restitution to the death penalty.

A careless reading of the study to this point may allow one to think
that the study seeks to validate the entirety of Old Covenant law.
Nothing could be further from the truth. Many changes were made, but
they did not pertain to morality.

Some had to do with the temporary measures developed so the Old
Covenant could deal with sin, other changes were deletions of regulations for Israel's movement in their desert wanderings, selection of a
king, and administration of a theocratic national government.

Those Old Covenant provisions *for dealing with sin* were temporary
provisions, temporary measures looking forward to permanent resolu-
tion of the sin problem, with changes in the law to accommodate the
permanent solution. These changes are most clearly stated in the book
of Hebrews.   ---o-O-o---

Prologue to the Needed Changes

*"We must pay more careful attention, therefore, to what we have
heard, so that we do not drift away. For if the message spoken by
angels was binding, and every violation and disobedience received*

---

[49] Romans 7:13: "Did that which is good, then, become death to me? By no means!
But in order that sin might be recognized as sin, it produced death in me through
what was good, so that through the commandment sin might become utterly sinful."

its just punishment, how shall we escape if we ignore such a great salvation?

"This salvation, which was first announced by the Lord, was confirmed to us by those who heard him. God also testified to it by signs, wonders and various miracles, and gifts of the Holy Spirit distributed according to his will" (Hebrews 2:1-4).

It is fitting that we begin this section with a reaffirmation of the vital role played by the Son of God:

"In the past God spoke to our forefathers through the prophets at many times and in various ways, but in these last days he has spoken to us by his Son, whom he appointed heir of all things, and through whom he made the universe.

"The Son is the radiance of God's glory and the exact representation of his being, sustaining all things by his powerful word. After he had provided purification for sins, he sat down at the right hand of the Majesty in heaven. So he became as much superior to the angels as the name he has inherited is superior to theirs" (Hebrews 1:1-4).

The Son is the radiance of God's glory and the exact representation of his being – and thus He was able to die in the place of His Father, as the Covenant Maker, through Whose death the Covenants, Old and New, have been validated and sealed forever in their effectiveness.

Therefore Christ, as Covenant Maker, could enunciate such changes in the law as are found in the Sermon on the Mount. It is here we find some fulfillment of the prophesied magnification of the law. Notice the preamble to those changes:

"Do not think that I have come to abolish the Law or the Prophets; I have not come to abolish them but to fulfill them. I tell you the truth, until heaven and earth disappear, not the smallest letter, not the least stroke of a pen, will by any means disappear from the Law until everything is accomplished.

"Anyone who breaks one of the least of these commandments and teaches others to do the same will be called least in the kingdom of heaven, but whoever practices and teaches these commands will be called great in the kingdom of heaven.

"For I tell you that unless your righteousness surpasses that of the Pharisees and the teachers of the law, you will certainly not enter the kingdom of heaven" (Matthew 5:17-20).

Reading this passage one would not expect to find *any* New Covenant *changes* in the law, were it not for the statement, *"I tell you the truth, until heaven and earth disappear, not the smallest letter, not the least stroke of a pen, will by any means disappear from the Law **until everything is accomplished."***

The implication is that as some things are accomplished, those things would disappear from the law. And indeed, those changes began immediately to take place.

Keep in mind, as these changes are made, that *until the death of the Will Maker,* the death of the One stating the conditions of inheritance, the Maker of the will has *every right* to change the provisions of the will, and make changes He did! All throughout the wilderness journey under Moses, and in the leadership of Joshua, additions were made to the book of the Covenant.

Even through the prophets, before and after the Babylonian and Assyrian exiles, God continued to refine the Old Covenant with explanations and revisions.

It should not, therefore, be considered illogical for the Covenant Maker Himself, Jesus Christ, to personally revise the Old Covenant as He did in the Sermon on the Mount. In view of a Covenant Maker's right to revise His Last Will and Testament *until the time of His death* (this is true of human wills as well as divine wills or covenants), we should not be surprised to notice the following changes Jesus announced and put into effect:

Isaiah prophesied, *"The LORD is well pleased for his righteousness' sake; he will magnify the law, and make it honourable"* (Isaiah 42:21).

Note the following refinements and modifications:

1) *"You have heard that it was said to the people long ago, 'Do not murder,' and anyone who murders will be subject to judgment.' But I tell you that anyone who is angry with his brother will be subject to judgment.*

2) *"Again, anyone who says to his brother, 'Raca,' is answerable to the Sanhedrin. But anyone who says, 'You fool!' will be in danger of the fire of hell.*

3) *"Therefore, if you are offering your gift at the altar and there remember that your brother has something against you, leave your gift there in front of the altar. First go and be reconciled to your brother; then come and offer your gift."*

4) *"You have heard that it was said, 'Do not commit adultery.' But I tell you that anyone who looks at a woman lustfully has already committed adultery with her in his heart"* (Matthew 5:21, 22b-24, 27, 28).

One meaning of "honourable" is "obeyable." The law becomes obeyable by the indwelling of the Holy Spirit, by being born again, by the law being written in our hearts and minds, by God making a way of escape from every temptation, not allowing them to be more than we can resist.   ---o-O-o---

Did Jesus Have the Authority to Change Law?

As you ponder whether these things are true or not, consider this statement of Jesus: *"Then Jesus came to them and said, 'All authority in heaven and on earth has been given to me'"* (Matthew 28:18). Really? Indeed! And just when was all that "authority" given to Jesus? While He was the Son of Man, or when He did the following:

"For by him were all things created, that are in heaven, and that are in earth, visible and invisible, whether they be thrones, or dominions, or principalities, or powers: all things were created by him, and for him" (Colossians 1:16).

"In the past God spoke to our forefathers through the prophets at many times and in various ways, but in these last days he has spoken to us by his Son, whom he appointed heir of all things, and through whom he made the universe.

"The Son is the radiance of God's glory and the exact representation of his being, sustaining all things by his powerful word. After he had provided purification for sins, he sat down at the right hand of the Majesty in heaven" (Hebrews 1:1-3).

Is it possible we still do not believe these truths? Did Jesus create the covenants? Are they included in "all power," in the visible and invisible elements of Creation? We must decide!

Yes, Jesus had the power and authority! Immediately after the Sermon on the Mount, during which these changes in the Old Covenant were effected, it is written that *"When Jesus had finished saying these things, the crowds were amazed at his teaching, because he taught as one who had authority, and not as their teachers of the law"* (Matthew 28, 29).

The same Greek word for "authority" means "power." Indeed, He did have the "authority," the power! In contrast, what Scribe, Priest or Pharisee could make such pronouncements? Not one! Jesus was challenged because of such pronouncements:

"Jesus entered the temple courts, and, while he was teaching, the chief priests and the elders of the people came to him. 'By what authority are you doing these things?' they asked. 'And who gave you this authority?'" (Matthew 21:23).

Their question was not just "Who told you could do these things?" It included, "Where did the power come from?" We may be tempted to ask the same question! Did Jesus the Christ indeed have such authority? Do we *now* know the answer? Indeed we do!

If he had all authority in heaven and earth, if He was Creator of all things in heaven and earth, if He was the Old Covenant Maker *and* the New Covenant Maker, and in each instance was acting in His Father's stead, Jesus had the perfect right to make such covenant changes before His death.

This is clearly affirmed by our Lord: "Jesus came to them and said, *"All authority in heaven and on earth has been given to me"* (Matthew 28:18). *"All things have been committed to me by my Father"* (Luke 10:22).

The Jews did not believe it – *do we?* We must, if we believe the Scriptures! These things are part of the mysteries hidden through the ages, but they were made known through the revelation of Jesus Christ as the Son of God.

It was the perfect right of the Covenant Maker to change His will, old or new, anytime before they both were sealed by His death. Thereafter neither the old nor the new could be modified, for both were made immutable by the death of our Lord, by Whose blood the work of both the Old and New Covenants were forever validated and sealed.

Therefore, whatever changes are revealed in the Holy Scriptures *after the cross* were already ordained *before the cross* and sealed forever *by the cross: "All inhabitants of the earth will worship the beast – all whose names have not been written in the book of life belonging to the Lamb that was slain from the creation of the world"* (Revelation 13:8).

---o-O-o---

In Exercise of His Authority
He Negated Portions of Previous Covenant Law

Comparison 1:

New: *"It has been said, 'Anyone who divorces his wife must give her a certificate of divorce.' But I tell you that anyone who divorces his wife, except for marital unfaithfulness, causes her to become an adulteress, and anyone who marries the divorced woman commits adultery"* (Matthew 5:31, 32).

Old: *"When a man hath taken a wife, and married her, and it come to pass that she find no favour in his eyes, because he hath found some uncleanness in her: then let him write her a bill of divorcement, and* *give it in her hand, and send her out of his house. And when she is departed out of his house, she may go and be another man's wife"* (Deuteronomy 24:1, 2, KJV).

Comparison 2:

New: *"Again, you have heard that it was said to the people long ago, 'Do not break your oath, but keep the oaths you have made to the Lord.' But I tell you, Do not swear at all: either by heaven, for it is God's throne; or by the earth, for it is his footstool; or by Jerusalem, for it is the city of the Great King.*

"And do not swear by your head, for you cannot make even one hair white or black. Simply let your 'Yes' be 'Yes,' and your 'No,' 'No'; anything beyond this comes from the evil one" (Matthew 5:33-37).

Old: *"Thou shalt fear the LORD thy God, and serve him, and shalt swear by his name"* (Deuteronomy 6:13, KJV). *"Fear the LORD your God, serve him only and take your oaths in his name"* (Deuteronomy 6:13).

Comparison 3:

New: *"You have heard that it was said, 'Eye for eye, and tooth for tooth.' But I tell you, Do not resist an evil person. If someone strikes you on the right cheek, turn to him the other also. And if someone wants to sue you and take your tunic, let him have your cloak as well. If someone forces you to go one mile, go with him two miles. Give to the one who asks you, and do not turn away from the one who wants to borrow from you"* (Matthew 5:38-42).

Old: *"If anyone injures his neighbor, whatever he has done must be done to him: fracture for fracture, eye for eye, tooth for tooth. As he has injured the other, so he is to be injured"* (Leviticus 24:19, 20).

Comparison 4:

Old: "You have heard that it was said, 'Love your neighbor and hate your enemy.'

New: "But I tell you: Love your enemies and pray for those who persecute you, that you may be sons of your Father in heaven" (Matthew 5:43-45a).

Did Jesus have the right, the power, to say such things? Were they "authoritative"? The Jews wondered that also!

Many clarifications of the workings of the New Covenant relate to changes in the office of the priesthood and the making of sacrifices. Notice these clarifications in the book of Hebrews:

Change in the Priesthood:

The following passages are a thorough explanation of this change in the covenants, From the Old to the New:

"Therefore, since we have a great high priest who has gone through the heavens, Jesus the Son of God, let us hold firmly to the faith we profess. For we do not have a high priest who is unable to sympathize with our weaknesses, but we have one who has been tempted in every way, just as we are – yet was without sin. Let us then approach the throne of grace with confidence, so that we may receive mercy and find grace to help us in our time of need" (Hebrews 7:14-16 NIV).

"For every high priest taken from among men is ordained for men in things pertaining to God, that he may offer both gifts and sacrifices for sins: Who can have compassion on the ignorant, and on them that are out of the way; for that he himself also is compassed with infirmity. And by reason hereof he ought, as for the people, so also for himself, to offer for sins.

"And no man taketh this honour unto himself, but he that is called of God, as was Aaron. So also Christ glorified not himself to be made an high priest; but he that said unto him, Thou art my Son, today have I begotten thee. As he saith also in another place, Thou art a priest for ever after the order of Melchisedec" (Hebrews 5:1-6 KJV).

"We have this hope as an anchor for the soul, firm and secure. It enters the inner sanctuary behind the curtain, where Jesus, who went before us, has entered on our behalf. He has become a high priest forever, in the order of Melchizedek" (Hebrews 6:19 NIV).

"If perfection could have been attained through the Levitical priesthood (for on the basis of it the law was given to the people), why was there still need for another priest to come – one in the order of Melchizedek, not in the order of Aaron?

"For when there is a change of the priesthood, there must also be a change of the law. *He of whom these things are said belonged to a different tribe, and no one from that tribe has ever served at the altar. For it is clear that our Lord descended from Judah, and in regard to that tribe Moses said nothing about priests"* (Hebrews 7:11-14 NIV).

It is important to note that these are "changes" in the law; the law remained that there must be a High Priest; but who could officiate as High Priest and the instructions for the high priest's duties were changed in the ways outlined above.

---o-O-o---

Why Change, if Abolished?

One problem with the concept of "abolishing" the Old Covenant is repudiation of the good that was accomplished by the Old Covenant. Imperfect though it was, there was no other approach to God in those days, and that which God accomplished through the Old Covenant stands. The work accomplished under the Old Covenant was ratified by the death of Christ just as surely as the work of the New Covenant was ratified by His death.

What we find in Hebrews 9:15 is this: *"For this reason Christ is the mediator of a New Covenant, that those who are called may receive the promised eternal inheritance –* ***now that he has died as a ransom to set them free from the sins committed under the first covenant."***

Let's consider the case of a Jew or Gentile who under the Old Covenant "joined (or "bound," NIV) themselves to the Lord,"[50] who took hold of God's Old Covenant.

If the blood of Jesus had not also applied to them, if the Old Covenant were "abolished," or just disappeared without confirmation of the Old Covenant through the blood of Christ, *since the blood of bulls, goats, heifers etc. cannot take away sin, what would have been the fate of the Jews and Gentiles who were faithful to the Old Covenant in order to be reconciled to God?*

If Jesus had not "fulfilled" the Old Covenant rather than abolishing it, those who came to God under the Old Covenant would still be guilty of their sins and ineligible to enter the kingdom of God, because the blood of bulls and goats cannot take away sin!

By His death and cleansing blood Jesus not only ratified and sealed the Old Covenant, He also freed from guilt those who came to God under the Old Covenant.

So as an operative system, the Old Covenant disappeared; but as a means of bringing all the faithful of the Old Covenant to Christ for salvation, it was the valid connecting link to the sacrifice *that could take away sin – the crucifixion of our Lord and Savior, Jesus Christ!*

"But the ministry Jesus has received is as superior to theirs (the priests of the Old Covenant) as the covenant of which he is mediator is superior to the old one, and it is founded on better promises.

"For if there had been nothing wrong with that first covenant, no place would have been sought for another."

"By calling this covenant 'new,' he has made the first one obsolete; and what is obsolete and aging will soon disappear" (Hebrews 8:6, 7, 13).

"When Christ came as high priest of the good things that are already here, he went through the greater and more perfect taberna-

---

[50] "And foreigners who bind themselves to the LORD to serve him, to love the name of the LORD, and to worship him, all who keep the Sabbath without desecrating it and who hold fast to my covenant – these I will bring to my holy mountain and give them joy in my house of prayer" (Isaiah 56:6, 7)..

cle that is not man-made, that is to say, not a part of this creation. He did not enter by means of the blood of goats and calves; but he entered the Most Holy Place once for all by his own blood, having obtained eternal redemption.

"The blood of goats and bulls and the ashes of a heifer sprinkled on those who are ceremonially unclean sanctify them so that they are outwardly clean. How much more, then, will the blood of Christ, who through the eternal Spirit offered himself unblemished to God, cleanse our consciences from acts that lead to death, so that we may serve the living God!" (Hebrews 9:11-14).

Of all the biblical passages dealing with the transition from the Old to the New Covenant, those in the book of Hebrews deal more specifically with the differences between the two covenants relating to priesthood and sacrifice for sin – the "new and better" to be found in the New Covenant.   ---o-**O**-o---

Hebrews, A Book of Comfort for Israel

Hebrews is a book which brings comfort to Israel in particular, for consider how it would be for such saints of the Old Covenant who were faithful and obedient, if their system of atonement and approach to worship were simply abolished, the blood of bulls and goats declared incapable of taking away sin, and no note were ever made in the New Covenant with reference to the results of their faithful obedience!

There *were* some who obeyed God (contrary to the popular claim that no person can keep or has kept the law of God!).[51] The book of Hebrews pointedly explains that their faithfulness was brought to fruition in Christ *("And for this cause he is the mediator of the new testa-*

---

[51] "Though I might also have confidence in the flesh. If any other man thinketh that he hath whereof he might trust in the flesh, I more: Circumcised the eighth day, of the stock of Israel, of the tribe of Benjamin, an Hebrew of the Hebrews; as touching the law, a Pharisee; Concerning zeal, persecuting the church; touching the righteousness which is in the law, blameless" (Phil. 3:4-6 KJV).

ment, that by means of death, for the redemption of the transgressions that were under the first testament, they which are called might receive the promise of eternal inheritance" [Hebrews 9:15, KJV]),

Hebrews explicitly names many of the Old Testament saints as awaiting the resurrection, that they with the New Testament Saints may receive the inheritance together (see Hebrews chapters 11, 12). Jesus affirmed the same when He spoke of Abraham, Isaac, Jacob and all the prophets being seen in the Kingdom of God (Luke 13:8).

It is to be noted also that Hebrews chapter eleven very carefully documents *the role of faith in the Old Covenant,* and it must of necessity be concluded that faith has *always* been the effective means of establishing a solid relationship with God, and works have *never* been effective in establishing a relationship with God!

Resumption of obedience after disobedience has never atoned and can never atone for previous lapses in obedience. Faith in the means of atonement provided by God, Old Covenant or New, is and always has been the means of establishing relationships. Unbelief, the opposite of faith, has always guaranteed estrangement from God.

Faith in the means of atonement was not the only role played by faith under the old covenant. It had an every day application, as seen when under King Hezekiah's reign the Ammonites and Moabites came against Israel:

"Early in the morning they left for the Desert of Tekoa. As they set out, Jehoshaphat stood and said, 'Listen to me, Judah and people of Jerusalem! Have faith in the LORD your God and you will be upheld; have faith in his prophets and you will be successful.'

"After consulting the people, Jehoshaphat appointed men to sing to the LORD and to praise him for the splendor of his holiness as they went out at the head of the army, saying: "Give thanks to the LORD, for his love endures forever"' (Chronicles 20:21).

---o-O-o---

Breaking Covenant Still a Problem

The applied blood of Jesus Christ is the only complete answer to sins committed under either the Old or New Covenants.

But, having entered into covenant with God – either Old or New, having accepted His means of atonement, *the means of destroying that relationship* remains the same, loss of faith and disobedience. Consider these advantages and warnings:

"You have not come to a mountain that can be touched and that is burning with fire; to darkness, gloom and storm; to a trumpet blast or to such a voice speaking words that those who heard it begged that no further word be spoken to them, because they could not bear what was commanded: 'If even an animal touches the mountain, it must be stoned.' The sight was so terrifying that Moses said, 'I am trembling with fear.'

"But you have come to Mount Zion, to the heavenly Jerusalem, the city of the living God. You have come to thousands upon thousands of angels in joyful assembly, to the church of the firstborn, whose names are written in heaven. You have come to God, the judge of all men, to the spirits of righteous men made perfect, to Jesus the mediator of a New Covenant, and to the sprinkled blood that speaks a better word than the blood of Abel.

"See to it that you do not refuse him who speaks. If they did not escape when they refused him who warned them on earth, **how much less will we, if we turn away from him who warns us from heaven?** *At that time his voice shook the earth, but now he has promised, 'Once more I will shake not only the earth but also the heavens.' The words 'once more' indicate the removing of what can be shaken – that is, created things – so that what cannot be shaken may remain"* (Hebrews 12:18-27).

Some of the most stern warnings of the New Testament are found in the book of Hebrews:

"It is impossible for those who have once been enlightened, who have tasted the heavenly gift, who have shared in the Holy Spirit, who have tasted the goodness of the word of God and the powers of the coming age, if they fall away, to be brought back to repentance, because to their loss they are crucifying the Son of God all over again and subjecting him to public disgrace (Hebrews 6:4-6).

*"'This is the covenant I will make with them after that time,' says the Lord. 'I will put my laws in their hearts, and I will write them on their minds.' Then he adds: 'Their sins and lawless acts I will re-member no more.' **And where these have been forgiven, there is no longer any sacrifice for sin.***

"Therefore, brothers, since we have confidence to enter the Most Holy Place by the blood of Jesus, by a new and living way opened for us through the curtain, that is, his body, and since we have a great priest over the house of God, let us draw near to God with a sincere heart in full assurance of faith, having our hearts sprinkled to cleanse us from a guilty conscience and having our bodies washed with pure water.

"Let us hold unswervingly to the hope we profess, for he who promised is faithful. And let us consider how we may spur one an-other on toward love and good deeds. Let us not give up meeting together, as some are in the habit of doing, but let us encourage one another – and all the more as you see the Day approaching.

"If we deliberately keep on sinning after we have received the knowledge of the truth, no sacrifice for sins is left, but only a fearful expectation of judgment and of raging fire that will con-sume the enemies of God. Anyone who rejected the law of Moses died without mercy on the testimony of two or three witnesses.

"How much more severely do you think a man deserves to be punished who has trampled the Son of God under foot, who has treated as an unholy thing the blood of the covenant that sancti-fied him, and who has insulted the Spirit of grace?

"For we know him who said, 'It is mine to avenge; I will repay,' and again, 'The Lord will judge his people.' It is a dreadful thing to fall into the hands of the living God" (Hebrews 10:16-31).

This is a continuation of the theme of chapters three and four, a warning not to break covenant with God as Israel did, only with a more stern message, since we are dealing with Jesus Christ *the Son of God,* and not with Moses, *the servant-friend of God* – (Hebrews 3:5, 6).

So the two covenants have this in common, that in each covenant, faith is essential to establish oneself in the position of an heir, to establish family relations with God; while loss of faith and disobedience are the means of becoming one of the disinherited:

*"And the LORD said unto Moses, How long will this people provoke me? and how long will it be ere they believe me, for all the signs which I have shown among them? I will smite them with the pestilence, **and disinherit them,** and will make of thee a greater nation and mightier than they"* (Numbers 14:11, 12, KJV).

Paul says of Israel:
*"Well; because of unbelief they were broken off, and thou standest by faith. Be not highminded, but fear: **For if God spared not the natural branches, take heed lest he also spare not thee.** Behold therefore the goodness and severity of God: on them which fell, severity; but **toward thee, goodness, if thou continue in his goodness: otherwise thou also shalt be cut off.** And they also, if they abide not still in unbelief, shall be grafted in: for God is able to graft them in again"* (Romans 11:20-23, KJV).

The following are truths common to both Covenants:
"Do you not know that the wicked will not inherit the kingdom of God? Do not be deceived: Neither the sexually immoral nor idolaters nor adulterers nor male prostitutes nor homosexual offenders nor thieves nor the greedy nor drunkards nor slanderers nor swin-

dlers will inherit the kingdom of God" (1 Corinthians 6:9, 10); and again:

"The acts of the sinful nature are obvious: sexual immorality, impurity and debauchery; idolatry and witchcraft; hatred, discord, jealousy, fits of rage, selfish ambition, dissensions, factions and envy; drunkenness, orgies, and the like. I warn you, as I did before, that those who live like this will not inherit the kingdom of God" (Galatians 5:19-21).   ---o-O-o---

Abolished, Disappeared, or Changed?
The Meaning of "It Is Finished"

One common assumption is that all Old Covenant law was abolished on the cross of Christ, and new principles were established for the conduct of God's people. In spite of the fact Jesus said not to think it, another common assumption is that all Old Covenant law was abolished but parts of the old law were reestablished in the New, as New Covenant law.

In-depth discussions with some Bible Students make it apparent that this maneuvering is mainly for the purpose of disposing of the seventh day Sabbath, since the rest of the Ten Commandments are not objected to, neither are quite an additional list of moral commands from the Book of the Law.

According to the usual interpretation of Paul's writings, some or all Old Covenant commandments were "abolished" or modified, deleted or replaced, as the case may be. What Paul has to say must be understood in the light of Jesus' own clear declaration:

*"**Do not think** that I have come to abolish the Law or the Prophets; **I have not come to abolish them** but to fulfill them. I tell you the truth, until heaven and earth disappear, not the smallest letter, not the least stroke of a pen, will by any means disappear from the Law until everything is accomplished.*

"Anyone who breaks one of the least of these commandments and teaches others to do the same will be called least in the kingdom of heaven, but whoever practices and teaches these commands will be called great in the kingdom of heaven.

"For I tell you that unless your righteousness surpasses that of the Pharisees and the teachers of the law, you will certainly not enter the kingdom of heaven" (Matthew 5:17-20).

Since Jesus *commanded* that His listeners *not even think* He came to abolish the law and stated plainly that He did not come to do that, one must consider whether Paul contradicted Jesus. One must also consider whether we, modern students of the Word, disobey Christ's command!

Do some translators misunderstand Paul's intention and consequently misconstrue and mistranslate what He wrote about *abolishing* the law of commandments contained in ordinances (Ephesians 2:15, KJV)?

It will be assumed here that since Jesus came neither to *abolish* the law nor the Prophets, then *He didn't abolish* any part of either, but that He did intentionally fulfill parts of both!

If we couple *"not the least stroke of a pen, will by any means disappear from the Law until everything is accomplished"* with John 19:30: *"When he had received the drink, Jesus said, "It is finished." With that, he bowed his head and gave up his spirit"* – what is suggested?

When the thoughts are coupled, some come to the conclusion that Jesus saying on the cross, *"It is finished,"* denotes the point in time when *everything was accomplished;* and that at that point, *not just the least stroke of a pen disappeared from the law, but the entire law* disappeared because *"everything was accomplished."*

But is that a true interpretation? Does that interpretation agree with Paul's statement that by faith we establish or uphold the law? No, for by faith we establish, by faith we uphold the same law that is unable to save us, the same law which is holy, just, good and spiritual, the same law Paul says the carnal mind cannot obey, but the Spiritual mind can – this is the same law about which Paul wrote:

*"For what the law could not do, in that it was weak through the flesh, God sending his own Son in the likeness of sinful flesh, and for sin, condemned sin in the flesh: **That the righteousness of the law might be fulfilled in us,** who walk not after the flesh, but after the Spirit.*

*"For they that are after the flesh do mind the things of the flesh; but they that are after the Spirit the things of the Spirit. For to be carnally minded is death; **but to be spiritually minded is life and peace. Because the carnal mind is enmity against God: for it is not subject to the law of God, neither indeed can be"** (Romans 8:3-7).*

It is obvious by the context of that passage that:

1) The law could not produce righteousness in sinful, carnal man.

2) Sin in the flesh is condemned by the coming of Christ in the flesh.

3) The Son of God was sent to accomplish what the law could not accomplish – fulfilling the righteousness of the law *in us.*

4) To be carnally minded is death because the carnal mind is not subject to the law, and cannot be subject to the law.

5) We become spiritually minded *so as to become able to be subject to the law of God* – subject in the sense of obedience to, guided by, not in the sense of being condemned by it.

If God sent His son for that purpose, then that law which the Spirit enables us to obey did not cease to exist when Jesus said, "It is finished." What was finished? His earthly ministry, His mission of dying in our place, His sacrifice to pay the death penalty for our sins; termination of the old system of sacrifices and the old priesthood – thus making it possible for the righteousness of the law to be fulfilled in us.

---o-O-o---

"Until All Be Fulfilled"
Or, "Everything Is Accomplished"

There are two meanings to "fulfill," and it is assumed in this study that both meanings of "fulfill" are intended in the words of Jesus:

1) *Fulfill the law and prophets:* in the sense of accomplish their intended purpose, or perform a predicted act: *"This was to fulfill the word of Isaiah the prophet: 'Lord, who has believed our message and to whom has the arm of the Lord been revealed?'"*

2) *Live in accordance with the instructions of:* as in Galatians 6:2: *"Carry each other's burdens, and in this way you will fulfill the law of Christ."*

This does not intend to say we may carry someone's burdens once and never be expected to carry any more burdens. It is a way of life, to be practiced continually. This is the intent of God sending His Son as an atonement for our sins, that the righteous requirements of the law may be fulfilled in us. The law's righteousness becomes our way of life.

These two assumptions are necessary because some parts of the law were only intended to last until they were replaced, as for example the Levitical high priest's office replaced by Christ as High Priest. The sons of Aaron were not intended to continue in that office after the crucifixion of Christ.

By then they had fulfilled their roles as priests and the law appointing them to that office ceased to be a valid law because that law's purpose, its term of service was fulfilled, completed, and as part of the Old Covenant, it "was made obsolete" and what was obsolete and aging was "soon to disappear" (Hebrews 8:13).

At the time the book of Hebrews was written, the priesthood had already become obsolete, but it hadn't disappeared. It "soon" disappeared completely, with the destruction of the Temple in the 70's A.D., and the Levitical Priesthood has not functioned since.

Additionally, many provisions of the law and prophets did not become obsolete. They continue to function as guides to morality and to what the future holds.

So let's examine the Greek words which are translated "abolish."

Matthew 5:17: "Μὴ νομίσητε ὅτι ἦλθον **καταλῦσαι** τὸν νόμον ἢ τοὺς προφήτας· **οὐκ ἦλθον καταλῦσαι ἀλλὰ πληρῶσαι**."

Matthew 5:17: "Do not think that I have come to **abolish** the Law or the Prophets; I have **not come to abolish them but to fulfill them.**"

The word "**καταλῦσαι**" means "to dissolve, destroy, demolish, overthrow, throw down, nullify, or abrogate" *(Harper's Analytical Greek Lexicon).*

This, then, is what we must keep in mind as we read Paul's theological explanations: Jesus did not come to dissolve, destroy, demolish, overthrow, throw down, nullify or abrogate the law or the prophets. He said not to think it, and that He did not come to do it!

Paul's conclusion in Romans 3:31 agrees perfectly: *"Do we, then, nullify the law by this faith? Not at all! Rather, we uphold the law."* The Greek text for the passage reads: "Νόμον οὖν **καταργοῦμεν** διὰ τῆς πίστεως; μὴ γένοιτο, ἀλλὰ νόμον **ἱστάνομεν**."

The Greek word the NIV translates "we nullify" is **καταργοῦμεν**. Paul says οὖν **καταργοῦμεν** the law through faith – *we do not nullify, cause the law to fade away or disappear through faith,* is the meaning. Rather, through faith, we make the law to stand (ἀλλὰ νόμον **ἱστάνομεν**).

What we do not do to the law through faith (οὖν **καταργοῦμεν**), Paul affirms did happen to the radiance of Moses' face: *"We are not like Moses, who would put a veil over his face to keep the Israelites from gazing at it while the radiance was **fading away"** (2 Corinthians 3:13). The Greek of the passage reads:

"Καὶ οὐ καθάπερ Μωϋσῆς ἐτίθει κάλυμμα ἐπὶ τὸ πρόσωπον αὐτοῦ, πρὸς τὸ μὴ ἀτενίσαι τοὺς υἱοὺς Ἰσραὴλ εἰς τὸ τέλος τοῦ **καταργουμένου**."

So what *did happen* to the radiance of Moses' face as the radiance of Christ's ministry took center stage, *did not happen* to the law as faith takes center stage!

Since Paul affirms that we do not nullify the law through faith, but rather by faith we cause the law to stand, we must conclude that the function of the law, defining and condemning sin and leading us to Christ, are still valid functions, *and the purpose of the law is still being fulfilled* by God having sent His Son in the flesh to make it possible for those who live according to the Spirit to obey the righteousness of God's law.

The same Greek word used for "fading away" in 2 Corinthians 3:13 is used in Ephesians 2:15, and the NIV translates it "abolishing" and reads: "... by **abolishing** *in his flesh the law with its commandments and regulations. His purpose was to create in himself one new man out of the two, thus making peace.*"

In effect, the NIV stands the 2 Corinthians 3:13 on its head, and says the whole was abolished, therefore the parts were abolished – "by abolishing in his flesh the law," whereas the passage actually says that in His flesh, Christ caused the "law of commandments contained in ordinances" to fade away – the Greek uses a possessive form of "commandments," which is properly translated "of commandments," not "with its commandments."

The difference is that a part of the whole faded away, not the whole law faded away, which is contrary to the rest of the teachings of Christ, Paul and the book of Hebrews.

"Fade away" is a compatible meaning with the statement of Christ that HE DID NOT come to *abolish law*. "Fading away" rather suggests completion in stages of intended purposes. As we have seen, some of the "fading" occurred even during the Sermon on the Mount.

The KJV translates the passage: *"Having abolished in his flesh the enmity, even the law of commandments contained in ordinances; for to make in himself of twain one new man, so making peace."* It is evident that "abolished" cannot agree with Christ's denial of His having come to abolish the law, nor with Paul's denial that by faith we destroy the law.

---o-O-o---

How Is This Reconciled?

What was abolished was the *enmity* caused by a part of the law, commandments contained in ordinances, which enforced separation between Jew and Gentile.

This part of the law faded away because it was the purpose of God to make one body of two bodies – the body of believing Jews combined with the body of believing Gentiles to produce one new body, the Church of Christ, God's firstborn.

We notice that "fading" in the instructions of Jesus: *"These twelve Jesus sent out with the following instructions: 'Do not go among the Gentiles or enter any town of the Samaritans'"* (Matthew 10:5); compared with their work after the cross, *"Then Paul and Barnabas answered them boldly: 'We had to speak the word of God to you first. Since you reject it and do not consider yourselves worthy of eternal life, we now turn to the Gentiles'"* (Acts 13:46).

The important thing to note here is that what was abolished was enmity caused by the "law of injunctions, commands, orders," which had the result of making a separation between Jew and Gentile. Such an order or command would include circumcision and any other order which made a separation between Jews and other ethnic groups.

There are no such barriers, for example, in the two greatest commandments, Love God with your whole being and your neighbors as yourself; nor are there such barriers in the Ten Commandments. But, such barriers *are found* in the *law of commandments contained in ordinances*.

What was effected by "καταργήσα" (He brought it to an end) was this specific kind of "νόμον τῶν ἐντολῶν ἐν δόγμασιν," law of commands in doctrines (judgments, opinions, ordinances, decrees) – in this case those which specifically dealt with making differences between Jews and Gentiles.

The passage is in Greek: "τὸν νόμον τῶν ἐντολῶν ἐν δόγμασιν καταργήσα", [He brought to an end the law of commands con-

tained in ordinances] ἵνα τοὺς δύο κτίσῃ ἐν αὐτῷ εἰς ἕνα καινὸν ἄνθρωπον ποιῶν εἰρήνης **[in order that the two bodies may become one in peace]** (Ephesians 2:15).

These ordinances had fulfilled, served their purposes in full, and the Law of Moses was changed to delete these commands so as no longer to make such antagonising distinctions.

In contrast to simply being terminated, some parts of the law were replaced, the Levitical priesthood and the sacrificial system of animal slaughter for atonement for sin *would be most clearly understood to have been terminated by being replaced.*

How then does one account for the fact that the Old Covenant is spoken of as obsolete? *"By calling this covenant 'new,' he has made the first one obsolete; and what is obsolete and aging will soon disappear"* (Hebrews 8:13)?

Note: "Will soon disappear" – in the book of Hebrews many things about the priesthood were said to be in practice, which they were, decades after their ministry ceased to have God's sanction. They had not yet "disappeared" although disappearance was in process, and was consummated when the Temple was destroyed and the priesthood with its sacrificial system was forcibly terminated.

For example: "For if he [Jesus] were on earth, he should not be a priest, seeing that *there **are** priests* that **offer** *gifts according to the law"* (Hebrews 8:4); priests were still offering gifts according to the law, although without any spiritual validity.

In fact the Old Covenant as an instrument of the Father's will has indeed disappeared; but like man-made rewritten wills before the death of the will-maker, they often contain many of the same provisions; some provisions are changed to account for the behavior of the heirs in the time before the death of the will-maker, and other provisions are deleted.

Consequently, in contrast to the law, the entire old will is null and void, *even if it did contain many of the same provisions as those stated in the new,* including the law which we establish by faith. The Old Will is replaced, but in the case of God's will, the definitions of unacceptable immoral behavior and required moral behavior – the details of God's law of righteousness – are re-affirmed.

In this particular instance, the Old Covenant to New Covenant changes are analogous to the changed human wills. God's New Covenant is a brand-new instrument; however, within each instrument are what the Bible calls the law of God, or sometimes "the law of Moses."

There is not necessarily a distinction between the two terms "law of God" and "law of Moses," because both were from God delivered through Moses, and both were written in the Book of the Law before the Ten Commands were written on stone (refer again to Exodus chapters 20-24).   ---o-O-o---

Changes in the Whole? Or, the Whole Replaced?

The Old Covenant contained the law of God. The New Covenant contains the law of God. The entire Old Covenant was replaced, but not the entire law of the Old Covenant. In this sense, "the law" is not synonymous with "covenant."

If it be the case that all Old Covenant law ceased, why change a law and ratify that "change" by the death of Christ on the cross, if the whole law was abolished? Or, conversely, why make a change in the law, then abolish the whole law of which the change has become a part?

As we have seen, provision for such change has to be stipulated in the will of the Will Maker before the Will-Maker's death. So, if a change was made in the law, and then the entire law of which the change was a part was then abolished by the death of the Will-Maker, why make a *change* in the law?

Why would you modify or make changes in that which is no longer to exist? What purpose is served in rewriting laws and bylaws, perfecting their wording, adding and subtracting provisions, if in the final analysis the entirety is abandoned and nullified? It is not logical, and it just did not happen that way!

"Changes," in general, describe *the differences in law* found in the Old and New Covenants. That which remained unchanged constitutes a continuum from the Old Covenant to the new. That which continues is the part which remains holy, just, good, magnified, honourable, and established – made to stand – by faith.

The following laws were changed:

1) The Old Covenant required a son of Aaron, a Levite, to be high priest. The New Covenant requires Jesus Christ of the tribe of Judah, to be High Priest (forever: Hebrews 7:4-18).

2) The Old Covenant required animal sacrifices to atone for sin, but they could not perfect the job they began. The New Covenant required the death of the Covenant Maker, Jesus Christ, the Son of God, which could and does take away sin (Hebrews 9:11-14).

3) The Old Covenant required the High Priest to minister in the earthly tabernacle or temple; the New Covenant requires the High Priest, Jesus, to minister in the heavenly sanctuary, in the presence of God (Hebrews 9:1-14).

4) Because the blood of bulls and goats cannot remove sin, consciences were not cleared; but because the blood of Christ does remove sin, His blood confirms through faith the complete removal of guilt, and consciences are cleared (Hebrews 9:9,14).

5) Because the Old Covenant was broken, God's people could not enter into rest. Through the New Covenant God's people do enter into rest (see Hebrews chapters 3, 4).

Then there is this commonality: all saints of both covenants, whose worship of God and atonement are confirmed in the death of Christ, all must wait the return of their Lord to be resurrected from the dead to become immortal and receive their inheritance (Hebrews 11:13-16, 39-40).   --o-O-o---

These Issues Were Raised – Are They Resolved?

Have we then resolved the issues raised at the outset of the study? We will indicate the answers given to each of the issues raised.

1) *What constituted the Old Covenant? A Verbal Agreement Between Israel and God? The Ten Commandments? The Law of Moses? The books of the Bible, Genesis through Malachi? All of these elements and more?*

The answer to these questions is found within the record of God's dealings with His chosen people, Abraham and his descendants. It is not a theoretical matter, but a matter of recorded history.

God approached Abraham and made promises to him that he and his descendants would inherit *"... this land, from the river of Egypt to the great river, the Euphrates – the land of the Kenites, Kenizzites, Kadmonites, Hittites, Perizzites, Rephaites, Amorites, Canaanites, Girgashites and Jebusites"* (Genesis 15:18b-21).

The covenant with Abraham and Abraham's seed, was renewed with Isaac, Jacob, the twelve tribes, and with Christians (through Christ). That covenant has never ceased, was not replaced either by the Sinai covenant nor the Mt. Zion covenant – the latter two are referred to as the Old and New covenants.

The covenant with Abraham was amended, however; first to include circumcision, then to include the covenants made with Israel, then the new covenant made with Israel, Judah, and all of God's children, including the Christian Church, the Church of God; but the covenant with Abraham and his offspring stands regardless of amendments.

As amendments were replaced, the covenant with Abraham always remained valid. Requiring circumcision was such an amendment to the covenant with Abraham, and the amendment being replaced with circumcision of the heart does not nullify the Covenant with Abraham.

Thus, more than one covenant has been in operation between God and His people ever since God with Moses[52] led Israel in the Exodus

Paul speaks of "covenants" (plural) in two pertinent passages:

"For I could wish that I myself were cursed and cut off from Christ for the sake of my brothers, those of my own race, the people

---

[52] Jer. 31:32: "'It will not be like the covenant I made with their forefathers when I took them by the hand to lead them out of Egypt, because they broke my covenant, though I was a husband to them,' declares the LORD."

*of Israel. Theirs is the adoption as sons; theirs the divine glory, **the covenants,** the receiving of the law, the temple worship and the promises"* (Romans 9:3,4).

*"Therefore, remember that formerly you who are Gentiles by birth and called "uncircumcised" by those who call themselves "the circumcision" (that done in the body by the hands of men) – remember that at that time you were separate from Christ, excluded from citizenship in Israel **and foreigners to the covenants of the promise,** without hope and without God in the world"* (Ephesians 2:12).

By speaking of "covenants," Paul is not referring to the "Old Covenant" and the "New Covenant" in either of these passages. *Old Covenant* and *New Covenant* is not the basis of the word being plural – rather Paul is speaking of more than one covenant before the New Covenant was established, *the covenants of the promise.*

Through Christ, we Gentiles are no longer *foreigners to the **covenants** of promise.* These "covenants" of promise existed before the cross.

As members of the Body of Christ, and therefore seed of Abraham, we are beneficiaries of the same covenant with Abraham, and if we do not fall after the example of rebellious disbelief by which most of Israel fell, we will enjoy the inheritance promised Abraham and his seed, an inheritance called the "covenants of promise."[53] The covenant with Abraham could not be superseded by any subsequent covenant or by someone else's commission of sin.[54]

So before Israel had the law explained to them, they made a basic covenant with God, to be His obedient people, and He would be their God. This agreement for us to obey and Yahweh to be our God was

---

[53] "Remember that at that time you were separate from Christ, excluded from citizenship in Israel and foreigners to the covenants of the promise, without hope and without God in the world" (Ephesians 2:12).

[54] Gal. 3:17: "What I mean is this: The law, introduced 430 years later, does not set aside the covenant previously established by God and thus do away with the promise."

God's basic covenant not only with Israel, but also with Gentile Christians, God's adopted children:

"Not everyone who says to me, 'Lord, Lord,' will enter the kingdom of heaven, **but only he who does the will of my Father who is in heaven"** *(Matthew 7:21).*

"Now **if you obey me fully and keep my covenant,** *then out of all nations you will be my treasured possession. Although the whole earth is mine, you will be for me a kingdom of priests and a holy nation.' These are the words you are to speak to the Israelites.'*

"So Moses went back and summoned the elders of the people and set before them all the words the LORD had commanded him to speak. The people all responded together, "We will do everything the LORD has said." So Moses brought their answer back to the LORD " (Exodus 19:5-8).

That is the basic agreement made repeatedly between God and Israel:

"I will walk among you and be your God, and you will be my people" (Leviticus 26:12).

"... I gave them this command: Obey me, and I will be your God and you will be my people. Walk in all the ways I command you, that it may go well with you" (Jeremiah 7:23).

"... the terms I commanded your forefathers when I brought them out of Egypt, out of the iron-smelting furnace.' I said, 'Obey me and do everything I command you, and you will be my people, and I will be your God" (Jeremiah 11:4).

"'So you will be my people, and I will be your God'" (Jeremiah 30:22).

"You will live in the land I gave your forefathers; you will be my people, and I will be your God" (Ezekiel 36:28).

God began revealing, in addition to already given instructions to obey the Sabbath and observe the Passover, what Israel would be required to obey by identifying who He was. He then spoke the Ten Commandments to the entire congregation of Israel, and continued speaking with Moses, giving the basics of the sacrificial system and other social regulations governing relationships between the people themselves. As shown, He continued His instructions from between the cherubim over the ark in the tabernacle.

God had Moses write it all, including the Ten Commandments, in the book of the law. The congregation of Israel heard the book read, and again agreed to be God's obedient people.

Thereupon it was sealed by the offering of animal sacrifices and blood being sprinkled on the all the people (Exodus chapters 20-24).

Some may not have been aware; but the Ten Commandments not only were spoken to all of Israel before being written on stone, but also were written in the Book of the Law and read to the people, then Israel agreed to obey them before they were written on stone by the finger of God.

---

2) *Was the Old Covenant a static document or a growing body of law?*

The communications between God and Israel at Sinai did not end the development of the Old Covenant, which was not a static covenant, but a growing and changing set of instructions to Israel.

This did not end the matter of commands which Israel had to obey. After the covenant was ratified, God told Moses: *"Place the cover on top of the ark and put in the ark the Testimony, which I will give you. There, above the cover between the two cherubim that are over the ark of the Testimony, I will meet with you and give you all my commands for the Israelites"* (Exodus 25:2). These continuing commands were additions to the Old Covenant.

Throughout the leadership of Moses and Joshua, additions to the Book of the Law were made, which became the reference book for the kings of Israel, who were commanded to make and keep a reference copy of the Book of the Law by which they were to govern and judge.

Even the pronouncements of the prophets contained elements which became part of the covenant law, as God continued to unfold His statutes and judgments. This continued even through the ministry of John the Baptist and Christ, as some previous commands were amplified and even terminated, for they had served the extent of their intended purpose.

3) *Did Israel make the old covenant with God before knowing its contents?*

The "Old Covenant" which faded away began as a verbal agreement between Israel and God, that He would be their God and they would be His people *if* they believed and obeyed Him.

God offered the covenant through Moses to the congregation of Israel, and the whole congregation verbally agreed without having heard the whole of what they were to obey (Exodus 19). The Passover and Sabbath observance had already been commanded (Exodus 12-16).

4) *Are the books of the Bible, Genesis through Malachi, the "Old Covenant," and the Books of the Bible Matthew through Revelation the "New Covenant"?*

The Books of the Bible, Genesis through Malachi, do not equate with "the Old Covenant," which was to disappear. This is evident since the Old Scriptures continued to be taught by Christ and the Apostles. Since Paul affirmed they continued able to make one wise unto salvation, and since whatever was written "aforetime" was written for our learning, the law continued to function for sinners and the teaching of sound doctrine (1 Timothy 1).

5) *What was the attitude of Jesus and the Apostles toward use of the Old Scriptures, those formulated before John the Baptist, for teaching Faith and Practice?*

Paul taught that the Old Scriptures, which we call the Old Testament, were written for our learning. Peter indicated that we could twist the old Scriptures to our own destruction. Many ministers from different Christian fellowships correctly preach moral concepts liberally from the Old Scriptures. Paul taught that the kingdom of God was founded on the Apostles, the Prophets, and Jesus Christ – the chief Cornerstone.

6) *Are the "Gospels," Matthew through John, Old Covenant or New Covenant? Do they teach New Covenant or Old Covenant doctrine? Do they teach both?*

The Gospels, writings of Matthew, Mark, Luke and John, tell the story of the ministry of Christ and the very beginning ministry of the Apostles. It was a time of transition, correcting misconceptions in faith and practice among the people of God.

Until His death, provisions of the Old Covenant continued, correctly so, even as Jesus was Himself circumcised the eighth day in compliance with the Old Covenant that the seed of Abraham be circumcised; obedience to the priesthood and making of sacrifices continued to be valid requirements until the crucifixion.

Traditions of Israel which nullified the commands of God were denounced, the identity of Jesus was revealed, the Kingdom of God was proclaimed. The gospel was preached first to Israel, and only by Christ's death and resurrection were the Gentiles welcomed by breaking down the middle wall of partition between the faithful of Israel and the faithful of the Gentiles.

There were elements of both the old and new covenants in effect during the ministry of Christ, but in the main, He explained Christian behavior, and those explanations do not abolish the law. He commanded not to think that!

7) *Was Jesus a "Gospel" Preacher and Teacher, or an Old Covenant Prophet, or both?*

Jesus was a prophet like Moses; Moses prophesied of the coming Prophet who would be like himself.[55] The earthly ministry of Jesus

---

[55] Deut. 18:15: "The LORD your God will raise up for you a prophet like me from among your own brothers. You must listen to him." Interestingly, the recent "Jesus Seminar" took note of their similarity, and concluded that Jesus was "trying to be another Moses"!

Acts 3:22-26: "For Moses said, `The Lord your God will raise up for you a prophet like me from among your own people; you must listen to everything he tells

proclaimed many prophecies of the same nature as given through earlier prophets, regarding Israel losing control of the kingdom, and the ultimate establishment of the kingdom of God on earth.

It also contained teachings about proper conduct, ordinances of the Church, proper Sabbath keeping, and the importance of the smallest of God's commandments. A Prophet like Moses, He was an Old Covenant prophet *and* a proclaimer of the Gospel and bringer of the New Covenant.

8) *What part does law play in God's covenant-making with His people?*

"Law" is basically a declaration of what it is that God's people are to obey, whether in the New Covenant or the Old. The basic element of the prophesied new covenant was God writing His law in the hearts of His people.

The law continues as a definition of sin, a "tutor-mentor" that leads to Christ, a reminder to careless believers what they once were and what they should not become again. It was made for sinners (which means it was made for all of us); it continues as the strength of sin, the basis of a sinner's condemnation and need of a Savior.

9) *Is the New Covenant about law, about Christ, or about both law and Christ?*

It is plainly stated in the promise of the new covenant (Jeremiah 31) that it was about law; but in its fuller revelation, the New Covenant focuses on Jesus, the author and finisher of our salvation.

The more closely one draws to Christ, the less one needs the law, which was not made for a righteous man, but for sinners. We all begin our relations with God under the condemnation of the law. The New Covenant is about both, the law and Christ.

---

you. Anyone who does not listen to him will be completely cut off from among his people.' "Indeed, all the prophets from Samuel on, as many as have spoken, have foretold these days. And you are heirs of the prophets and of the covenant God made with your fathers. He said to Abraham, `Through your offspring all peoples on earth will be blessed.' When God raised up his servant, he sent him first to you to bless you by turning each of you from your wicked ways."

10) *Do passages of the new scriptures which affirm the validity of "law," speak of old scriptures law, or new scriptures law?*

Indeed, the New Scriptures affirm both, for both old and new scriptures speak of the same law. Old scripture "law" is the new scripture "law" **with changes**. Neither Jesus nor Paul speak of a new and different "law" as they disclose the role and effectiveness of law.

In his discussions of law, works, and grace, it is not a new law that is declared by Paul to be holy, just, good, and established by faith. It is the same law which he declares unable to save.

11) *Could God change His covenant with His chosen people, His church, after the Cross? Did He?*

No – by His own choice; not by lack of power. The new Scriptures state emphatically that a will or testament (same as "covenant") cannot be changed after the death of the Will-Maker: *"Brothers, let me take an example from everyday life. Just as no one can set aside or add to a human covenant that has been duly established, so it is in this case"* (Galatians 3:15). Applied to God's will, the rule applies by His choice.

12) *Was Jesus the "Testator" of both the Old and New Covenants?*

Jesus died for the sins committed under both the Old and the New Covenants. The evidence presented of His role in creation, His being Creator of all things visible and invisible; the evidence of all power and authority having been vested in Him; the Covenant-Maker at Sinai being seen by the 70 elders of Israel and Moses, His form being seen between the cherubim by Moses and His continued giving commands from there to Israel, the fact that God the Father has never been seen nor heard at any time, Paul stating Christ was the Rock in the wilderness with Israel, all affirm the role of His Son Jesus as Covenant-Maker, both old and new.

13) *Was there more than one covenant in operation at the same time? Is there more than one in operation at this time?*

The covenants with which we are concerned are these:

(1) God's Covenant with Abraham, which has always been in operation since God made it with Abraham, and always will be in operation;

(2) The covenants with Israel at Sinai and during the leadership of both Moses and Joshua, and

(3) The Covenant with all the people of God at Mt. Zion, validated by the death of Jesus on the cross.

The covenant God made with Abraham continued valid along with the covenants God made later with His people. We, ourselves, are included in the covenant made with Abraham. All God's people, old covenant and new, are covered by the blood of the new covenant.[56]

14) *Is the law God writes on the hearts of His people under the new covenant a continuing law, a changed law, a new law formulated for the New Covenant, a definable law, or a different law for every believer as the Spirit impresses individual hearts?*

One may find the answer to that important question in a very simple concept: *"For God is not the author of confusion, but of peace, as in all churches of the saints"* (1 Corinthians 14:33). *"For where envying and strife is, there is confusion and every evil work"* (James 3:16).

That is, God has a reason not to be the author of confusion because it originates in envy and strife, not in the peace of God which passes understanding!

The law written on our hearts is an integral part of the new covenant (God's "last will and testament"); and since a covenant – will – cannot be changed after the death of the one making out the Covenant (or "Will"), and since the Maker of the will (Christ) has already died, the New Covenant law does not change and cannot change. This is related to the closing of the canon of the Bible.

God's calling is not to confusion. He does not have a different law for different people, Jew, Gentile, male, female. His Holy Spirit may

---

[56] Gal. 3:17, 26-29: "What I mean is this: The law, introduced 430 years later, does not set aside the covenant previously established by God and thus do away with the promise." "You are all sons of God through faith in Christ Jesus, for all of you who were baptized into Christ have clothed yourselves with Christ. There is neither Jew nor Greek, slave nor free, male nor female, for you are all one in Christ Jesus. If you belong to Christ, then you are Abraham's seed, and heirs according to the promise."

lead us into different *areas of service,* but it does not teach one child of God a different law, a different truth. Paul has a stern warning against the modern notion that "your truth may not be my truth":

> *"I am astonished that you are so quickly deserting the one who called you by the grace of Christ and are turning to a different gospel – which is really no gospel at all. Evidently some people are throwing you into confusion and are trying to pervert the gospel of Christ. But even if we or an angel from heaven should preach a gospel other than the one we preached to you, let him be eternally condemned!"* (Galatians 1:6-8).
>
> *"You were running a good race. Who cut in on you and kept you from obeying the truth? That kind of persuasion does not come from the one who calls you. 'A little yeast works through the whole batch of dough.' I am confident in the Lord that you will take no other view. The one who is throwing you into confusion will pay the penalty, whoever he may be"* (Galatians 5:7-10).

While Paul, in Galatians 5, was not addressing specifically the issue of "law" continuing or changing, he does address the issue of confusion, as he also did in his first letter to the Corinthians: *"For God is not the author of confusion, but of peace, as in all churches of the saints"* (1 Corinthians 14:33, KJV). God's consistency in dealing with man is upheld.

To answer the questions specifically: The law God writes in the hearts of His people is a continuing, changed law.[57] The law which led people to Christ still leads people to Christ: *"So the law was put in charge to lead us to Christ that we might be justified by faith"* (Galatians 3:24). The law still operates to lead people to Christ.

15) *When Paul wrote, "And so he condemned sin in sinful man, in order that the righteous requirements of the law might be fully met in*

---

[57] Hebr. 7:12: "For when there is a change of the priesthood, there must also be a change of the law."

us, who do not live according to the sinful nature but according to the Spirit," what law did Paul have reference to?

Paul referred to the same law to which He referred in most of his writings. It is the same law which no longer condemns the saved; it is the same law that continues to identify sin; it is the law to which Jesus referred when He said he did not come to abolish the law, it is the law about which Paul wrote, *"For it is not those who hear the law who are righteous in God's sight, but it is those who obey the law who will be declared righteous"* (Romans 2:13).

16) *When Paul wrote, "Do we, then, nullify the law by this faith? Not at all! Rather, we uphold the law," what law did Paul have reference to?*

Paul referred to the same law that He, James, John and the other apostles taught as the "oracles of God," which were spoken to Israel and Moses, and upheld by the prophets of old. It was a *changed law* after the cross, but still valid as changed.

17) *What is the role of the Cross in covenant matters?*

The role of the cross is to validate the covenants God made with His chosen people, old and new covenants. The fact that it is not possible for the blood of animals to take away sin was not a new truth – it was always true. Therefore, the cross validated the work of the old covenant as well as the new:

"For this reason Christ is the mediator of a new covenant, that those who are called may receive the promised eternal inheritance – now that he has died as a ransom to set them free from the sins committed under the first covenant" (Hebrews 9:15).

"For you know that it was not with perishable things such as silver or gold that you were redeemed from the empty way of life handed down to you from your forefathers, but with the precious blood of Christ, a lamb without blemish or defect" (1 Peter 1:18, 19). **---o-O-o---**

The New Covenant *Not About Behavior* Examined

"The first covenant prescribes a behavior. The second covenant describes a relationship. Those two statements refer to categorically different phenomena. They cannot compare. They do not contrast. They operate in different realms" – a minister.

"As adults in a marriage, the essence of our relationship is not about rules – it's about love, commitment, appreciation, and caring. The foundation of the relationship is not adherence to a whole set of rules."

"But the focus is not on the rules we learned as children, rather the focus is on building the relationship."

"But still, the focus is not the keeping of rules. Likewise, the relationship I have with God through Jesus Christ isn't about keeping laws" – a minister[58]

These words above were written in response to a study on the law by the author. It was suggested that we need a new paradigm through which to view the concept of "law" in the Bible. It was sent mostly to ministers and leaders of the Church of God (Seventh Day).

It helps to read and repeat what "thus saith the Lord," but some responses theorized and analogized, not quoting the Bible to support the concepts presented. It isn't as though the Bible has nothing to say – which should be seen as much more important than "How I like to look at" things.

The author affirms in his book, *"Paul, New Testament Lawyer and Advocate of Grace,"* that unrepentant sinners are married to the law as they become aware of the will of God through the law (Romans 7), and

---

[58] I wish to affirm that although differences of opinion surface quite regularly among us, I for one do not hold brethren in low esteem because of it. Our differences are sometimes quite serious, but because we are brethren, and because we wish to ferret out misunderstandings of each other and of the Bible, in order to come to greater unity, we find ourselves contending with each other in order to "contend for the faith." Our prayer is that we are on the move, not just spinning our wheels as we sink in the sand.

that children of God are married to Christ, having died to the law. Then born again as Christians, they are married to a new husband, Christ.

In fact, even though the law of God is written in the minds and hearts of His children, the law did not arise for the righteous, but for sinners:

"As I urged you when I went into Macedonia, stay there in Ephesus so that you may command certain men not to teach false doctrines any longer nor to devote themselves to myths and endless genealogies.

"These promote controversies rather than God's work --which is by faith. The goal of this command is love, which comes from a pure heart and a good conscience and a sincere faith. Some have wandered away from these and turned to meaningless talk. They want to be teachers of the law, but they do not know what they are talking about or what they so confidently affirm.

"We know that the law is good if one uses it properly. We also know that law is made not for the righteous but for lawbreakers and rebels, the ungodly and sinful, the unholy and irreligious; for those who kill their fathers or mothers, for murderers, for adulterers and perverts, for slave traders and liars and perjurers – and for whatever else is contrary to the sound doctrine" (1 Timothy 1:3-9).

It is conceivable that at some point in our disagreements we would be tempted to concentrate more on Paul's statement, *"They want to be teachers of the law, but they do not know what they are talking about or what they so confidently affirm,"* than to concentrate on the portion that says the law is good *"for whatever else is contrary to sound doctrine."*

The law is not limited to "you must" and "you must not." It also teaches sound doctrine (1 Timothy 1:10), and love (James 2:8). Paul says, *"The law is not made for the righteous but for lawbreakers and rebels." "We are not under the law, but under grace."* Nonetheless, it is still true that God expects us to submit to His law:

"For what the law was powerless to do in that it was weakened by the sinful nature, God did by sending his own Son in the likeness of sinful man to be a sin offering.

*"And so he condemned sin in sinful man, **in order that the righteous requirements of the law might be fully met in us,** who do not live according to the sinful nature but according to the Spirit.*

"Those who live according to the sinful nature have their minds set on what that nature desires; but those who live in accordance with the Spirit have their minds set on what the Spirit desires.

"The mind of sinful man is death, but the mind controlled by the Spirit is life and peace; the sinful mind is hostile to God. It does not submit to God's law, nor can it do so.

"Those controlled by the sinful nature cannot please God. You, however, are controlled not by the sinful nature but by the Spirit, if the Spirit of God lives in you. And if anyone does not have the Spirit of Christ, he does not belong to Christ" (Romans 8:3-9).

One must factor in somewhere recognition of the fact that the law was made for us all, because *we all began this life as sinning, rebellious lawbreakers.* We all must also factor in the prophecy of God through Jeremiah that He would write His law on the hearts and in the minds of His people.

So even though the law was not made for righteous people, it has a very close and meaningful relationship to us if it is written on our hearts. It also has a close and meaningful relationship because the law leads us to Christ.

By the law is the knowledge of sin and knowledge of the punishment for sin. It is how we became aware of our need for Christ. If we suppose that we have no further need of the law once we have become Christians, we fool ourselves.

*"Do not merely listen to the word, and so deceive yourselves. **Do what it says.** Anyone who listens to the word but does not do what it says is like a man who looks at his face in a mirror and, after*

looking at himself, goes away and immediately forgets what he looks like.

*"But **the man who looks intently into the perfect law that gives freedom, and continues to do this**, not forgetting what he has heard, but doing it – he will be blessed in what he does. If anyone considers himself religious and yet does not keep a tight rein on his tongue, he deceives himself and his religion is worthless"* (James 1:22-25).

*"If you really keep the royal law found in Scripture, "Love your neighbor as yourself," you are doing right. **But if you show favoritism, you sin and are convicted by the law as lawbreakers.** For whoever keeps the whole law and yet stumbles at just one point is guilty of breaking all of it.*

"For he who said, "Do not commit adultery," also said, "Do not murder." If you do not commit adultery but do commit murder, you have become a lawbreaker. Speak and act as those who are going to be judged by the law that gives freedom, because judgment without mercy will be shown to anyone who has not been merciful. Mercy triumphs over judgment!" (James 2:8-13).

Do you know any Christians who show favoritism? Was it Christians or unbelievers to whom James and Paul wrote their epistles, warning of the result of continued practice of sin? Paul wrote:

"Do you not know that the wicked will not inherit the kingdom of God? Do not be deceived: Neither the sexually immoral nor idolaters nor adulterers nor male prostitutes nor homosexual offenders" (1 Corinthians 6:9).

" ... and envy; drunkenness, orgies, and the like. I warn you, as I did before, that those who live like this will not inherit the kingdom of God" (Galatians 5:21).

Do we understand why Paul warned *born-again believers* of these dangers? Were they not beyond rules and regulations? Didn't they have a "relationship" with God and His son Jesus?

Is the reason that such sinners will not be in the kingdom of God the fact they do not submit to the law of God? In part, yes, but first they must die to the law that they may be married to Christ! Otherwise they cannot submit to the law of God (see Romans 8).

Those well acquainted with Paul's writings recognize that one of his prominent themes is defining the role of law and the relationship of sinners and the relationship of God's people to the law. Christ also dealt in depth with matters of biblical law, particularly in His *Sermon on the Mount.*

If then time is spent exploring what Jesus and Paul have to say about the law in a prayerful endeavor to understand and share their teachings, any criticism of *wanting to be teachers of the law, without knowing what we are talking about or what we so confidently affirm,* may not in fairness be applied to those who seek to follow Paul's example by spending considerable time discussing matters of godly, biblical law.

Is such exercise a waste of time? Not according to James: *"But the man who looks intently into the perfect law that gives freedom, and continues to do this, not forgetting what he has heard, but doing it – he will be blessed in what he does."*

Neither is it a waste of time according to Ezekiel: *"I will remove from them their heart of stone and give them a heart of flesh.* **Then they will follow my decrees and be careful to keep my laws. They will be my people, and I will be their God"** (Ezekiel 11:19, 20). God said this twice to the prophet Ezekiel:

> *"I will show the holiness of my great name, which has been profaned among the nations, the name you have profaned among them. Then the nations will know that I am the LORD, declares the Sovereign LORD, when I show myself holy through you before their eyes. "'For I will take you out of the nations; I will gather you from all the countries and bring you back into your own land.*
>
> *"I will sprinkle clean water on you, and you will be clean; I will cleanse you from all your impurities and from all your idols. I will give you a new heart and put a new spirit in you;* **I will remove**

from you your heart of stone and give you a heart of flesh. And I will put my Spirit in you and move you to follow my decrees and be careful to keep my laws" (Ezekiel 36:23-27).

Let's observe two things about the matter:

1) These are obviously New Covenant developments when God gives His people new hearts and *moves them* to follow His decrees and to be careful to keep His laws.

2) God did not change His mind: *"Think not that I am come to destroy the law, or the prophets: I am not come to destroy, but to fulfil"* (Matthew 5:17 KJV).

Therefore, one of the intents of the coming of Christ was to work in behalf of this statement of His Father through the Prophet Ezekiel! We would be very ill-advised to teach that under the guidance of the Holy Spirit we do not even need to refer to the laws of God! Some have headed down that wrong path!

We can learn much sound doctrine about "relationships" from the law itself, doctrine which Paul expounds, even from the law:

"What agreement is there between the temple of God and idols? For we are the temple of the living God. As God has said: "I will live with them and walk among them, and I will be their God, and they will be my people. Therefore come out from them and be separate, says the Lord. Touch no unclean thing, and I will receive you" (2 Corinthians 6:16).

Here, Paul teaches sound doctrine from the law, as he cites Leviticus 26:12: *"I will walk among you and be your God, and you will be my people."* He also teaches from the book of Isaiah in the same passage: *"Depart, depart, go out from there! Touch no unclean thing! Come out from it and be pure, you who carry the vessels of the* LORD *"* (Isaiah 52:11).

In the Old Covenant temple, the servants of the Lord who carried the holy vessels were to be sanctified and not touch unclean things.

How much more are we to be sanctified as the very vessels in which God dwells:

"Nevertheless the foundation of God standeth sure, having this seal, The Lord knoweth them that are his. And, Let every one that nameth the name of Christ depart from iniquity." "If a man therefore purge himself from these, he shall be a vessel unto honour, sanctified, and meet for the master's use, and prepared unto every good work" (2 Timothy 2:19, 21).

We are to become "blameless and pure, children of God without fault in a crooked and depraved generation" (from Philippians 2:15).

---o-O-o---

Various Biblical "Relationships" with God

The Servant Relationship:

Paul termed us *servants of God: "Rather, as servants of God we commend ourselves in every way: in great endurance; in troubles, hardships and distresses"* (2 Corinthians 6:4). *"Live as free men, but do not use your freedom as a cover-up for evil; live as servants of God"* (1 Peter 2:16).

Our being "servants" of God is one aspect of our *relationship* with God. It is not a newly conceived relationship with God:

"Because the Israelites are my servants, whom I brought out of Egypt, they must not be sold as slaves" (Leviticus 25:42).
" ... for the Israelites belong to me as servants. They are my servants, whom I brought out of Egypt. I am the LORD your God" (Leviticus 25:55).

What we do and teach must enhance this *servant relationship.*

The "People of God" Relationship:

In the Bible, God's goal for us is that He be our God and we be His obedient people: *"I gave them this command: Obey me, and I will be your God and you will be my people. Walk in all the ways I command you, that it may go well with you"* (Jeremiah 7:23). *"My people"* is one aspect of *our relationship with God.* What we do and teach must also enhance this **people of God relationship**.

God, being *"our God"* is another aspect of *our relationship with Him.* Yahweh being our God, we being His people, is an oft repeated theme of the Old Covenant. It was the theme of the Exodus, "Let *My people* go."

This relationship of being God's people was conditional: "... the terms I commanded your forefathers when I brought them out of Egypt, out of the iron-smelting furnace.' I said, *'Obey me and do everything I command you,* and you will be *my people,* and I will be *your God'"* (Jeremiah 11:4).

"The LORD Is Our God" Relationship:

God's being our God has the same conditions, the same terms. The results are expressed in Zechariah 13:9: *"This third I will bring into the fire; I will refine them like silver and test them like gold. They will call on my name and I will answer them; **I will say, 'They are my people,' and they will say, 'The LORD is our God.'"***

Over and over this relationship, "He is our God, we are His people," is described in the Old Testament, and it is defined also to be the New Testament relationship of God with His people:

"This is the covenant I will make with the house of Israel after that time," declares the LORD. "I will put my law in their minds and write it on their hearts. I will be their God, and they will be my people" (Jeremiah 31:33).

This was a prediction of the New Covenant. This is a very special relationship, that we are His people, and He is our God. It is a relationship common to both covenants. It is reiterated over and over again, dozens of times, when God speaks of His people – even more in the old scriptures than in the new.

When we speak of having a "relationship with Christ," or a "relationship with God," this is part of the picture of relationships.

---o-O-o---

Covenants Were Always About Relationships

Having a relationship with God is not a new concept. ***What we do and teach must enhance these relationships, that He is our God, and we are His people.***

Whatever erodes or tends to erode these relationships must be avoided. Disobeying the law which He has written in our hearts erodes our relationship with God and with His Son.

With these passages in mind, we must recognize that there is limited if any truth in saying our relationship with deity is not a law relationship, or that our relationship with deity is not about rules.

Pray tell, what is the law of God doing in our hearts and our minds, written there by God Himself, if it has nothing to do with our relationships with Him? Or do we affirm that the law written in our hearts and minds is itself not about law? Are the decrees of this law in our hearts and minds not rules of behavior?

The Father-Child Relationship:

In Jesus' discussions with Jewish leaders, it becomes very apparent that the father-child relationship we enjoy with God is tied closely to obedient behavior:

"You are doing the things your own father does," (Jesus said to the Jews).

"We are not illegitimate children," they protested. 'The only Father we have is God himself.'

"Jesus said to them, 'If God were your Father, you would love me, for I came from God and now am here. I have not come on my own; but he sent me.'

"'You belong to your father, the devil, and you want to carry out your father's desire. He was a murderer from the beginning, not

- 172 -

holding to the truth, for there is no truth in him. When he lies, he speaks his native language, for he is a liar and the father of lies'" (John 8:41, 42, 44).

"Not everyone who says to me, 'Lord, Lord,' will enter the kingdom of heaven, but only he who does the will of my Father who is in heaven" (Matthew 7:21). (

Does God's law written in our hearts and minds express His will? If not, why is it written there?

"This is how we know who the children of God are and who the children of the devil are: Anyone who does not do what is right is not a child of God; nor is anyone who does not love his brother" (1 John 3:10).

We *"... receive from him anything we ask, because we obey his commands and do what pleases him"* (1 John 3:22).

"This is how we know that we love the children of God: by loving God and carrying out his commands. This is love for God: to obey his commands. And his commands are not burdensome" (1 John 5:2, 3).

Those commands we carry out, are they law or just individual instructions given each of us?

The Father-child relationship continues Covenant to Covenant:

*"They will come with weeping; they will pray as I bring them back. I will lead them beside streams of water on a level path where they will not stumble, because I am Israel's father, and Ephraim is my **firstborn son***" Jeremiah 31:9).

*"For to us a child is born, to us a son is given, and the government will be on his shoulders. And he will be called Wonderful Counselor, Mighty God, **Everlasting Father**, Prince of Peace"* (Isaiah 9:6).

*"**My children**, I will be with you only a little longer. You will look for me, and just as I told the Jews, so I tell you now: Where I am going, you cannot come"* (John 13:33).

*"Yet to all who received him, to those who believed in his name, he gave **the right to become children of God**"* (John 1:12).

*" ... and not only for that nation but also for the **scattered children of God,** to bring them together and make them one"* (John 11:52).

*"Do everything without complaining or arguing, so that you may become blameless and pure, **children of God without fault** in a crooked and depraved generation, in which you shine like stars in the universe"* (Philippians 2:14, 15).

*"How great is the love the Father has lavished on us, that we should be called **children of God!** And that is what we are! The reason the world does not know us is that it did not know him. Dear friends, **now we are children of God,** and what we will be has not yet been made known. But we know that when he appears, we shall be like him, for we shall see him as he is"* (1 John 3:1, 2).

*" ... because those who are led by the Spirit of God **are sons of God"*** (Romans 8:14).

*"**You are all sons of God through faith** in Christ Jesus"* (Galatians 3:26).

*"'Therefore come out from them and be separate, says the Lord. Touch no unclean thing, and I will receive you.' '**I will be a Father to you, and you will be my sons and daughters,** says the Lord Almighty.' Since we have these promises, dear friends, let us purify ourselves from everything that contaminates body and spirit, perfecting holiness out of reverence for God"* (2 Corinthians 6:17-7:1:).

*"I will say to the north, 'Give them up!' and to the south, 'Do not hold them back.' Bring **my sons from afar and my daughters from the ends of the earth** – everyone who is called by my name, whom I created for my glory, whom I formed and made"* (Isaiah 43:6,7:).

This Father-child relationship is a very special relationship. What we do must enhance that relationship.

The Lord and Teacher – Servants Relationship:

*"You call me 'Teacher' and 'Lord,' and rightly so, for that is what I am. Now that I, your Lord and Teacher, have washed your feet, you also should wash one another's feet." "I tell you the truth, **no servant is greater than his master, nor is a messenger greater than the one who***

sent him. *Now that you know these things, you will be blessed if you do them"* (John 13:13, 14, 16, 17).

What we do and say must enhance this "Jesus is Lord and Teacher," "We are His servants" relationship.

---o-**O**-o---

Summary of Relationships

We have pointed out these relationships: the Lord and Teacher – servants relationship; the Father-child relationship; the LORD is our God" relationship; the "People of God" relationship; the Servants of God relationship.

We could speak of other relationships: the people which are called by My Name relationship; the heirs of God; the Mediator between God and man relationship; the God-Christ-Holy Spirit dwelling in us relationship; the Jehovah-Jireh (our provider) relationship; the King and subjects relationship; the High-Priest work of mediation relationship; the Savior-saved relationship; and even "husband and wife" (Jer. 3:8; Eph. 5:21-30) – still not an exhaustive list of relations, all of which are both Old and New Covenant concepts.

So what are we saying if we declare: *The first covenant prescribes a behavior. The second covenant describes a relationship. Those two statements refer to categorically different phenomena – ?* Quite clearly the statement is saying that:

1) The first covenant does not describe a relationship.

2) The second covenant does not prescribe a behavior.

Well, Brethren, not I, but the entire teachings of the Old and New Covenants declare these statements to be patently false, and on their face, a complete misunderstanding of the Word of God.

"Nevertheless, God's solid foundation stands firm, sealed with this inscription: 'The Lord knows those who are his,' and, 'Everyone who confesses the name of the Lord must turn away from wickedness'" (2 Timothy 2:19).

"Do you not know that the wicked will not inherit the kingdom of God? Do not be deceived: Neither the sexually immoral nor idolaters nor adulterers nor male prostitutes nor homosexual offenders" (1 Corinthians 6:9).

" ... and envy; drunkenness, orgies, and the like. I warn you, as I did before, that those who live like this will not inherit the kingdom of God" (Galatians 5:21).

"I urge you, brothers, to watch out for those who cause divisions and put obstacles in your way that are contrary to the teaching you have learned. Keep away from them" (Romans 16:17).

Is *turning away from wickedness* behavior? Are sexual immorality, idolatry, adultery, male and female prostitution, homosexuality, envy, drunkenness, orgies, avoiding those who cause division – are these *behavior?* Indeed, are these New Covenant or Old Covenant declarations?

Jesus said, *"If you love me, you will obey what I command"* (John 14:15). Is obeying our Lord and Savior *behavior?* As said earlier, some responses we get come from "how I like to look at it" rather that "Thus saith the Lord" followed by quoting His Word.

---o-O-o---

Unrepentant Disobedience
Severs Relationships with God

In the Old Testament, that Israel obey God was a contingency of their covenant relationship. If they did not obey Him, He would not be their God, and they would not be His people. Is this also a contingency in the New Covenant? That it would be is shown clearly in Ezekiel's prophecy:

"Therefore say: 'This is what the Sovereign LORD says: I will gather you from the nations and bring you back from the countries where you have been scattered, and I will give you back the land of

Israel again.' "They will return to it and remove all its vile images and detestable idols.

"I will give them an undivided heart and put a new spirit in them; I will remove from them their heart of stone and give them a heart of flesh. Then they will follow my decrees and be careful to keep my laws. They will be my people, and I will be their God" (Ezekiel 11:17-20).

The elements of this Old Scripture passage show its fulfillment to be a New Covenant event. A different heart, in which the law of God is written, is New Covenant. It is also New Covenant to follow God's decrees and be careful to keep His laws! Do the New Scriptures affirm the same? Indeed they do!

If we say our relationship is with God is not rules and law oriented, we may be telling the truth. But if we are telling the truth, we need to ask ourselves whether we are His people and whether He is our God!

God declared that when we receive our heart of flesh instead of a heart of stone that His law would be written in our minds and our hearts and that, ***"Then they will follow my decrees and be careful to keep my laws."*** Being God's people and God being *our God* is predicated on our following His decrees and being careful to keep His laws.

In reading this prediction of God through Ezekiel, there ought to be just a twinge of conscience in the hearts of those who minimize rather than magnify the law of God! Jesus did not magnify the law just to have us turn around and deny we need to follow God's decrees and be careful to keep His laws!

Jesus verified the very same concept: *"Anyone who breaks one of the least of these commandments and teaches others to do the same will be called least in the kingdom of heaven, but whoever practices and teaches these commands will be called great in the kingdom of heaven"* (Matthew 5:19).

The least of what commandments? Those embodied in His statement, *"Do not think that I have come to abolish the Law or the Prophets; I have not come to abolish them but to fulfill them"* (Matthew

5:17). The concept is rather lasting: *"Heaven and earth will pass away, but my words will never pass away"* (Luke 21:33).

There is a solid connection between God promising under His new Covenant to write His law in the hearts and minds of His people and the New Covenant statements of the outward means of identifying the children of God – they love God and obey His commands.

It is not just a corporate relationship, but a very personal relationship as shown in the passage from Ezekiel: *"I will give them an undivided heart and put a new spirit in them; I will remove from them their heart of stone and give them a heart of flesh. Then they will follow my decrees and be careful to keep my laws. They will be my people, and I will be their God."*

An "undivided heart" speaks of complete devotion to God. It did not happen under the Old Covenant, and whether it happens in our day becomes questionable among some who name the name of Christ. This is a New Covenant prophecy, and in this undivided condition the people of God follow God's decrees and are careful to keep his laws.

As Paul stated, there is something for us to learn in what was written "aforetime (KJV)." Consider these statements from David:

> *"Oh, how I love your law! I meditate on it all day long"* (Psalm 119:97).
> *"I hate double-minded men, but I love your law"* (Psalm 119:113).
> *"I hate and abhor falsehood but I love your law"* (Psalm 119:163).
> *"Great peace have they who love your law, and nothing can make them stumble"* (Psalm 119:165).

David's attitude toward God's law resulted in his being chosen king of Israel. Samuel said to Saul: *"But now thy kingdom shall not continue: the LORD hath sought him **a man after his own heart**, and the LORD hath commanded him to be captain over his people, because thou (Saul) hast not kept that which the LORD commanded thee"* (1 Samuel. 13:14 KJV).

This was cited in Acts 13:22: *"And when he had removed him (Saul), he raised up unto them David to be their king; to whom also he gave testimony, and said, I have found David the son of Jesse, **a man after mine own heart, which shall fulfil all my will**"* (Acts 13:22).

Compare Paul's feelings with David's feelings about the law of God:

"For in my inner being I delight in God's law; but I see another law at work in the members of my body, waging war against the law of my mind and making me a prisoner of the law of sin at work within my members.

"What a wretched man I am! Who will rescue me from this body of death? Thanks be to God – through Jesus Christ our Lord! So then, I myself in my mind am a slave to God's law, but in the sinful nature a slave to the law of sin" (Romans 7:22-25).

Can we say that the law of Paul's mind was a different law than the law God promised to write in the hearts and minds of His people? Paul says that *in his mind he is a slave to God's law.* That is an interesting contrast to the concept that our relationship with God "is not about law and rules."

No matter how you define "law" or what set of principles you decide Paul refers to here, no matter what "law" God declared "His" that He would write in the minds of His people, how can we declare that our relationship with God and His Son is not about law and rules? If we declare that, we must recognize the limits of the meaning intended.

---o-**O**-o---

Summary Observations

The New Covenant being a matter of "relationships" is not a new concept – the Old Covenant also was a matter of relationships. That God was "King" over Israel until Israel demanded a human king was a relationship. That God was Savior and Israel the saved was a relationship.[59] That Israel were the "children of God" was a parent-child relationship. That they covenanted with God to be His people and He covenanted with them to be their God was a relationship.

That Jesus is our redeemer, our Savior, our King, our Mediator with God is a relationship. That Jesus was the Presence in the Wilderness that went with Israel in the wilderness and walked among them is evident, and that was a relationship:

"For I do not want you to be ignorant of the fact, brothers, that our forefathers were all under the cloud and that they all passed through the sea. They were all baptized into Moses in the cloud and in the sea. They all ate the same spiritual food and drank the same spiritual drink; for they drank from the spiritual rock that accompanied them, and that rock was Christ"[2] (1 Corinthians 10:1).

Jesus was that Spiritual Rock, they *ate and drank* of that Spiritual Rock – and that is a very special kind of relationship *established in the old covenant, and fulfilled in the words and sacrament of Jesus:*

"Whoever eats my flesh and drinks my blood has eternal life, and I will raise him up at the last day. For my flesh is real food and my blood is real drink" (John 6:54, 55).

Jesus is our Rock, our firm foundation on which we are built as a holy temple for the Lord to dwell in. The Lord is our Anchor, to which we are bound by strong cords of love – love for Him, His people, and His law.

Both the Old and the New covenants were and are about relationships with God and the Son of God, and in both covenants we evidence

---

[59] Deut. 32:15: "Jeshurun grew fat and kicked; filled with food, he became heavy and sleek. He abandoned the God who made him and rejected the Rock his Savior."
2 Sam. 22:3: " ... my God is my rock, in whom I take refuge, my shield and the horn of my salvation. He is my stronghold, my refuge and my savior-- from violent men you save me."
2 Sam. 22:47: "The LORD lives! Praise be to my Rock! Exalted be God, the Rock, my Savior!"

that relationship by obeying the law of God, and by our very attitudes toward the law of God:

"I will give them an undivided heart and put a new spirit in them; I will remove from them their heart of stone and give them a heart of flesh. Then they will follow my decrees and be careful to keep my laws. They will be my people, and I will be their God."

Are we, professed children of God, careful to keep God's laws? Do we follow his decrees? Or do we speak disparagingly of His "rules" and "regulations" and assume that no carefulness to keep His laws is called for on our parts?

When brethren speak of rules and law as an inferior kind of relationship with God, a type of relationship which we have outgrown, one must ask what scripture they used to come to such conclusions.

One also must wonder what kind of conflicts must swirl in their thinking when they reflect on the fact that God promised under the New Covenant to write His law on the hearts and minds of His people.

Perhaps we forget that we are still children of God, and not yet grownups:

"Not as though I had already attained, either were already perfect: but I follow after, if that I may apprehend that for which also I am apprehended of Christ Jesus" (Philippians 3:12, KJV).

"If any man speak, let him speak as the oracles of God; if any man minister, let him do it as of the ability which God giveth: that God in all things may be glorified through Jesus Christ, to whom be praise and dominion for ever and ever. Amen" (1 Peter 4:11 KJV).

---o-O-o---

What Gave Rise to these Discussions?

At some point, we need to take a breathing spell, sit back and reflect on what initiated such discussions as these. It was not disagreement on whether we ought to love God with our all, and our neighbors as ourselves; it was not that any of us advocated killing, stealing, adultery, covetousness, disrespect for our parents, or idolatry.

It had much to do with a rather popular phrase which began to be repeated in Sabbath observing circles that keeping the Sabbath won't save us. It also related to the fact that *it was not being said* that refraining from adultery won't save us, and that obeying the commands found in the New Scriptures will not save us either!

God's covenant making with mankind is understood in the simple concept of God choosing a people with whom He has made the agreement that He will be our God if we believe and obey Him. He has given the basics of what we are to obey in what He calls His "law."[60] Law is a simplified expression of God's righteousness, in both the Old and New covenants. Learning obedience is a necessary discipline. In several ways David was a type of Christ:

> *"It was good for me to be afflicted so that I might learn your decrees"* (Psalm 119:71).
>
> *"Although he was a son, he learned obedience from what he suffered"* (Hebrews 5:8).

God's ultimate aim is that He may have an obedient people to inherit eternal life and inhabit His eternal Kingdom with Him.[61]

---

[60] Jer. 31:33: "'This is the covenant I will make with the house of Israel after that time,'" declares the LORD. 'I will put my law in their minds and write it on their hearts. I will be their God, and they will be my people.'"

Hebr. 8:10: "This is the covenant I will make with the house of Israel after that time, declares the Lord. I will put my laws in their minds and write them on their hearts. I will be their God, and they will be my people."

Hebr. 10:16: "This is the covenant I will make with them after that time, says the Lord. I will put my laws in their hearts, and I will write them on their minds."

[61] Rev. 21:1-4: "Then I saw a new heaven and a new earth, for the first heaven and the first earth had passed away, and there was no longer any sea. I saw the Holy City, the new Jerusalem, coming down out of heaven from God, prepared as a bride beautifully dressed for her husband. And I heard a loud voice from the throne saying, "Now the dwelling of God is with men, and he will live with them. They will be his people, and God himself will be with them and be their God. He will wipe every tear from their eyes. There will be no more death or mourning or crying or pain, for the old order of things has passed away"

"The Lord is not slack concerning his promise, as some men count slackness; but is longsuffering to us-ward, not willing that any should perish, but that all should come to repentance." "Nevertheless we, according to his promise, look for new heavens and a new earth, wherein dwelleth righteousness" (2 Peter 3:9, 13).

---o-O-o---

Unless otherwise noted, Scripture quotations are New International Version, used by permission of Zondervan Bible Publishers, Grand Rapids, Michigan.

APPENDICES

APPENDIX A

Heir, Heirs, Inherit, Inheritance

Covenants inextricably entwined with inheritance because we are "children of God":

Genesis 15:7, 8: "And he said unto him, I am the LORD that brought thee out of Ur of the Chaldees, to give thee this land to inherit it. And he said, Lord GOD, whereby shall I know that I shall inherit it?'

Genesis 28:4: "And give thee the blessing of Abraham, to thee, and to thy seed with thee; that thou mayest inherit the land wherein thou art a stranger, which God gave unto Abraham."

Genesis 15:3, 4: "And Abram said, Behold, to me thou hast given no seed: and, lo, one born in my house is mine heir. And, behold, the word of the LORD came unto him, saying, This shall not be thine heir; but he that shall come forth out of thine own bowels shall be thine heir."

Genesis 21:10: "Wherefore she said unto Abraham, Cast out this bondwoman and her son: for the son of this bondwoman shall *not be heir* with my son, even with Isaac."

Exodus 15:17: "Thou shalt bring them in, and plant them in the mountain of thine inheritance, in the place, O LORD, which thou hast made for thee to dwell in, in the Sanctuary, O LORD, which thy hands have established."

Matthew 5:5: "Blessed are the meek: for they shall inherit the earth."

Matthew 19:29: "And every one that hath forsaken houses, or brethren, or sisters, or father, or mother, or wife, or children, or lands, for my name's sake, shall receive an hundredfold, and shall inherit everlasting life."

Matthew 25:34: "Then shall the King say unto them on his right hand, Come, ye blessed of my Father, inherit the kingdom prepared for you from the foundation of the world."

Mark 10:17: "And when he was gone forth into the way, there came one running, and kneeled to him, and asked him, Good Master, what shall I do that I may inherit eternal life?"

Luke 10:25: "And, behold, a certain lawyer stood up, and tempted him, saying, Master, what shall I do to inherit eternal life?"

Luke 18:18: "And a certain ruler asked him, saying, Good Master, what shall I do to inherit eternal life?"

Acts 7:5: "And he gave him none inheritance in it, no, not so much as to set his foot on: yet he promised that he would give it to him for a possession, and to his seed after him, when as yet he had no child."

Acts 20:32: "And now, brethren, I commend you to God, and to the word of his grace, which is able to build you up, and to give you an inheritance among all them which are sanctified."

Acts 26:18: "To open their eyes, and to turn them from darkness to light, and from the power of Satan unto God, that they may receive forgiveness of sins, and inheritance among them which are sanctified by faith that is in me."

Romans 4:13, 14: "For the promise, that he should be the heir of the world, was not to Abraham, or to his seed, through the law, but through the righteousness of faith. For if they which are of the law be heirs, faith is made void, and the promise made of none effect."

Romans 8:17: "And if children, then heirs; heirs of God, and joint-heirs with Christ; if so be that we suffer with him, that we may be also glorified together."

1 Corinthians 6:9, 10: "Know ye not that the unrighteous shall not inherit the kingdom of God? Be not deceived: neither fornicators, nor idolaters, nor adulterers, nor effeminate, nor abusers of themselves with mankind, Nor thieves, nor covetous, nor drunkards, nor revilers, nor extortioners, shall inherit the kingdom of God."

1 Corinthians 15:50: "Now this I say, brethren, that flesh and blood cannot inherit the kingdom of God; neither doth corruption inherit incorruption."

Galatians 3:18: "For if the inheritance be of the law, it is no more of promise: but God gave it to Abraham by promise."

Galatians 3:29: "And if ye be Christ's, then are ye Abraham's seed, and heirs according to the promise."

Galatians 4:1, 7, 30: "Now I say, That the heir, as long as he is a child, differeth nothing from a servant, though he be lord of all;" "Wherefore thou art no more a servant, but a son; and if a son, then an heir of God through Christ." "Nevertheless what saith the scripture? Cast out the bondwoman and her son: for the son of the bondwoman shall not be heir with the son of the freewoman."

Galatians 5:21: "Envyings, murders, drunkenness, revellings, and such like: of the which I tell you before, as I have also told you in time past, that they which do such things shall not inherit the kingdom of God."

Ephesians 1:11: "In whom also we have obtained an inheritance, being predestinated according to the purpose of him who worketh all things after the counsel of his own will."

Ephesians 1:14: "Which is the earnest of our inheritance until the redemption of the purchased possession, unto the praise of his glory."

Ephesians 1:18: "The eyes of your understanding being enlightened; that ye may know what is the hope of his calling, and what the riches of the glory of his inheritance in the saints."

Ephesians 5:5: "For this ye know, that no whoremonger, nor unclean person, nor covetous man, who is an idolater, hath any inheritance in the kingdom of Christ and of God."

Colossians 1:12: Giving thanks unto the Father, which hath made us meet to be partakers of the inheritance of the saints in light."

Colossians 3:24: "Knowing that of the Lord ye shall receive the reward of the inheritance: for ye serve the Lord Christ."

Titus 3:7: "That being justified by his grace, we should be made heirs according to the hope of eternal life."

Hebrews 1:2, 4; 14:2: "Hath in these last days spoken unto us by his Son, whom he hath appointed heir of all things, by whom also he made the worlds; Being made so much better than the angels, as he hath by inheritance obtained a more excellent name than they. 14 Are they not all ministering spirits, sent forth to minister for them who shall be heirs of salvation?"

Hebrews 6:12: "That ye be not slothful, but followers of them who through faith and patience inherit the promises."

Hebrews 6:17: "Wherein God, willing more abundantly to show unto the heirs of promise the immutability of his counsel, confirmed it by an oath."

Hebrews 9:15: "And for this cause he is the mediator of the new testament, that by means of death, for the redemption of the transgressions that were under the first testament, they which are called might receive the promise of eternal inheritance."

Hebrews 11:7-9: "By faith Abraham, when he was called to go out into a place which he should after receive for an inheritance, obeyed; and he went out, not knowing whither he went. By faith he sojourned in the land of promise, as in a strange country, dwelling in tabernacles with Isaac and Jacob, the heirs with him of the same promise."

James 2:5: "Hearken, my beloved brethren, Hath not God chosen the poor of this world rich in faith, and **heirs of the kingdom** which he hath promised to them that love him?"

1 Peter 1:4: "To an inheritance incorruptible, and undefiled, and that fadeth not away, reserved in heaven for you."

1 Peter 3:7: "Likewise, ye husbands, dwell with them according to knowledge, giving honour unto the wife, as unto the weaker vessel, and as being heirs together of the grace of life; that your prayers be not hindered."

1 Peter 3:9: "Not rendering evil for evil, or railing for railing: but contrariwise blessing; knowing that ye are thereunto called, that ye should inherit a blessing."

Revelation 21:7: "He that overcometh shall inherit all things; and I will be his God, and he shall be my son."

(This series of Scripture References are from the KJV.)

---o-O-o---

APPENDIX B

COVENANTS

Comparing "Ber-eeth '" and "Dia-thay'-kay"

Background:

About three hundred years before the birth of Christ a group of Jewish scholars were commissioned to translate the Hebrew Scriptures into Greek. In doing so, they used the Greek word "διαθήκη" (dee-uh-thay'kay) to translate the Hebrew word "**ber-eeth'**." This Greek word διαθήκη is the same Greek word in the New Scriptures translated either "testament," "covenant," or "will."

Translators interpret διαθήκη as either a "covenant," "testament," or "will," when translating the Book of Hebrews, according to their understanding of the context. In the sense of a document defining what ones heirs are to inherit after the will-maker dies, or a "covenant" in any sense used in the Old Scriptures, the same Greek word "διαθήκη" is used. This is true of the Old Scriptures. "Διαθήκη" is always used to translate the Hebrew into Greek, in the Septuagint.

Keep in mind that these translators from Hebrew into the Greek Septuagint were all Hebrew speaking Jews.

The "blood of the covenant," whether Old Covenant or New, old Scriptures or New, in the Greek is the same:

Exodus 24:8: "And Moses took the blood, and sprinkled it on the people, and said, Behold **the blood of the covenant**, which the LORD hath made with you concerning all these words,"

Exodus 24:8 λαβὼν δὲ Μωυσῆ" τὸ αἷμα κατεσκέδασεν τοῦ λαοῦ καὶ εἶπεν Ἰδοὺ **τὸ αἷμα τῆς διαθήκης**, ἧς διέθετο κυ-'ριος πρὸς ὑμᾶς περὶ πάντων τῶν λόγων τούτων,...

Hebrews 10:29: "Of how much sorer punishment, suppose ye, shall he be thought worthy, who hath trodden under foot the Son of God,

and hath counted *the blood of the covenant,* wherewith he was sanctified, an unholy thing, and hath done despite unto the Spirit of grace?"

Hebrews 10:29 πόσῳ δοκεῖτε χείρονος ἀξιωθήσεται τιμωρίας
ὁ τὸν υἱὸν τοῦ θεοῦ καταπατήσας, καὶ **τὸ αἷμα τῆς**
διαθήκης κοινὸν ἡγησάμενος ἐν ᾧ ἡγιάσθη, καὶ τὸ πνεῦμα
τῆς χάριτος ἐνυβρίσας,...

In a very real sense, the effective blood of both covenants was the
blood of our Lord Jesus Christ: "And for this cause he is the mediator
of the new testament (new διαθήκη), *that by means of death, for the*
redemption of the transgressions that were under the first testament
(first διαθήκη), they which are called might receive the promise of
eternal inheritance" (Hebrews 9:15). The blood of Christ was the effective activator and guarantee of the inheritance of all the "Israel of God,"
in both covenants.

If they are both blood of the *"διαθήκη,"* then it is legitimate to ask
whether the "διαθήκη" God made with Abraham is also a "will" like
the new covenant made with the "Israel of God" is a "will."

Some pertinent examples follow:

Genesis 17:2 καὶ θήσομαι τὴν **διαθήκην** μου ἀνὰ μέσον
ἐμοῦ καὶ ἀνὰ μέσον σοῦ καὶ πληθυνῶ σε σφόδρα.

Genesis 17:2 And I will make my covenant between me and thee,
and will multiply thee exceedingly.

Genesis 17:7 καὶ στήσω τὴν **διαθήκην** μου ἀνὰ μέσον ἐμοῦ
καὶ ἀνὰ μέσον σοῦ καὶ ἀνὰ μέσον τοῦ σπέρματός σου μετὰ
σὲ εἰς γενεὰς αὐτῶν εἰς **διαθήκην** αἰώνιον εἶναί σου θεὸς καὶ
τοῦ σπέρματός σου μετὰ σέ.

Genesis 17:7: "And I will establish my covenant between me and
thee and thy seed after thee in their generations for an everlasting covenant, to be a God unto thee, and to thy seed after thee."

As one compares the basic meaning of "ber-eeth '" with "διαθήκη,ς
their word origins do not seem to be the same. Does that invalidate, for
example, the idea of a "ber-eeth '" being a "will"? Could we assume, for
example, that God's "ber-eeth '" with Abraham was equal to a "will"?

Since Abraham and his seed were to "inherit" the earth as a result of this covenant, the basic concept that God's covenant with Abraham and his seed is equal in some respects to a will seems impossible to rule out.

Consider:

Exodus 32:13: "Remember Abraham, Isaac, and Israel, thy servants, to whom thou swarest by thine own self, and saidst unto them, I will multiply your seed as the stars of heaven, and all this land that I have spoken of will I give unto your seed, and **they shall inherit** it for ever."

Hebrews 9:15: "And for this cause he is the mediator of the new testament, that by means of death, for the redemption of the transgressions that were under the first testament, they which are called might receive the promise of **eternal inheritance.**"

---o-O-o---

"Blessed are the undefiled in the way, who walk in the law of the LORD. *Blessed are they that keep his testimonies, and that seek him with the whole heart. They also do no iniquity: they walk in his ways. Thou hast commanded us to keep thy precepts diligently.*

"O that my ways were directed to keep thy statutes! Then shall I not be ashamed, when I have respect unto all thy commandments. I will praise thee with uprightness of heart, when I shall have learned thy righteous judgments. I will keep thy statutes: O forsake me not utterly.

"Wherewithal shall a young man cleanse his way? by taking heed thereto according to thy word. With my whole heart have I sought thee: O let me not wander from thy commandments. Thy word have I hid in mine heart, that I might *not sin against thee"* (Psalm 119:1-11 KJV).

Part II

The "Rest" of the Story

A Study of Hebrews Chapters 3, 4

Part II

The "Rest" of the Story

A Study of Hebrews Chapters 3, 4

Purpose of the Study

The issue joined here is the historic debate among Sabbatarians as to whether support for Sabbath observance is or is not found in Hebrews chapter 4, and whether "rest in Jesus" replaces Sabbath-observance. Some individuals have been on both sides, at one time affirming one way, at another time the other.

This ambivalence is reflected in the inconsistent use of Hebrews four as support in various editions of Church of God (Seventh-day) doctrinal belief booklets and tracts, which have vacillated from printing to printing, at times using Hebrews four as support, and at other times making no reference to the passage, with each change irritating opposing camps of thought. It is also seen in the variant wording of different translations of the Bible, footnotes in study Bibles, and Commentary analyses.

One conclusion says there is *nothing* in Hebrews four to support Sabbath observance and another affirms there is a clear-cut affirmation. In between, some affirm there is a "by-product" affirmation of Sabbath observance, while that was not the primary intent of the passage.

There also is a view that the rest we enter is a replacement of Sabbath rest by "rest in Christ." An adjunct position affirms *Sabbath* rest in Christ means a cessation of trying to save ourselves by good works, having "ceased from our own works as God did from His," a position requiring a special interpretation of how God rested.

There is also a question whether the passage is mainly an affirmation of Promised Land rest for the people of God, basically fulfillment of the covenant of promise made with Abraham.

Perhaps none of us have a complete or even adequate grasp of the total picture in Hebrews 3, 4. It isn't hard to arrive at some truth regarding the two chapters, but it is evident that some very basic and fundamentally wrong conclusions are commonly drawn.

Some view the rest we enter as accepting the invitation of Jesus: *"Come to me, all you who are weary and burdened, and I will give you rest"* (Matthew 11:28). We should consider whether this invitation refers to rest in Himself, or rest in the kingdom of God which accompanies salvation, a parallel perhaps to Exodus 33:14: *"The LORD replied, 'My Presence will go with you, and I will give you rest.'"*

Exodus 33:14 was God's promise to Moses, when Moses pled with God to make the journey to Canaan with him. Canaan, the Promised Land, is the promised rest spoken of in Hebrews 3. Is it also the promised rest spoken of in Hebrews 4, but modified to encompass several phases of the kingdom of God?

Paul wrote of Israel in the wilderness, *"They all ate the same spiritual food and drank the same spiritual drink; for they drank from the spiritual rock that accompanied them, and that rock was Christ"* (1 Corinthians 10:3, 4).

Moses wrote in the song God gave him: *"I will proclaim the name of the LORD. Oh, praise the greatness of our God! He is the Rock, his works are perfect, and all his ways are just. A faithful God who does no wrong, upright and just is he"* (Deuteronomy 32:3, 4).

In other words, Christ was God's Presence, the Rock, that went with Moses and Israel in the wilderness. His Presence was to give comfort and encouragement on the way, then to assure rest in the Promised Land.

Why, then, would not Jesus' invitation to come to Him, and He would give rest to those who came, refer to faith in Himself, resulting in comfort, companionship and encouragement along the journey to rest in the kingdom of God, rather than spiritual rest in Himself? Or, are they one and the same thing?

It is assumed in one view that the *promised* "rest" in Hebrews 3, 4 equates with a "spiritual" rest and *not* the rest promised Israel. If true, it requires evidence the topic of those chapters changes subjects. The beginning is a discussion of the people of God not finding rest in the Promised Land, and how Christians are to avoid the same mistake.

Does the topic change to a discussion of finding or failing to find rest in Christ? This depends on whether a change of subjects can be demonstrated to occur in the passage, not on what we may conjecture.

It is one matter to find rest *through* Christ, to enter the Kingdom of God *through Christ,* and quite another to substitute rest *in Christ* for the rest God promised His people. It is biblical and sound theology to speak of the saved being *in Christ;* and if one who *was not* in Him *is now* "in Christ" that one must have entered in order to be "in." But, is *"entering Christ"* the "entering rest" spoken of in Hebrews 4:1, 3? Not if the passage itself does not demonstrate it.

Our being "in Christ" is an oft repeated phrase in Paul's writings and a few times in Peter's writings; but is it biblical or sound theology to interpret being *in Christ* as the rest promised to the people of God spoken of in Hebrews chapters 3, 4?[62] It may be logical, if we interpret entering Christ as entering the kingdom of God; but being logical does not prove it is the meaning of Hebrews chapter 4.

The beginning discussion of rest in Hebrews three and four concerns God's promise of "rest" to the seed of Abraham in a country of their own, and their failure to enter and maintain that rest under the leadership of Moses and Joshua.

The basic premise of the chapters is that the promise to the seed of Abraham must be fulfilled, and since it had not been, it was yet to happen. Since the unfulfilled promise was rest in a homeland, do the

---

[62] Nuances of expression and meaning sometimes form the basis of entire doctrinal positions. For example the wording of Romans 6:23 in the NIV, "For the wages of sin is death, but the gift of God is eternal life *in Christ Jesus* our Lord," compared with the KJV: "For the wages of sin is death; but the gift of God is eternal life *through Jesus Christ* our Lord."

Is eternal life *"in Christ* Jesus our Lord" different than eternal life *"through Jesus* Christ our Lord"? Yes! Both are true concepts, but which does the text speak of, eternal repose in Christ, or the means of gaining eternal life?

chapters continue to speak of the same promise? Is that same promise what the saints ought still to anticipate as their inheritance?

Whereas the promise to Israel of rest referred to the Promised Land, we should consider whether entering that promised rest in this era refers to entering the kingdom of God, in its various forms of existence.

In other words, do Hebrews three and four speak of entering the Kingdom of God as the fulfillment of the promise of rest to the seed of Abraham, or do Hebrews 3 and 4 speak of being spiritually comforted and at ease in Christ as the fulfillment of the promise of rest to the seed of Abraham?

To believe that the subject changes from a Promised Land rest to "rest in Christ," one must define "rest in Christ," and illustrate *where,* in Hebrews 3 and 4, the discussion of a Promised Land rest changes to a discussion of "rest in Christ," a spiritual condition and not a physical kingdom.

What in the passage indicates "His rest" (Hebrews 4:1) switches from the previous discussion of failure to enter the Promised Land to a discussion of salvation rest? How is such a transition indicated?

The concept that Hebrews 4 upholds seventh-day Sabbath observance also requires a sound rationale for mentioning Sabbath rest in the midst of a different discussion, an exhortation not to fail to enter the promised rest, a rest which "remains" and is not fulfilled.

When the subject had been fulfilling the promise of rest in the Promised Land, why would there be such a sudden injection of a different "rest" subject matter?

Many Sabbath-observing believers consider Sabbath observance to be a sign of the people of God, as it was in the Old Covenant: *"It will be a sign between me and the Israelites forever, for in six days the LORD made the heavens and the earth, and on the seventh-day he abstained from work and rested"* (Exod. 31:17).

One must at least consider whether it continues in the New Covenant to be a sign as it was in the old: *"... anyone* who enters God's rest also rests from his own work, just *as God did from his"* (Hebrews 4:10b).

If it is literally true that "*anyone* who enters God's rest also rested from his own work, just as God did from his" (and why would it not be literal?) can a person identify those who enter God's promised rest by whether they observe the Sabbath? If Sabbath observance remains a sign between God and His chosen people, you can!

---o-**O**-o---

The Position Taken Here

Jesus said, "Blessed are the meek, for they will inherit the earth" (Matthew 5:5). The position taken here is that the meek inheriting the earth is the promised rest of Hebrews 4, in fulfillment of God's promise of rest to Abraham and his offspring; that the rest we enter now is the spiritual phase of "the kingdom of heaven," or the "Kingdom of God." We enter the kingdom of God during this life, by faith.

We enter God's kingdom now, instead of the land of the Philistines, Moabites, Amorites and Canaanites – the old "Promised Land." But the kingdom of God is not just a status of being in Christ. It is not just the Church. It involves inheritance, a location, which *is now the earth.* Our inherited place of rest will still be the earth during the reign of Christ, and it will still be the earth, made new, throughout eternity.

But although the earth *is now our inheritance,* and *it is now where the kingdom of God is to be found,* it is now occupied and ruled by spiritual Philistines, spiritual Moabites, Amorites and Canaanites! We are pilgrims in our own land! When Jesus returns, rule will be returned to the heirs.[63]

But, there is a means of entering God's spiritual kingdom *now.* The way of entering is comprehended in these sayings of Jesus:

---

[63] Rev. 5:9, 10, KJV: "And they sung a new song, saying, Thou art worthy to take the book, and to open the seals thereof: for thou wast slain, and hast redeemed us to God by thy blood out of every kindred, and tongue, and people, and nation; And hast made us unto our God kings and priests: *and we shall reign on the earth."*

"Jesus answered, 'I am the way and the truth and the life. No one comes to the Father except through me'" (John 14:6).

"I tell you the truth, the man who does not enter the sheep pen by the gate, but climbs in by some other way, is a thief and a robber" (John 10:1).

"Therefore Jesus said again, 'I tell you the truth, I am the gate for the sheep'" (John 10:7).

How do these concepts mesh with the discussion of "rest" in Hebrews chapters three and four? This study addresses those and other issues. May the Spirit of God dwell in us richly as we assess the matter.   ---o-O-o---

What God Promised

Hebrews 10:36 reflects the constant message of the book to the Hebrews: ***"You need to persevere so that when you have done the will of God, you will receive what he has promised."*** What had God promised? He said to Abraham:

"I will establish my covenant as an everlasting covenant between me and you and your descendants after you for the generations to come, to be your God and the God of your descendants after you. The whole land of Canaan, where you are now an alien, I will give as an everlasting possession to you and your descendants after you; and I will be their God" (Genesis 17:7, 8).

The promise was repeated to Isaac, Jacob, and their descendants: "The land I gave to Abraham and Isaac I also give to you, and I will give this land to your descendants after you" (Genesis 35:12).

Finally, the promise is repeated to all believers. It is this inheritance that constituted the promise referred to in Galatians 3:29, which declares the promise is also to believing Gentiles: *"If you belong to Christ, then you are Abraham's seed, and heirs according to the promise."*

"Heirs" refers to inheriting the earth. This promise to Abraham and his posterity is the background of the statement of Jesus: *"Blessed are the meek, for they will inherit the earth"* (Matthew 5:5), and such passages as the following:

> *"What man is he that feareth the LORD? him shall he teach in the way that he shall choose.* **His soul shall dwell at ease;** *and* **his seed shall inherit the earth"** (Psalm 25:12, 13).
> *"But the meek shall inherit the earth; and shall delight themselves in the abundance of peace." "For such as be blessed of him shall inherit the earth; and they that be cursed of him shall be cut off"* (Psalm 37:11, 22 – series from KJV).

---o-O-o---

The Gospel of the Kingdom Was Preached to Israel

According to Hebrews 4:2, Israel heard the gospel, the good news of what the land of Canaan was like; good news, even though some painted an evil picture and stated it was impossible to take what God offered. But, ancient Israel did not believe their "gospel," their "good news."

The same issue is at stake today, inheriting the kingdom of God or not inheriting the kingdom, with the same problems determining the issue – unbelief and disobedience – lack of faith and sin!

In Hebrews 4:2, the meaning of the "gospel" Israel heard is the "gospel of the kingdom": "For unto us *was the gospel preached, as well as unto them....*" It is what Jesus spoke of when He said, *"And this gospel of the kingdom will be preached in the whole world as a testimony to all nations, and then the end will come"* (Matthew 24:14).

For us, "today" is when we receive the gospel – the "good news" of the kingdom of God and what it is like. We are privileged to enter and "inherit the kingdom," but like in the wilderness when the ten spies gave an evil report and wanted to return to Egypt, so it has been ever since Jesus preached the gospel of the kingdom:

"But woe to you, scribes and Pharisees, hypocrites, because you shut off the kingdom of heaven from men; for you do not enter in yourselves, nor do you allow those who are entering to go in" (Matthew 23:13).

Our "today" (when we individually hear the gospel) is the *"another day"* of Hebrews 4:8: *"For if Joshua had given them rest, He would not have spoken of another day after that."* Who is this "He" who spoke "after that" of *another day* after Israel made God angry in the wilderness?

"He" refers to the Holy Spirit speaking through David: *"Therefore, just as the Holy Spirit says, 'Today if you hear his voice'"* (Hebrews 3:7). *"He again fixes a certain day, 'Today,' saying through David after so long a time just as has been said before, today if you hear his voice, do not harden your hearts'"* (Hebrews 4:7).

---o-**O**-o---

A Previous Phase of the Kingdom of God

It is worthwhile to reiterate the point that we enter the kingdom of God when we are born again and become a Christian. By faith we lay hold on the promise of rest. The Church of God teaches that there are three phases or eras to the kingdom of God:

1. The *spiritual phase* (some equate with "the church phase," or era) which began when Jesus and His disciples began to preach the Gospel of the kingdom, an era which continues until the resurrection at the return of Christ.

2. We then speak of the *millennial phase* or era, during which Christ and His saints rule the earth for 1000 years, ending with the destruction of the wicked in the lake of fire.

3. These are followed by the *eternal phase,* beginning with the cleansing of the heavens and earth by fire and establishment of the new heavens and new earth: *"Nevertheless we, according to his promise, look for new heavens and a new earth, wherein dwelleth righteousness"*

(2 Peter 3:13 KJV). "Wherein dwelleth righteousness" includes God Himself dwelling in the new earth:

"And I saw a new heaven and a new earth; for the first heaven and the first earth passed away, and there is no longer any sea. And I saw the holy city, new Jerusalem, coming down out of heaven from God, made ready as a bride adorned for her husband. And I heard a loud voice from the throne, saying, 'Behold, the tabernacle of God is among men, and He shall dwell among them, and they shall be His people, and God Himself shall be among them'" (Revelation 21:1-3).

But is the "three phases" model adequate? Even though Luke 16:16 says, *"The Law and the Prophets were proclaimed until John; since then the gospel of the kingdom of God is preached, and everyone is forcing his way into it,"* the Bible reveals that the gospel of the kingdom had already been preached to Israel in the wilderness:

"For we also have had the gospel preached to us, just as they did; but the message they heard was of no value to them, because those who heard did not combine it with faith" (Hebrews 4:2).
"It still remains that some will enter that rest, and those who formerly had the gospel preached to them did not go in, because of their disobedience" (Hebrews 4:6:).

The Bible also reveals that the kingdom of God already existed before our redemption bought on the Cross, as seen in the declaration of Christ to the Jews: *"Therefore I say to you, the kingdom of God will be taken away from you, and be given to a nation producing the fruit of it"* (Matthew 21:43).

As seen in Matthew 21:43 the kingdom of God was already in existence and recognized by Jesus to have been under the management of the Jews. The evidence shows that the kingdom of God under Israel was a different "phase" of the kingdom of God.

The elements of such thinking lead some people to the concept of "dispensationalism," which has some credence, depending on which brand of dispensationalism one is considering.

Consider again: ***"For unto us was the gospel preached, as well as unto them:*** *but the word preached did not profit them, not being mixed with faith in them that heard it"* (KJV). The gospel was preached to Israel in the wilderness, and *unto us was the gospel preached,* ***as well as unto them.***

The gospel was preached both to Israel of the desert and to Israel of the New Testament – the Israel addressed as "Hebrews" in the book to the Hebrews. What gospel was preached to "them" and to "us"? It was the gospel of the kingdom, the rest promised to the seed of Abraham.

The "us" and "them" both refer to Hebrew people (the book is to the Hebrews). It is not contrasting Jew and Gentile. But, thanks be to God and our Savior Jesus Christ, provision was made for Gentiles as well, for if we belong to Christ we are a part of the Israel of God and Abraham's seed and heirs according to the promise.

---o-O-o---

Scriptures Illustrating the Four Phases

The purpose of this section is two-fold. First, to illustrate from Scriptures that the promise of a place of rest in the kingdom of God is a continuation of the promise of rest to the people of God from age to age. The promise was first made to Abraham, and it continues to this day.

Second, to illustrate from the Scriptures that there are not just *three* phases to the kingdom of God, but four, as the following scriptures illustrate:

The Old Covenant Kingdom:
"Therefore now, LORD God of Israel, keep with thy servant David my father that thou promisedst him, saying, There shall not fail thee a man in my sight to sit on the throne of Israel; so that thy

children take heed to their way, that they walk before me as thou hast walked before me" (1 Kings 8:25, KJV).

Jesus said to the Jewish leaders, *"Therefore I say to you, the kingdom of God will be taken away from you, and be given to a nation producing the fruit of it"* (Matthew 21:43).

The Transition from the Old to the Spiritual:
This transition comes through the "seed of David," that is, Jesus:

"Behold, the days come, saith the LORD, that I will raise unto David a righteous Branch, and a King shall reign and prosper, and shall execute judgment and justice in the earth" (Jer. 23:5 KJV).

"He will be great and will be called the Son of the Most High. The Lord God will give him the throne of his father David" (Luke 1:32).

"It is he who will build the temple of the LORD, and he will be clothed with majesty and will sit and rule on his throne. And he will be a priest on his throne. And there will be harmony between the two" (Zechariah 6:13).

"And we declare unto you glad tidings, how that the promise which was made unto the fathers, God hath fulfilled the same unto us their children, in that he hath raised up Jesus again; as it is also written in the second psalm, Thou art my Son, this day have I begotten thee.

"And as concerning that he raised him up from the dead, now no more to return to corruption, he said on this wise, I will give you the sure mercies of David" (Acts 13:32-34).

The Spiritual Era of the Kingdom:
"Now having been questioned by the Pharisees as to when the kingdom of God was coming, He answered them and said, 'The kingdom of God is not coming with signs to be observed; nor will they say, "Look, here it is!" or, "There it is!" For behold, the kingdom of God is in your midst'" (Luke 17:20, 21). This passage speaks of the spiritual phase of

the kingdom, already existing among the Jews as Jesus spoke – before the cross.

"...For the kingdom of God is not eating and drinking, but right-eousness and peace and joy in the Holy Spirit" (Romans 14:17). This scripture also speaks of the spiritual phase of the kingdom, which was being entered even before the cross.

"But woe to you, scribes and Pharisees, hypocrites, because you shut off the kingdom of heaven from men; for you do not enter in yourselves, nor do you allow **those who are entering** *to go in"* (Matthew 23:13). This verse reflects the same truth already in operation before the cross, as also after the cross, referred to in Hebrews 4:3: *"For we who have believed enter that rest."*

The Transition from the Spiritual Era to the Millennial Era:

"For since death came through a man, the resurrection of the dead comes also through a man. For as in Adam all die, so in Christ all will be made alive. But each in his own turn: Christ, the firstfruits; then, when he comes, those who belong to him" (1 Corinthians 15:21-23.).

"I saw thrones on which were seated those who had been given authority to judge. And I saw the souls of those who had been be-headed because of their testimony for Jesus and because of the word of God. They had not worshipped the beast or his image and had not received his mark on their foreheads or their hands. They came to life and reigned with Christ a thousand years" (Revelations 20:4).

The Millennial Era of the Kingdom:

"And while they were listening to these things, He went on to tell a parable, because He was near Jerusalem, and they supposed that the kingdom of God was going to appear immediately" (Luke 19:11).

What they expected to appear immediately equates with the millennial reign. They expected the physical kingdom of God with the Messiah as King to replace Roman domination at that time.

Daniel gave credence to such expectations:

"Then the sovereignty, power and greatness of the kingdoms under the whole heaven will be handed over to the saints, the people of the Most High. His kingdom will be an everlasting kingdom, and all rulers will worship and obey him" (Daniel 7:27).

"So when they met together, they asked him, "Lord, are you at this time going to restore the kingdom to Israel?[64] He said to them: 'It is not for you to know the times or dates the Father has set by his own authority'" (Acts 1:6, 7).

This also speaks of the rule of Jesus during the Millennium, as do the following passages:

"Jesus said to them, 'I tell you the truth, at the renewal of all things, when the Son of Man sits on his glorious throne, you who have followed me will also sit on twelve thrones, judging the twelve tribes of Israel'" (Matthew 19:28).

"You have made them to be a kingdom and priests to serve our God, and they will reign on the earth" (Revelations 5:10).

The Transition from the Millennial Reign to the Eternal:

"Then the end will come, when he hands over the kingdom to God the Father after he has destroyed all dominion, authority and power. For he must reign until he has put all his enemies under his feet. The last enemy to be destroyed is death" (1 Corinthians 15:24-26).

The Eternal Era of the Kingdom:

"Behold, I will create new heavens and a new earth. The former things will not be remembered, nor will they come to mind" (Isaiah 65:17).

"'As the new heavens and the new earth that I make will endure before me," declares the LORD, 'so will your name and descendants endure'" (Isaiah 66:22).

---

[64] This question indicates the questioner's complete lack of comprehending of the statement of Jesus that the kingdom was to be taken from Israel and given to a more fruitful people (Mt. 21:43).

"But in keeping with his promise we are looking forward to a new heaven and a new earth, the home of righteousness" (2 Peter 3:13).

"Then I saw a new heaven and a new earth, for the first heaven and the first earth had passed away, and there was no longer any sea. I saw the Holy City, the new Jerusalem, coming down out of heaven from God, prepared as a bride beautifully dressed for her husband.

"And I heard a loud voice from the throne saying, 'Now the dwelling of God is with men, and he will live with them. They will be his people, and God himself will be with them and be their God.

"He will wipe every tear from their eyes. There will be no more death or mourning or crying or pain, for the old order of things has passed away'" (Revelations 21:1-4).

This is the setting in which Isaiah 66:22, 23 is to occur:

"As the new heavens and the new earth that I make will endure before me," declares the LORD, *"so will your name and descendants endure. From one New Moon to another and from one Sabbath to another, all mankind will come and bow down before me,"* says the LORD."*

There Is a Unity in All Phases of God's Kingdom:

*"All you have made will praise you, O LORD; your saints will extol you. They will tell of the glory of your kingdom and speak of your might, so that all men may know of your mighty acts and the glorious splendor of your kingdom. **Your kingdom is an everlasting kingdom, and your dominion endures through all generations.** The LORD is faithful to all his promises and loving toward all he has made"* (Psalm 145:10-13).   ---o-**O**-o---

Entering God's Kingdom Before the Cross

It is apparent from Matthew 23:13 that believers already were entering the kingdom of God during the ministry of Jesus on earth: *"But woe to you, scribes and Pharisees, hypocrites, because you shut off the kingdom of heaven from men; for you do not enter in yourselves, nor do you allow **those who are entering** to go in."*

This verse reflects the same "entering" the kingdom of God before the cross referred to in Hebrews 4:3: *"For we who have believed enter that rest."*

So we see that the kingdom already existed with subjects in and subjects entering the kingdom. Jesus said to the Jewish leaders, *"Therefore I say to you, the kingdom of God will be taken away from you, and be given to a nation producing the fruit of it"* (Matthew 21:43).

The kingdom already existed, or it could not have been taken away from the Jews, and people were "entering" the kingdom of heaven, even as Jesus and His disciples preached the gospel of the kingdom.

The kingdom of God was taken away from Jewish leadership and given to a people who would produce its fruit. This roughly corresponds to what Jesus referred to in Luke 21:24 as "the times of the Gentiles": *"And they* (Israel) *shall fall by the edge of the sword, and shall be led away captive into all nations: and Jerusalem shall be trodden down of the Gentiles, until the times of the Gentiles be fulfilled."*

Was that kingdom *which was taken away from Israel,* the times of the Gentiles, the *promised rest for Israel?* The answer obviously is "no." That rest is yet to come.

The taking away refers to leadership in promulgating the gospel, not the exclusion of the seed of Abraham from their promised possession! This change of leadership began the spiritual era of the kingdom in which we find ourselves: "... we who have believed enter that rest." It is the spiritual phase (era) of the kingdom referred to in Hebrews four that we enter now in our "today."

But consider the kingdom, the one we are calling the "spiritual phase" of the kingdom, the one taken from Israel and given to a more worthy people – is *this* the rest promised to Abraham and his seed, Israel?

The incongruity of that ought to be obvious! How can it be taken away from those to whom it was promised and yet be the rest promised to them, and which is re-affirmed *to the Hebrews in the book to the Hebrews* as a fulfillment of the same promise made to them?

Our entering today is the time of hope, not the time of fulfillment. But we must understand this is our "Today" to enter. If we do not enter the kingdom through Jesus Christ in our "Today," we will never enter God's eternal inheritance-rest!

---o-**O**-o---

We Enter – But We Get no Rest!

Becoming part of the church, a part of the body of Christ, is concurrent with *entering* the kingdom of God; but entering the body of Christ, the church, does not produce the "rest" promised to Israel, nor does entering the spiritual phase of the kingdom fulfill the promise of rest to the Church. That "rest" will not be achieved until the saints are resurrected, and the seed of Abraham – both Jew and Gentile who belong to Christ – inherit the earth.

The physical kingdom, the earth, does not come under control of the saints when they enter the spiritual phase of the kingdom. We are not now kings and priests ruling over the earth. Being born a part of God's people, Israel, did not equate with entering God's promised rest, the land of Canaan. Israel were already God's chosen people *before they entered the promised rest.*

Israelites did not experience the promised "rest" by being a part of the people of God – *neither do we!* Believing, becoming a Christian, "joining the church," is only entering rest by faith.

The rest God promised Israel equated with dwelling in a homeland of their own ruled by God as their King. They were already His people, and becoming His people was not the rest God promised – Dwelling in Canaan was the rest He promised!

This is typical of our becoming a part of the people of God in our own era, entering the promised rest by faith, but not yet possessing the promised inheritance, the earth.

There is another parallel. Even Gentiles *became* a part of the people of God by laying hold on God's Old Covenant with Israel.[65] Those Gentiles entered the Promised Land with Israel, but none of the people of the Old Covenant really had rest while dwelling in the very land of promise! They all were strangers and pilgrims as was Abraham, to whom God said:

> *"The whole land of Canaan, where you are now an alien, I will give as an everlasting possession to you and your descendants after you; and I will be their God"* (Genesis 17:8).
>
> *"All these people were still living by faith when they died. They did not receive the things promised; they only saw them and welcomed them from a distance. And they admitted that they were aliens and strangers on earth. People who say such things show that they are looking for a country of their own"* (Hebrews 11:13, 14).

We, too, are part of the "people who say such things." We, in fact, like Abraham, *live in the promised possession* as aliens, and in this life we have no rest.

The Church has been in her "wilderness" experience[66] during these past two thousand years, during which we are tried, tempted, even martyred, and pass or fail to pass the tests of faith and obedience.

The Holy Spirit is the deposit guaranteeing our inheritance, *it is not the inheritance itself!* Although we have entered the kingdom (spiritual phase) we have not entered the rest to be achieved with the resurrection of the saints.

---

[65] See Isaiah 56.
[66] No reference to Rev. 12:6, 12:14, or 17:3; rather reference is to our individual spiritual travels.

*"And you also were included in Christ when you heard the word of truth, the gospel of your salvation. Having believed, you were marked in him with a seal, the promised Holy Spirit, **who is a deposit guaranteeing our inheritance** until the redemption of those who are God's possession – to the praise of his glory"* (Ephesians 1:13, 14, KJV).

Fulfillment of the promised rest awaits the resurrection when Revelation 5:9, 10 will be fulfilled:

"And they sang a new song: 'You are worthy to take the scroll and to open its seals, because you were slain, and with your blood you purchased men for God from every tribe and language and people and nation. You have made them to be a kingdom and priests to serve our God, and they will reign on the earth."

---o-**O**-o---

The Original Failure to Enter Rest

The basic premise of Hebrews chapters three and four is that Hebrew Christians were in danger of making the same mistakes made by their forefathers. The central theme of chapters three and four is not to miss out on the opportunity to enjoy the promised kingdom rest, a promise that remains valid.

Their forefathers had been called out of Egypt to a land God had promised to their ancestor, Abraham. With many miracles God delivered Israel from slavery in Egypt, and under the leadership of Moses, led them to Mount Sinai, where God made a covenant with them to be their God, if they would be His obedient people.

The twelve tribes of Israel agreed, and God began giving them instructions by talking directly to them from Mount Sinai, then continued His instructions through Moses, God's human mediator between Himself and His people. When they approached the Promised Land, spies were sent to see what the country was like.

Ten of twelve spies gave a bad report, and ignoring all the miracles God had performed to deliver Israel from Egypt, they declared it impossible to take the land.

Israel believed the bad report, but did not believe God, that He would deliver what He had promised. They began to measure the probability of successful conquest in terms of what they could do, rather than in terms of what God could and would do.

They threatened to appoint a new leader and return to Egypt! Because of this rebellion, God refused to allow that generation, all over 20 years old, to enter the Promised Land, the primary "rest" spoken of in Hebrews 3, 4.

The rebellion that prevented Israel from enjoying rest in the Promised Land was not just failure to enter caused by believing the bad report of the spies, it was *40 years* of seeing God in action and still not believing: *"...during the time of testing in the desert, where your fathers tested and tried me and for forty years saw what I did"* (Hebrews 3:8, 9).

The Oath God Swore in Anger Against Israel

"Nevertheless, as surely as I live and as surely as the glory of the LORD fills the whole earth, not one of the men who saw my glory and the miraculous signs I performed in Egypt and in the desert but who disobeyed me and tested me ten times – not one of them will ever see the land I promised on oath to their forefathers. No one who has treated me with contempt will ever see it" (Numbers 12:21-23).

"So, as the Holy Spirit says: 'Today, if you hear his voice, do not harden your hearts as you did in the rebellion, during the time of testing in the desert, where your fathers tested and tried me and for forty years saw what I did. That is why I was angry with that generation, and I said, 'Their hearts are always going astray, and they have not known my ways.' So I declared on oath in my anger, 'They shall never enter my rest.'" (Hebrews 3:7-11).

The rebellious nature that troubled the offending elders of Israel continued among the rest of Israel, resulting in Israel not continuing to enjoy rest once they had crossed Jordan and conquered its inhabitants.

Hundreds of rebellious years later, Jesus Christ the Messiah came on the scene, making a new covenant with Israel and Judah. He, like God through Moses, performed many miracles; He was ready, willing and able to save Israel from their slavery (to sin).

Some of the Hebrews, who even believed and embraced Him, were tempted to turn back into the Old Covenant system, which could not remove sin, and others needed faith to take hold of the New Covenant and its better promises.[67]

The book to the Hebrews was written in part to address these problems. Admonition not to repeat the mistakes of their forefathers is one of the basic messages of the book:

"Therefore, since the promise of entering his rest still stands, let us be careful that none of you be found to have fallen short of it." "Let us, therefore, make every effort to enter that rest, so that no one will fall by following their example of disobedience" (Hebrews 4:1, 11).

The means of entering and the means of success is made plain:

"Therefore, holy brothers, who share in the heavenly calling, fix your thoughts on Jesus, the apostle and high priest whom we confess." "See to it, brothers, that none of you has a sinful, unbelieving heart that turns away from the living God. But encourage one another daily, as long as it is called Today, so that none of you may be hardened by sin's deceitfulness" (Hebrews 3:1, 12-13).

Notice the two elements, "sinful" (disobedience) and "unbelieving" (lack of faith). After explaining the new and better system of worship and atonement for sin, the warning is repeated in chapter ten:

---

[67] Heb. 8:6: "But the ministry Jesus has received is as superior to theirs as the covenant of which he is mediator is superior to the old one, and it is founded on better promises."

- 212 -

"Anyone who rejected the law of Moses died without mercy on the testimony of two or three witnesses. How much more severely do you think a man deserves to be punished who has trampled the Son of God under foot, who has treated as an unholy thing the blood of the covenant that sanctified him, and who has insulted the Spirit of grace?' [Cf. Numbers 12:23: "No one who has treated me with contempt will ever see it."]

"For we know him who said, 'It is mine to avenge; I will repay,' and again, 'The Lord will judge his people.

"It is a dreadful thing to fall into the hands of the living God. Remember those earlier days after you had received the light, when you stood your ground in a great contest in the face of suffering. Sometimes you were publicly exposed to insult and persecution; at other times you stood side by side with those who were so treated.

"You sympathized with those in prison and joyfully accepted the confiscation of your property, because you knew that you yourselves had better and lasting possessions. So do not throw away your confidence; it will be richly rewarded. **You need to persevere so that when you have done the will of God, you will receive what he has promised"** (Hebrews 10:28-36).

We need to recognize the great contrast between the above passage, which lauds the great determination and zeal, the great effort to be faithful and obedient to God, in contrast with the interpretation some give to Hebrews 4:10: *"... for anyone who enters God's rest also rests from his own work, just as God did from his."* They interpret the passage to mean that we quit trying to save ourselves by good works.

Of course we cannot save ourselves by good works, but if ceasing from our works means no longer obeying law, what is it we are admonished to obey? If we think it means we cease either obedience or good works, we have read chapters 3 and 4 and 10:28-36 much too hastily! ---o-O-o---

- 213 -

What Moses Expected, Joshua and David Experienced

Moses took for granted the promised rest would be achieved:

"Therefore it shall come about when the LORD your God has given you rest from all your surrounding enemies, in the land which the LORD your God gives you as an inheritance to possess, you shall blot out the memory of Amalek from under heaven; you must not forget" (Deuteronomy 25:19).

But, Hebrews 4:8 *("For if Joshua had given them rest, He would not have spoken of another day after that")* seems to deny that Israel entered rest. Keep in mind, the rest Joshua expected to give Israel was *Promised Land rest.*

Israel did enter the Promised Land, but only had peace from their enemies sporadically. That does not fulfill the promise to Abraham and his seed, just as this life does not fulfill the promise of rest to the church. This life is not our inheritance!

Joshua and David believed the promised rest had been achieved:

"And the LORD gave them rest on every side, according to all that He had sworn to their fathers, and no one of all their enemies stood before them; the LORD gave all their enemies into their hand" (Joshua 21:44).

"Is not the LORD your God with you? And has He not given you rest on every side? For He has given the inhabitants of the land into my hand, and the land is subdued before the LORD and before His people" (1 Chronicles 22:18).

If Moses at the end of His leadership took it for granted that Israel would enter rest and gave Israel instructions what to do after entering, why does the Book of Hebrews indicate that Joshua did not give Israel rest? If Joshua and David believed Israel had entered the promised rest, why does the Book of Hebrews indicate Joshua did not give them rest?

One must recognize the similarity between what happened to back-sliding Israel who entered rest and got kicked out for disobedience[68] and what happens to backsliding Christians who enter the kingdom of God and "get kicked out" for the same problems of losing faith and disobedience (see Hebrews chapters 6, 10).

Israel did enter rest, but lost it from lack of faith and disobedience. Hebrews 3 and 4 are warnings to Christians who have entered rest (the spiritual kingdom of God) not to lose their rest as Israel did, through loss of faith and disobedience.

The message is the same in 1 Corinthians 10:1-13:

"For I do not want you to be ignorant of the fact, brothers, that our forefathers were all under the cloud and that they all passed through the sea. They were all baptized into Moses in the cloud and in the sea. They all ate the same spiritual food and drank the same spiritual drink; for they drank from the spiritual rock that accompanied them, and that rock was Christ.

"Nevertheless, God was not pleased with most of them; their bodies were scattered over the desert. Now these things occurred as examples to keep us from setting our hearts on evil things as they did. Do not be idolaters, as some of them were; as it is written:

"'The people sat down to eat and drink and got up to indulge in pagan revelry.' We should not commit sexual immorality, as some of them did – and in one day twenty-three thousand of them died. We should not test the Lord, as some of them did – and were killed by snakes. And do not grumble, as some of them did – and were killed by the destroying angel.

"These things happened to them as examples and were written down as warnings for us, on whom the fulfillment of the ages has come. So, if you think you are standing firm, be careful that you don't fall!

"No temptation has seized you except what is common to man. And God is faithful; he will not let you be tempted beyond what you

---

[68] Assyrian and Babylonian captivities.

can bear. But when you are tempted, he will also provide a way out so that you can stand up under it."

---o-O-o---

Barriers to Rest

When David said, *"My soul finds **rest in God alone**; my salvation comes from him"* (Psalm 62:1), and *"He who dwells in the shelter of the Most High will rest in the shadow of the Almighty"* (Psalm 91:1), he was neither disdaining Promised Land rest, nor Sabbath rest. He enjoyed both while his soul found rest *in God alone.* Apostle John wrote:

"Dear children, let us not love with words or tongue but with actions and in truth. This then is how we know that we belong to the truth, and how we set our hearts at rest in his presence whenever our hearts condemn us.

"For God is greater than our hearts, and he knows everything. Dear friends, if our hearts do not condemn us, we have confidence before God and receive from him anything we ask, because we obey his commands and do what pleases him" (1 John 3:18-20).

It is important to keep in mind the relationships that tie together being obedient and having rest. These were the same issues in relation to "rest" in the Promised Land. Rest in the Presence of God is impossible without faith, obedience and a clear conscience.

"We set our hearts at rest in His presence" – we are still children, children of God, and disobedient children cannot be at rest in the presence of their parents without confessing their disobedience, repenting, and making a new commitment to obey. We cannot be at ease in the presence of those whom we offend without correcting the offense.

How do we set our hearts at rest in God's presence when our hearts condemn us? *How* do we know we belong to the truth? *By loving with actions and in truth rather than in words or tongue!*

How do we have confidence before God and receive what we ask of Him? *Why* do our hearts not condemn us? *Because we obey his commands and do what pleases him!*

Is obeying God's commands and doing what pleases God "ceasing to work" in order to rest in Jesus? Sometimes we build up dichotomies impossible to resolve in the discordant positions we take. The very intent of Hebrews three and four is to admonish *faithful obedience* and avoid disobedience, because *faithless disobedience* prevents entering God's rest. The very purpose of the chapter is to point out what causes failure to enter God's rest, and that cause of failure is stated to be two-fold, unbelief and disobedience.

This purpose would be sidetracked by teaching just the opposite, that obedience is equated with good works (which of course it is!) and that we, by ceasing to work as God ceased working, stop our good works, relying only on faith. There is no basis for faith in disobedience!

The message of the chapters is that disobedience prevents entering or continuing in God's rest. Again, we affirm that good works are not the means of salvation, but evil works, disobedience, are the very reason we need salvation!

Of course, some would affirm that we should continue doing good works, but just cease doing them for the purpose of influencing our relationship with God! But, evil conduct and disobedience *always have and always will influence our relations with God and His Son.* If the book of Hebrews is clear on anything, it is clear on this point!

---o-O-o---

Ancient Israel Barred from Being Saved?
Then Why Sacrifice?

Again, one proposition to which we are responding is this: *This Sabbath rest is not related to either possession of the land or the seventh-day Sabbath. This rest refers to a blessing of spiritual rest in Christ resulting from belief* (referring to Hebrews 4:3).

If the promised rest were rest in Christ, that would mean those Israelites over twenty years of age were barred forever from being saved, that there was no forgiveness possible for them, for God swore they could not enter His rest.

We may address this matter again, but think of the implications. While they still lived and wandered in the desert, they were required to make sacrifices for sin. To what purpose? While they still lived, they were required to observe the seventh-day Sabbath. To what purpose?

The Sabbath was a time for a holy convocation, a time of worship, a time for relaxation. If they were eternally doomed, why were those who were eternally doomed required to make sacrifices for sin and worship God, from Whom they were eternally separated? What was their relationship with God? Had they no relationship with God whatsoever?

Are the Scriptures silent on the matter? The Bible says if they made those sacrifices for sin, their sin would be forgiven: *"He shall burn all the fat on the altar as he burned the fat of the fellowship offering. In this way the priest will make atonement for the man's sin, **and he will be forgiven"** (Lev. 4:26).

When the elders of Israel brought sin offerings during those 40 years, were they forgiven as promised? When the Levites over 40 years old served in making sacrifices, were they eternally doomed and separated from God?

Ten of the twelve spies gave a bad report of the land of Canaan and persuaded the congregation of Israel it was not possible to conquer Canaan. Instead of believing with God's help they were able, they believed the bad report, and believed the spies assessment that they were unable.

Thereupon God proposed to Moses that He, God, would destroy Israel with a plague, and start over with Moses to build a stronger and greater people than Israel (Numbers 14:12).

Moses pled with God, and pointed out the effect it would have on other nations if God were to destroy all Israel at one time, and that it would be interpreted by other nations that God was unable to protect His people and give what He had promised. Moses pled:

"'In accordance with your great love, forgive the sin of these people, just as you have pardoned them from the time they left Egypt until now.' **The LORD replied, 'I have forgiven them, as you asked.** *Nevertheless, as surely as I live and as surely as the glory of the LORD fills the whole earth, not one of the men who saw my glory and the miraculous signs I performed in Egypt and in the desert but who disobeyed me and tested me ten times – not one of them will ever see the land I promised on oath to their forefathers. No one who has treated me with contempt will ever see it'"* (Numbers 14:19-23).

God thereupon destroyed the ten rebellious spies, *but he forgave the rest!* They were forgiven, but nonetheless still punished by not allowing them to enter into Canaan. This is similar to Hebrews 12:8: *"If you are not disciplined (and everyone undergoes discipline), then you are illegitimate children and not true sons."*

Those over 20 died in the wilderness, but it appears that except for the ten spies who rebelled, their status before God does not preclude their being resurrected to life and participating in the inheritance promised to the saints of old, *if they were subsequently obedient until death.*

Otherwise, to what avail would their continued sacrifices for sin have been? Keep Hebrews 9:15 in mind: *"For this reason Christ is the mediator of a new covenant, that those who are called may receive the promised eternal inheritance – now that* **he has died as a ransom to set them free from the sins committed under the first covenant.**"

---o-O-o---

The "Rests" of Hebrews 3, 4

What becomes of particular interest and poses a problem for Bible students is the mixture of kinds of rest spoken of in these chapters. Ten times in the third and fourth chapters of Hebrews the writer speaks of "rest." "Rest" refers variously to God resting at the end of creation week, some of Israel failing to find rest in the Promised Land, seventh-day Sabbath rest, and entering rest through faith in Christ.

Since these chapters warn against making the same mistakes of faithlessness and disobedience, we must be concerned with what sort of disobedience disqualifies us to enter the promised rest.

It is plain our endeavor to enter involves obedience – does obedience include the command to observe the Sabbath? Does disobeying the Sabbath command jeopardize entering God's rest?

Answers to these questions hinge greatly on interpreting the meaning of "rest." In the Greek text of Hebrews 3 and 4, the noun and verb forms for "rest" combined occur 11 times. They refer to "rest" as a place of rest and the act of resting. These noun and verb forms are all from the same word stem.

In the Septuagint *(Alexandrian)* Greek Old Testament one meaning of the same word refers to the act of God discontinuing to create at the end of six days work and His not working the seventh-day:

"And God finished [συνετε'λεσεν] *on the sixth day his works which he made and he ceased* [κατε'παυσε] *on the seventh-day from all his works which he made. And God blessed the seventh-day and sanctified it because in it he ceased* [κατε'παυσεν] *from all his works which God began to do"* (Genesis 2:2, 3 Brenton trans).

God "finished" His work on the sixth day, and "rested" the seventh. The meaning is clear. However, much confusion exists over the statement that God "ceased" on the seventh-day. Some see an implication that God was working into the seventh-day, then during the seventh-day God stopped creating. However, the verb "κατε'παυσε" not only means stopped, it means "paused" or took time out.

It is a cessation without stating anything pro or con about resumption of activity, and thus it properly refers to a "pause" such as a twenty-four hour Sabbath cessation or pause from work. This is not intended to imply God resumed creation on the beginning of the next week.

"Συνετε'λεσεν" (he ended) indicates what man is to do at the end of six days of work (end the week's work) and "κατε'παυσε" (rest, or take time out, pause) indicates what man is intended to do from the beginning to the end of the seventh-day, and in the Maccabees (shown later) even to the period of rest on the seventh-day.

The noun form, "καταʹπαυσις," refers to the place of rest in the promise to Israel that they would be given "rest" in Canaan. The noun also refers to what Christians enter when they become children of God. Hence, the logic some see in our being "baptized into Christ" or entering Christ as being and providing the rest spoken of in Hebrews 4.

The English words from this Greek word for "rest" occur 10 times in chapters 3, 4 of Hebrews in the King James Version of the Bible, all from 3:11 to 4:11 – nine times in the New International." It occurs 11 times in the Greek text. The difference occurs between the KJV and the NIV in 4:4 where the KJV says "did rest" and the NIV says "rested." It is the word translated "rest" and "ceased" in the KJV for Hebrews 4:10: "For he that is entered into his rest (κατάπαυσιν – ka-tah'pau-seen, a noun), he also hath ceased (κατέπαυσεν, – ka-teh'pau-sin, a verb) from his own works, as God did from his."

Since the same Greek word in noun and verb form refers to the Sabbath and what a person does (ceases work or rests) on the Sabbath, since it also refers to the Promised Land and Israel resting in the Promised Land, and to what believers enter on becoming children of God, use of the word in Hebrews 4 allows for much theological speculation.

The word "σαββατισμοσ" (sabbatismos – "sabbath rest," NIV) is also used in Hebrews 4:9 referring to the rest Joshua failed to provide. That usage of "sabbatismos," with verses 3, 4 referring to God resting the seventh-day from His work, adds to the potential for misunderstanding. So, when the author speaks of "rest," to what does he refer, the Promised Land, the Kingdom of God, the seventh-day Sabbath, or some new concept such as "rest in Christ"?

---o-O-o---

"Sabbatidzo," "Baptidzo," and "Katartidzo"

"There remains, then, a Sabbath-rest (Greek, "σαββατισμος" – "sabbatismos") for the people of God. For anyone who enters God's rest also rests from his own work, just as God did from his" (Verses 9, 10).

The word "sabbatismos" is the noun form of the verb "sabbatidzo," which means the act of "sabbath-keeping." "Sabbath" is the name of the day, while "sabbatismos" is the name of the act of sabbath-keeping.

The same Greek word forms can be seen in another biblical institution, "baptism." The word "baptism" is the name of a biblical institution parallel to the word "sabbath."

The verb which means to baptize has the same verb form as the verb to keep sabbath. Like the verb "sabbatidzo," which means to observe the Sabbath, there is a parallel verb "baptidzo" which means to baptize; and like the noun form "sabbatismos" that names the action of keeping Sabbath, there is a similar noun "baptismos" to name the action of baptizing.

This construction is also found in the verb "katartid'zo," the "knit together" of 1 Corinthians 1:10, which has the same noun form "katartismos" to name the action.

This is explained to illustrate that there was nothing strange or new about such a word as "sabbatismos." The ending "-ismos" is not a new word ending invented for Hebrews 4:9. Its meaning and use would be immediately recognized by those who spoke and wrote the Greek of the day.

The ending "-ismos" on verbs which end with "-idzo" was used much like our English grammar's gerund, in such sentence structures as "Fighting is not allowed in this school."

If we were to say, "The problem of fighting continues among students," it would be parallel to saying "sabbath-keeping continues among the people of God." But, the statement that a "sabbatismos" remains to the people of God refers to the fact that the children of God still have an inheritance.   ---o-O-o---

The Application of "Sabbatismos"

The first impression from saying "there remains a sabbath-keeping for the people of God," would be that God's people continue keeping the sabbath. The idea would seem reinforced by the statement that "anyone who enters God's rest *also rests* from his own work, just as God did from His." God rested from His work by working six days, then remained at rest throughout the seventh-day, pronounced a blessing on the day, and hallowed or made holy the seventh-day.

However, two different rests are referred to in verses 9 and 10, and the one using the word "sabbatismos" is referring to inheritance rest, rather than seventh-day Sabbath rest. Seventh-day Sabbath rest is the "also rests just as God did" of verse 10.

One of the meanings of "kata**paus**is" is to pause – we get our English word "pause" from the root (bold-face above) of this word. It does not of itself denote permanent cessation of activity, inasmuch as it is used to refer to weekly Sabbath rest, and for such temporary cessation of movement as the priests standing still in the Jordan river.[69]

This casts doubt on the interpretation some propose that God ceased forever from work as a meaning of Hebrews 4:3, 10, and therefore if we rest as God did, we also cease forever trying to save ourselves by works. The word "kata'pausis" has no such implication as permanent cessation.

---

[69] Josh. 3:13: καὶ ἔσται ὡς ἂν <u>καταπαύσωσιν</u> οἱ πόδες τῶν ἱερέων τῶν αι-ρόντων τὴν κιβωτὸν τῆς διαθήκης κυρίου πάσης τῆς γῆς ἐν τῷ ὕδατι τοῦ Ιορ-δάνου, τὸ ὕδωρ τοῦ Ιορδάνου ἐκλείψει, τὸ δὲ ὕδωρ τὸ καταβαῖνον στήσεται.

Josh. 3:13: "And it shall come to pass, as soon as the soles of the feet of the priests that bear the ark of the Lord of all the earth, shall rest in the waters of Jordan, that the waters of Jordan shall be cut off from the waters that come down from above; and they shall stand upon an heap."

The Greek of the Septuagint was written by Hebrews who translated the Old Testament from Hebrew into Greek. The word they chose (kata'pausis) suggests God "paused" or took time out on the seventh-day.

Let's consider further the question: Is "rest in Christ" mentioned or intended in Hebrews 3, 4? To suggest rest in Christ is meant by "sabbatismos" in Hebrews 4 would have been one big step further removed from the usual meaning of "sabbatismos."

"Kata'pausin" – rest – in the Promised Land was a common theme, but "sabbatismos" is not used for Promised Land rest in the Greek Old Testament, neither is "sabbath" used in English translations of the Old Testament to refer to rest in the Promised Land. Since it is not, some doubt *sabbatismos* means Promised Land rest in Hebrews 4.

When Jesus invites us to come unto Him and He will give us "rest," the Greek word for rest is *anapauso,* "κἀγὼ ἀναπαύσω ὑμᾶς" ("I will give rest to you")[70] This word "ἀναπαύσω" is used more frequently in the Septuagint OT to refer to sabbath rest than "κατάπαυσιν," the usual "rest" in reference to the promised land.

That would at first glance seem to limit "sabbatismos" to seventh-day Sabbath rest, unless the thesis is correct that the *sabbatismos* that remains is *rest in Christ.* But, **rest** *in Christ* is not a biblical theme, even though **being** "in Christ" is a theme found in Paul's and Peter's letters.

The nearest possibility in Hebrews would be 3:14: *"We have come to share in Christ if we hold firmly till the end the confidence we had at first";* but "sharing *in Christ"* is not the same language of "rest" or "sabbatismos" to which "rest" refers in the two chapters.

Sharing in Christ more logically refers to the same concept as found in Galatians 3:29: *"If you belong to Christ, then you are Abraham's*

---

[70] Matthew 11:28-30: Δεῦτε πρός με πάντες οἱ κοπιῶντες καὶ πεφορτισμένοι, **κἀγὼ ἀναπαύσω ὑμᾶς.** ἄρατε τὸν ζυγόν μου ἐφ᾿ ὑμᾶς καὶ μάθετε ἀπ᾿ ἐμοῦ, οτι πραΰς εἰμι καὶ ταπεινὸς τῇ καρδίᾳ, καὶ εὑρήσετε ἀνάπαυσιν ταῖς ψυχαῖς ὑμῶν· ὁ γὰρ ζυγός μου χρηστὸς καὶ τὸ φορτίον μου ἐλαφρόν ἐστιν.
Matthew 11:28-30: "Come to me, all you who are weary and burdened, and I will give you rest. Take my yoke upon you and learn from me, for I am gentle and humble in heart, and you will find rest for your souls. For my yoke is easy and my burden is light."

seed, and heirs according to the promise" – this refers to the very same promise discussed in Hebrews 3, 4. In Christ, *we share* the promise of rest in our inheritance, as seed of Abraham.

"That rest" in Hebrews 3 and 4 cannot be demonstrated to refer to "rest in Christ." Instead, it refers to the rest Israel did not receive under the leadership of Joshua. God did not swear that disobedient Israel could not enter Christ, He swore they could not enter the Promised Land. He held Israel in the desert until the disobedient elders all died so they *could not enter His rest* – the Promised Land.

When Hebrews 4:3 says, "Now we who have believed enter *that rest,"* it cannot refer to resting "in Christ," because being in Christ had not already been introduced as a "rest" in the Hebrews 3, 4 discussion – nor is it elsewhere in Hebrews! Jesus is not here nor elsewhere compared to the Promised Land. He is the Door to the Promised Land, He is the Gate to the kingdom of God – but He is the Shepherd, not the sheepfold!

> *"Jesus therefore said to them again, 'Truly, truly, I say to you, I am the door of the sheep. All who came before Me are thieves and robbers, but the sheep did not hear them. I am the door; if anyone enters through Me, he shall be saved, and shall go in and out, and find pasture'"* (John 10:7-9).

The disobedient of Israel who could not enter the Promised Land were the disobedient elders who died in the wilderness: *"And with whom was he angry for forty years? Was it not with those who sinned, whose bodies fell in the desert? And to whom did God swear that they would never enter his rest if not to those who disobeyed?"* (Hebrews 3:17).

"His rest" had no reference to Christ, even though Christ was the Rock in the Wilderness.[71] Scriptural "rest" is always something given to the people of God ("come unto me and I will give you rest"); it is never the God Who gives the rest.

---

[71] See 1 Cor. 10:1-5.

The "Rock," Jesus Christ, was already with Israel in the wilderness, in the very same way He was with Israel before and after the elders died and the survivors crossed Jordan into the land of Canaan ("The LORD replied, *'My Presence will go with you, and I will give you rest'"* – Exodus 33:14).

Compare the Exodus 33:14 promise to be with and give rest, to the Matthew 11:28 promise Jesus made to those who come to Him: *"Come to me, all you who are weary and burdened, and I will give you rest."*

Jesus is involved in both promises of rest: *"They all ate the same spiritual food and drank the same spiritual drink; for they drank from the spiritual rock that accompanied them, and that rock was Christ. Nevertheless, God was not pleased with most of them; their bodies were scattered over the desert"* (1 Corinthians 10:3-5).

When Hebrews 4 turns to a discussion of Christ as our High Priest, no reference is made to "resting" in Christ, nor does it refer to Him as a place of rest. The concept of "entering" plays a prominent role in the two questions, but there is no discussion of "entering Christ" in the two chapters (although entering Christ is a scriptural concept).

Let us be diligent to enter what rest? God's rest. What was God's rest that He swore "they shall not enter"? It was not seventh-day Sabbath rest. God was not saying, "I will not allow faithless, disobedient Israel to rest on the seventh-day Sabbath," for God enforced its observance before, during, and after the rebellion.

He continued the command to rest on the seventh-day Sabbath, and Jesus, even during His ministry on earth, was teaching its proper observance.[72]

If the above exposition is true, still to be understood is why the Holy Spirit even inspired this part of the passage: *"For He has thus said somewhere concerning the seventh-day, 'and God rested on the seventh-day from all his works'; and again in the passage, 'they shall not enter my rest'"* (Hebrews 4:4, 5).

---

[72] See Isaiah chapters 56, 58 for OT confirmation, Mark 3:4 for NT confirmation .

We also need more discussion of: *"There remains therefore a Sabbath rest (sabbatismos) for the people of God. For the one who has entered His rest has himself also rested from his works, as God did from His. Let us therefore be diligent to enter that rest, lest anyone fall through following the same example of disobedience"* (Hebrews 4:9-11).   ---o-O-o---

God's Work Finished
From the Foundation of the World

Let's factor in Hebrews 4:3: *"Now we who have believed enter that rest, just as God has said, 'So I declared on oath in my anger, "They shall never enter my rest." And yet his work has been finished since the creation of the world."*

Or as in the KJV: *"For we which have believed do enter into rest, as he said, As I have sworn in my wrath, if they shall enter into my rest: although the works were finished from the foundation of the world."*

Why does the text mention "his works were finished from the foundation of the world"? It is not a complicated concept. When God swore that the disobedient elders of Israel would never enter His rest, it was thousands of years after He created the place of rest, and yet the children of God had not been able to enjoy it.

The *place of God's rest* has existed since the creation of the world. God declaring "The meek shall inherit the earth" identifies the place of rest. The earth is the inheritance, the place of God's rest for His people. The place had been finished since creation. The place was ready, the people were not!

The purpose of speaking of God's work being finished from the end of creation week is directly related to the place of rest. God's entire plan of redemption and rest for the redeemed was a completed work of God by the end of creation week. Consider these "foundation of the world" texts:

1) *"Then the King will say to those on His right, 'Come, you who are blessed of My Father, inherit the kingdom prepared for you from the foundation of the world'"* (Matthew 25:34).

Notice the parallel "foundation of the world" concept found in the Hebrews 4:3 statement:

2) *"For we who have believed enter that rest, just as He has said, 'As I swore in My wrath, they shall not enter My rest,' although His works were finished from the foundation of the world."*

The kingdom of God, the promised rest, is the subject of "finished from the foundation of the world," and is what we now enter, in its spiritual phase, and what the Scribes and Pharisees refused to enter and hindered others from entering.

3) *"And all that dwell upon the earth shall worship him, whose names are not written in the book of life of the Lamb slain from the foundation of the world"* (Revelation 13:8).

4) *"According as he hath chosen us in him before the foundation of the world, that we should be holy and without blame before him in love"* (Eph. 1:4). *"... who has saved us and called us to a holy life – not because of anything we have done but because of his own purpose and grace. This grace was given us in Christ Jesus before the beginning of time..."* (2 Tim. 1:9).

These are the phrases to be compared: "... hath chosen us in him before the foundation of the world"; "...His works were finished from the foundation of the world;" and "the lamb was slain "from the foundation of the world"; "...inherit the kingdom prepared for you from the foundation of the world"; "This grace was given us in Christ Jesus before the beginning of time."

The Lamb was slain in the plan of God from the end of creation week – *This grace was given us in Christ Jesus before the beginning of time*. The people for the kingdom were chosen and known in the mind of God from before the foundation of the world. The saints' inheritance, the place of rest, was completed by the end of creation week.

This work of God appears to be the theme of and reason for Hebrews 4 mentioning *"... although His works were finished from the foundation of the world."*

So why does the passage say: *"... As I have sworn in my wrath, if they shall enter into my rest: although the works were finished from the foundation of the world"*? We need to remember what works were finished from the foundation of the world.

We have pointed out that:

1) *"... he hath chosen us in him before the foundation of the world, that we should be holy and without blame before him in love"* (Eph. 1:4 KJV); and

We have pointed out that:

2) The plan of salvation was finished from the time of creation: *"And all that dwell upon the earth shall worship him, whose names are not written in the book of life of the Lamb slain from the foundation of the world"* (Revelations 13:8 KJV); and

We have pointed out that:

3) The inheritance of the saints was finished from the time of creation: *"Then shall the King say unto them on his right hand, Come, ye blessed of my Father, inherit the kingdom prepared for you from the foundation of the world"* (Matthew 25:34 – KJV).

Number 3 appears to be the reason "although the works were finished from the foundation of the world" is brought up. The inheritance of the meek, the inheritance of the seed of Abraham, is the earth. The earth, which is the promised inheritance of the seed of Abraham, was completed from the foundation of the world.

"For since the beginning of the world men have not heard, nor perceived by the ear, neither hath the eye seen, O God, beside thee, what he hath prepared for him that waiteth for him" (Isaiah 64:4 KJV). Why had no man, since the beginning of the world, seen what God had prepared? Because man was driven from the Garden of Eden.

The place and the plan were ready at creation, the people were not. They had to be prepared: *"And he shall go before him in the spirit and power of Elias, to turn the hearts of the fathers to the children, and the disobedient to the wisdom of the just; to make ready a people prepared for the Lord"* (Luke 1:17).

In fact, in the meantime, the place itself has been degraded to the point a new heavens and new earth will finally replace the original place of rest, polluted and degraded by sinful mankind! Paul wrote:

"For the creation was subjected to frustration, not by its own choice, but by the will of the one who subjected it, in hope that the creation itself will be liberated from its bondage to decay and brought into the glorious freedom of the children of God. We know that the whole creation has been groaning as in the pains of child-birth right up to the present time.

"Not only so, but we ourselves, who have the firstfruits of the Spirit, groan inwardly as we wait eagerly for our adoption as sons, the redemption of our bodies. For in this hope we were saved. But hope that is seen is no hope at all. Who hopes for what he already has? But if we hope for what we do not yet have, we wait for it patiently" (Romans 8:20-25).

The key to understanding how this passage relates to our entering God's rest is in the last sentence of the passage: *"we hope for what we do not yet have!"* It is related to Matthew 10:22: *"All men will hate you because of me, but he who stands firm to the end will be saved."*

What we hope for but do not have yet is the promised rest in the kingdom of God.

So a contrast is drawn between God's readiness to give rest in the promised inheritance, and man's lack of readiness to enter God's promised inheritance. God's work was ready from the end of creation week.

The inheritance for His people was always available, the people were not prepared. But as the work of John the Baptist bore fruit, a people began to emerge that were ready, so the writer of Hebrews says:

"Now we who have believed enter that rest, just as God has said, 'So I declared on oath in my anger, "They shall never enter my rest." And

- 230 -

yet his work has been finished since the creation of the world. For somewhere he has spoken about the seventh-day in these words: 'And on the seventh-day God rested from all his work'" (Hebrews 4:3, 4).

---o-O-o---

The Fact God Rested
Proves He Had Finished His Work!

So a contrast is drawn between God's *readiness to give rest* in the promised inheritance, and *man's readiness to enter* God's promised inheritance. God's work was ready from the end of creation week. The inheritance for His people was always available, the people were not prepared.

But as the work of John the Baptist bore fruit, a people began to emerge [John's work was **to make ready a people prepared for the Lord"** – Luke 1:17]; a people that were ready.

So the writer of Hebrews says:

"Now we who have believed enter that rest, just as God has said, 'So I declared on oath in my anger, "They shall never enter my rest." And yet his work has been finished since the creation of the world. For somewhere he has spoken about the seventh-day in these words: 'And on the seventh-day God rested from all his work'" (4:3, 4).

God rested because His creation and the inheritance for His chosen people were completed; His plans for man's behavior and redemption for misbehavior were all finished; His plans for His kingdom, were finished. The fact God rested the seventh-day is offered by the writer of Hebrews as proof that God's place of rest, the inheritance for His chosen people, the created world, had been readied by the creation of the world.

Notice again what is happening in the passage: *"I declared on oath ... they shall never enter my rest ... and yet his work has been finished since the creation of the world"* (Hebrews 4:3). Relate that to the

- 231 -

statement of Matthew 25:34: *"Then the King will say to those on his right, 'Come, you who are blessed by my Father; take your inheritance, the kingdom prepared for you since the creation of the world."*

It is important to make the connection between the general subject of Hebrews 3 and 4 with this reference to the kingdom prepared "since the creation" (NIV)"; or "from the foundation" (KJV) of the world.

The place for the kingdom, the place for rest, had been prepared since creation week, and still God's chosen people were not ready to enter that which had been prepared at creation!

God *has always* had a chosen people, including you and me:

"For he chose us in him before the creation of the world to be holy and blameless in his sight" (Eph. 1:4); and *has always* had a kingdom prepared: *"Then the King will say to those on his right, 'Come, you who are blessed by my Father; take your inheritance, the kingdom prepared for you since the creation of the world"* (Matthew 25:34)!

The chosen people, the redeemed, are God's kingdom, and the earth is their promised inheritance, their place of rest.

Then the admonition comes: *"Let us, therefore, make every effort to enter that rest, so that no one will fall by following their example of disobedience"* (Hebrews 4:11).

It is the same as Paul's message to Titus:

"For the grace of God that brings salvation has appeared to all men.

"It teaches us to say 'No' to ungodliness and worldly passions, ***and to live self-controlled, upright and godly lives in this present age, while we wait for the blessed hope – the glorious appearing of our great God and Savior, Jesus Christ,*** *who gave himself for us to redeem us from all wickedness* ***and to purify for himself a people that are his very own, eager to do what is good.***

"These, then, are the things you should teach. Encourage and rebuke with all authority. Do not let anyone despise you" (Titus 2:11-15).   ---o-O-o---

Rest for the Soul

If a person becomes an obedient follower of Christ, then contrasts his life as a Christian with the turmoil caused by his former life of sin, he will rightly affirm a great peace in his soul.

There most certainly is a peace and rest that comes when a person accepts the invitation of Jesus to "come to Him." He then and there receives "rest *unto his soul."* But rest unto one's soul is not the kind spoken of in Hebrews 9:9, 10, 13, 14.

Contrast the inner peace, New Covenant compared with the Old:

a. Old Testament: *"Accordingly both gifts and sacrifices are offered which cannot make the worshiper perfect in conscience, since they relate only to food and drink and various washings, regulations for the body imposed until a time of reformation"* (vv. 9, 10). Feeling guilty is not rest for the soul!

b. New Testament: *"For if the blood of goats and bulls and the ashes of a heifer sprinkling those who have been defiled, sanctify for the cleansing of the flesh, how much more will the blood of Christ, who through the eternal Spirit offered Himself without blemish to God, cleanse your conscience from dead works to serve the living God?"* (vv. 13, 14).

A wonderful sense of relief comes with having resolved one's differences with the Lord. A cleansed conscience is rest to the soul!

c. New Testament: *"...for the kingdom of God is not eating and drinking, but righteousness and peace and joy in the Holy Spirit"* (Romans 14:17).

This is a kind of peace, a kind of rest, but it is not the rest God promised Israel, nor the promised rest that *remains,* referred to in Hebrews 3, 4. Knowing our sins are forgiven, knowing that all is right between us and the Lord, is a genuine, important kind of rest; but that is not really the intent of the "rest" spoken of in Hebrews three and four.

Hebrews three and four speak of the "rest" denied Israel when they disobeyed, did not believe, and were not allowed to enter Canaan; it should have been a permanent rest from their enemies in their own kingdom, which was a theocratic kingdom, a "kingdom of God."

Rest to their souls was not what God swore in His wrath that Israel could not enter.

We do *enter* rest now, for we enter the spiritual kingdom of God when we hear and believe the gospel of salvation and believe in Jesus Christ as Lord and Savior. As explained earlier, we enter the spiritual phase of the Kingdom of God now, in this life. And, inasmuch as we are "in Christ," we must of necessity have "entered Christ" to be in Him, but He is not the kingdom, the promised rest.

As stated in Romans 6:3: *"Or don't you know that all of us who were baptized into Christ Jesus were baptized into his death?"* and in 1 Corinthians 12:13: *"For we were all baptized by one Spirit into one body – whether Jews or Greeks, slave or free – and we were all given the one Spirit to drink."* We must have entered the kingdom of God through Christ, the Door to the kingdom, in order to be co-heirs with Him of the promised inheritance:

> *"You are all sons of God through faith in Christ Jesus, for all of you who were baptized into Christ have clothed yourselves with Christ. There is neither Jew nor Greek, slave nor free, male nor female, for you are all one in Christ Jesus. If you belong to Christ, then you are Abraham's seed, and heirs according to the promise"* (Galatians 3:26-29).

But even in this Galatians 3 passage, it is clear that the promised rest is not aimed at being in Christ, but rather, fulfilling the promise made to Abraham – inheriting the earth, the Kingdom of God, with Jesus as King of kings.   ---o-**O**-o---

Audience Considerations

Before we further consider the role played by references to the seventh-day Sabbath in Hebrews 4, let's do some background orientation. Instructors of the Bible frequently admonish us to take into consideration the cultural setting of biblical messages in order to understand what we are reading.

This takes into account the mindset, the mental framework of reference, of those for whom the message was originally intended, and the meaning of culturally charged expressions used in the Scriptures.

By "mindset," we mean how people of a culture and era look at things, what they mean by their expressions, how they would understand phrasing and sentence structure.

Sometimes such considerations play a very important part in exegesis. But, important as that is, in the guise of doing that, we may impose our own biases and fail to interpret correctly what we find, like an anthropologist mentally fleshing out an entire human body from a fossilized chimpanzee clavicle!

Such is the way some interpret the omission of the clause *"and the evening and the morning was the seventh-day"* in the Genesis account of creation week.

What marvelous imaginary doctrinal creations are invented from the omission! Whole doctrines are based on *what the passage doesn't say!* But there are legitimate bits of evidence in the Genesis account that bear on this subject. We will come to them.

The immediate audience to whom *Hebrews* was written, were Hebrews who believed in Christ as their Savior, and were people of God who potentially *could fall* after the same example of disobedience and unbelief – the causes of their ancestors being barred from entering the Promised Land rest.

They were mostly Christians,[73] who had already entered the spiritual kingdom of God. To understand the message of the book of Hebrews about entering rest, one must not overlook the fact that those who were entering rest were *yet to enter rest.* This reflects the fact that we are not now experiencing the promised rest, even though we have laid hold on it by faith.

How well did they understand the relationship between their having already entered the Kingdom of God and the fact *they still* must enter? By the time they had digested the epistle to them, it should have been quite clear! It should have also been quite clear that the promised rest was not immediate!

The admonition to the Hebrew Christians was that they take a lesson from their forefathers and remain obedient believers: *"For we also have had the gospel preached to us, just as they did; but the message they heard was of no value to them, because those who heard did not combine it with faith"* (Hebrews 4:2); *"Let us, therefore, make every effort to enter that rest, so that no one will fall by following their example of disobedience"* (Hebrews 4:11).

One of the expectations of the Hebrews was establishment of a literal kingdom of God on earth when the Messiah appeared. It prompted the following incidents:

"While they were listening to this, he went on to tell them a parable, because he was near Jerusalem and the people thought that the kingdom of God was going to appear at once" (Luke 19:11).
"So when they met together, they asked him, 'Lord, are you at this time going to restore the kingdom to Israel?' He said to them: 'It is not for you to know the times or dates the Father has set by his own authority'" (Acts 1:6).

This immediacy of their expectation was part of the mindset even of Christ's own disciples, a mindset He neither disputed nor corrected –

---

[73]Hebrews 3:1 makes it clear that the Hebrew recipients were mostly believers, as do chapters 5:12 – 6:6.

even though He would not set a date for the appearance of His literal kingdom, and He foretold events that had to occur before then.

"Are you at this time going to restore the kingdom to Israel?" was a legitimate question in their minds. A literal kingdom over which Jesus would be king was coming, even though Jesus had stated that the kingdom of God was within His followers and people were already entering the kingdom.[74]

Hebrews 4 is the same concept in different terms. The Hebrew *Christians* had already entered the "sheep pen" or "sheep-fold" (the spiritual kingdom of God) through the only legitimate means of entry, Jesus Christ, the Door or Gate to the kingdom – yet they were admonished to *"make every effort to enter,"* sounding almost as though they had not already entered!

We, too, have entered, but we must yet make every effort to enter! The concept embraces the statement: *"All men will hate you because of me, but he who stands firm to the end will be saved."*

---o-O-o---

Audience as It Pertains to the Sabbath

So as one reads through the book of Hebrews it is helpful to keep this audience in mind. They were not looking at the writer's message through eyes of two millennia of theological debate over whether one ought to observe Sabbath or Sunday.

Observing the first day of the week as the Lord's day in honor of the resurrection is not discussed in the Bible, and had not become a doctrinal discussion prior to the destruction of the temple.

---

[74] Luke 21:31: "So likewise ye, when ye see these things come to pass, know ye that the kingdom of God is nigh at hand."
Luke 16:16: "The law and the prophets were until John: since that time the kingdom of God is preached, and every man presseth into it."
Luke 17:21: "Neither shall they say, Lo here! or, lo there! for, behold, the kingdom of God is within you."

There is no record that such a discussion had even entered the minds of contemporary Hebrew Christians, nor Gentile Christians.[75] They were not even acquainted with what are called the writings of the *Early Church Fathers,* in which evidence of such considerations emerge, for most of those early writers had not yet been born, nor had they done their writing.

There is no *biblical* record of Christians or Jews debating such an issue as discontinuance of the Sabbath, like the debate over circumcision. An issue such as discontinuing the Sabbath would have loomed large in discussions between the Pharisees and Apostles, perhaps even larger than the matter of circumcision; and yet, not one instance is recorded in the Bible of such a discussion!

Without it being a topic of discussion or Apostolic teaching, neither the Hebrews nor other Christians could have understood that Hebrews 4 intends to teach that observing the Sabbath was to be replaced by rest in Christ. No such explanation is given in the Bible.

Neither the Hebrew nor Gentile Christians of the day were aware of such considerations, and this must be taken into account as one seeks to fathom the messages sent to them.

The book was written to Hebrews in a time when Hebrew Christians were continuing to observe the Sabbath. Modern theologians recognize this, as evidenced clearly in the writings of the "Early Church Fathers." Hebrews chapter four says a sabbath-keeping remains, and nothing in the entire book of Hebrews hints at *discontinuing* or *replacing* any kind of sabbath-keeping. Neither the Promised Land rest nor seventh-day Sabbath rest had become topics of dispute.

It is hard to perceive how the Hebrew Christians could understand from the message to them in Hebrews four that the Sabbath was being discontinued or replaced by a different kind of rest. Since they did not understand that, it is just as hard to perceive how other Christians of a later date manage to see that in the message. Polemics against Sabbath observance first appeared in writings of the second century.

---

[75] The wording of the book of Hebrews suggests that the temple sacrifices and Levitical priesthood were still in operation, the present tense always being used in discussing the temple, sacrifices and the priesthood.

How could Israel have reacted to the messages of chapters three and four except their being positive affirmation of both Sabbath observance and the yet to be fulfilled Promised Land inheritance?

Since the Hebrew Christians continued to observe the Sabbath after receiving this message, they obviously did not understand some other kind of rest to be replacing Sabbath rest.

Why, then, do some Christians see that in the passage? Does the understanding of the Hebrew Christian audience *count for anything* in our trying to see things through their eyes? Or should we in this instance reject what Hebrew Christians saw and didn't see?

Some 20th-21st century Christians see seventh-day Sabbath replacement in Hebrews 4, because they are seeing through the eyes of 1800 years of debate and biased opposition to "things Jewish." This first began to be apparent in 2nd century writings of church prelates.

Their bias was very strong, as seen shortly after the Apostolic writings, in the writings of the "Early Church Fathers." They discussed seventh-day Sabbath observance vs. "eighth-day" Sunday observance.

Whether to observe Sabbath or Sunday (or both!) was a common subject among the Church writers of the second, third, fourth and later centuries. Their condemnation of those who continued to observe the seventh-day Sabbath is ample proof that its continued observance was common among both Jews and Gentiles.

Consider also, it was not difficult for the author of the book to the Hebrews to state that a better sacrifice, a better High Priesthood, a better mediator and a better temple had been instituted.

Would it have been any harder for the author of Hebrews to simply state that seventh-day Sabbath rest was being replaced by a better rest, rest in Christ, if that were what the author intended?

In the same way, one should especially consider whether a Hebrew audience would see in the passage that rest in Christ replaces the promise to Abraham that he and his seed would inherit the earth. Can the wording of Hebrews 3, 4 accommodate such an interpretation? Attempts to show such a meaning fail utterly!

One more concern about audience – was the book also written to Gentiles? Are Gentiles intended to understand one message from the book to the Hebrews, and the Hebrews themselves understand a different message? Is the same admonition pertinent to Christians of Gentile origin? Paul taught:

"... There is no difference between Jew and Gentile – the same Lord is Lord of all and richly blesses all who call on him" (Romans 10:12). *"You are all sons of God through faith in Christ Jesus, for all of you who were baptized into Christ have clothed yourselves with Christ.*

"There is neither Jew nor Greek, slave nor free, male nor female, for you are all one in Christ Jesus. If you belong to Christ, then you are Abraham's seed, and heirs according to the promise" (Galatians 3:26-29).

The admonition in the book to the Hebrews is valid for all who would be heirs according to the promise; and being heirs, allowed to enter God's rest.

Consider the words of Christ, that the kingdom of God was being taken from the Jews, and the words of the Apostles that they were turning to the Gentiles. That was not a particularly heartening message to the Jews. The believing Hebrews needed reaffirmation, such as Paul gave in Romans 11.[76]

This book to the Hebrews, the book of James also, should be a special comfort to believing Jews. One could be tempted to dismiss the Hebrews from the kingdom of God without this special comfort that they still matter to God.   ---o-**O**-o---

---

[76] Romans 11:1-5: "I ask then: Did God reject his people? By no means! I am an Israelite myself, a descendant of Abraham, from the tribe of Benjamin. God did not reject his people, whom he foreknew. Don't you know what the Scripture says in the passage about Elijah – how he appealed to God against Israel: 'Lord, they have killed your prophets and torn down your altars; I am the only one left, and they are trying to kill me'? And what was God's answer to him? 'I have reserved for myself seven thousand who have not bowed the knee to Baal.' So too, at the present time there is a remnant chosen by grace."

Pray for no Flight on the Sabbath – Why?

The letter to the Hebrews was written after the cross, after the New Covenant had been confirmed with the Hebrews gathered in Jerusalem on the day of Pentecost, and after God had the Apostles turn to the Gentiles. Christians of the first century, Jew or Gentile, would have seen Sabbath affirmation in Hebrews 3, 4. Why?

The author of the book speaks of the temple, the priesthood, and the sacrifices as continuing,[77] therefore the book was written prior to destruction of the temple. Anticipating the time the temple would be destroyed, Jesus admonished, *"Pray that your flight will not take place in winter or on the Sabbath"* (Matthew 24:20).

It seems clear why Jesus would admonish they pray not to flee in the winter, but why would Jesus admonish His disciples to pray that their flight from Jerusalem not be on the Sabbath? Was He teaching that flight to safety on the Sabbath is wrong? Probably not, but flight on the Sabbath rather than the spiritual joy and fellowship intended for the Sabbath is rather dire tradeoff! It trades rest for turmoil.

In our modern minds, such a concern doesn't sound very convincing. A modern Christian's interpretation of Romans 14 would usually make the notion that Jesus cared about Sabbath keeping sound unthinkable!

We are not in the habit of thinking anything is that Holy, nor that God cares that much what we do on the Sabbath! We have no problem with fleeing to the mountains on Sabbath when we are not even being chased! Our modern mindset has difficulty with thinking Jesus was teaching concern for Sabbath observance.

It was no problem at all for a Hebrew audience to understand that intention!

So why pray their flight not be on the Sabbath? Theologians do not agree as to the reason for the advice Jesus gave about the Sabbath.

---

[77] See Hebrews 8:3-5.

They find it incredible Jesus could simply be teaching Sabbath observance.

The Pulpit Commentary remarks:

The Jewish Christians in those times of distress might pray that their flight should not be in the winter nor on the sabbath day. The Lord, indeed, had not encouraged the superstitious observance of the sabbath; Christians afterwards were to keep the first day of the week in place of the seventh. But the early Jewish Christians were "all zealous of the Law" (Acts xxi. 20), and the scrupulousness of those among whom they lived would cause many hindrances and difficulties. It was in the highest degree desirable that their flight should be unimpeded, for the misery of those days would be awful.

The Commentary says *"Jewish Christians might pray."* No command of the Lord that they do is acknowledged. It almost suggest Jews might do what Jesus commanded, but it sure wasn't likely Gentiles would obey!

The other comments suggest the problem would be zealous Sabbath observing Jewish Christians being hindered from fleeing by their zealous Sabbath observing non-Christian Jewish neighbors, who would impede their flight to prevent their breaking the Sabbath! A rather peculiar preoccupation for Jews facing an invasion by Titus!

Matthew Henry's commentary is equally confusing:

That it might not be on the sabbath day; not on the Jewish sabbath, traveling then would give offence to them; not on the Christian sabbath, that would be a grief to themselves. This intimates Christ's design, that a weekly sabbath should be observed in the church. We read not that Christ expressed care about any ceremonial ordinances of the Jews; but for the sabbath he often showed concern. It intimates likewise that it is very uncomfortable to a good man, to be taken by any work of necessity from the solemn service and worship, of God on the sabbath day. To flee in the winter is uncomfort-

*able to the body, but to flee on the sabbath day is more so to the
soul.*

Of interest is Henry's interpretation that the advice of Jesus was to
pray that *sabbath observance* not be hindered by having to flee that
day. Note Henry's recognition that those given the advice would be
Christians, with a dual concern:

a) Not to offend the Jews by traveling on their Sabbath, and

b) Not flee on "the Christian Sabbath, that would be a grief to themselves."

He sees concern in the advice of Jesus *for two sabbaths,* supposing
Jesus were referring to both Sabbath and Sunday in the one expression
to pray not to have to flee on the Sabbath!

Henry's confusion is seen most clearly in his saying, *It intimates
likewise that it is very uncomfortable to a good man, to be taken by any
work of necessity from the solemn service and worship, of God on the
sabbath day.*

Henry believed regulations for seventh-day Sabbath observance had
been transferred to the first day of the week – how quaint! It was,
however, a common view until recently, a view that continues in some
circles.

Our mindset, more modern than even Matthew Henry's! does not
accommodate rules from the Old Scriptures for observing the Sabbath
even to apply to observing the seventh-day of the week holy, much
less the first – even though Paul said everything written "aforetime"
was written for our learning! (See Romans 15:4.)

It may be hard to agree *why* Jesus advised to pray not to flee on the
Sabbath, but that the Sabbath would still exist and would be a factor of
some importance cannot be denied – Jesus advised prayer that flight
that day not happen!

Who would be answering those prayers? Would Jesus hear them and exert influence with the Father in the matter? Undoubtedly yes, seeing He is our Mediator with the Father![78] *But why?*

How would Hebrew listeners have understood Jesus' warning? Logically, Matthew 24:20 would have been interpreted by the Hebrews as admonition to be concerned with observing the seventh-day Sabbath past the time the book of Hebrews was written, for to that time, the imminent tribulation of Matthew 24 had not yet transpired.

It occurred in 70-71 A.D, and to that time, there had been no hint biblically or extra-biblically at replacing the Sabbath with another day of rest or another kind of rest. No subsequent scripture suggests a different interpretation.

Why would the Hebrews see Sabbath confirmation? *Because nothing* in Hebrews 3, 4 discusses *discontinuance* or replacement of *any* kind of rest, either seventh-day Sabbath rest or Promised Land rest; and Hebrews 4:9, 10 states: *"There remains therefore a Sabbath-rest for the people of God. For the one who has entered His rest has himself also rested from his works, as God did from His."*

The prima facie meaning of resting from one's own works "as God did from His" would be working six days and resting the seventh. Verse four affirms that resting the seventh-day is what God did: *"For He has thus said somewhere concerning the seventh-day, 'and God rested on the seventh-day from all his works.'"*

There certainly is nothing *negative* in relation to Sabbath observance in the text or context. There is no indication that the Sabbath was being suspended or superseded in any part of the book to the Hebrews!

This book is to the same Hebrew people to whom the New Covenant promise was originally made (Jeremiah 31; Ezekiel 36[79]). In New

---

[78] Tim. 2:5: "For there is one God and one mediator between God and men, the man Christ Jesus...."

Galatians 3:20: "A mediator, however, does not represent just one party; but God is one" – We are the other parties.

[79] Ezek. 36:24-27: "`For I will take you out of the nations; I will gather you from all the countries and bring you back into your own land. I will sprinkle clean water on you, and you will be clean; I will cleanse you from all your impurities and from all your idols. I will give you a new heart and put a new spirit in you; I will remove

Testament writings, that promise of a new covenant is mentioned directly only in the book to the Hebrews.

That fact has led some to claim the promise of a New Covenant was to the Hebrews and is not pertinent to the Gentiles, since it was promised to the House of Israel and the House of Judah.

This is similar to the claim that because the Ten Commandments and the Sabbath in particular were addressed specifically to Israel,[80] they therefore do not address Gentile relations with God, either in the Old or New Covenant.

Why not also oppose using the book of Hebrews for New Covenant theology for the Gentiles? Its preamble also is only to the Hebrews. Why not for the same reason oppose Gentiles using the book of James? Some writers would readily agree with those very suggestions!

Should we, since the Apostles had turned to the Gentiles, understand the letter to the Hebrews as "catch up" theology, affirming that all the Hebrews needed to do was what was required of the Gentiles, as determined by the Council of Elders in Jerusalem? It was decided there:

"Wherefore my sentence is, that we trouble not them, which from among the Gentiles are turned to God: But that we write unto them, that they abstain from pollutions of idols, and from fornication, and from things strangled, and from blood" (Acts 15:19, 20).

Is that all God requires of Gentile converts? Some theologians claim the Hebrews are still obligated to observe the Sabbath, based in part on the instructions about Gentiles converts in Acts 15,[81] which appears to

---

from you your heart of stone and give you a heart of flesh. And I will put my Spirit in you and move you to follow my decrees and be careful to keep my laws."

[80] Exod. 20:2: "I am the LORD your God, who brought you out of Egypt, out of the land of slavery."

Deut. 5:15: "Remember that you were slaves in Egypt and that the LORD your God brought you out of there with a mighty hand and an outstretched arm. Therefore the LORD your God has commanded you to observe the Sabbath day."

[81] Acts 15:16-21: "'After this I will return and rebuild David's fallen tent. Its ruins I will rebuild, and I will restore it, that the remnant of men may seek the Lord, and all the Gentiles who bear my name, says the Lord, who does these things' that have been

impose less on Gentile Christians than on Hebrew Christians, as some also claim the Hebrews are still obligated to be circumcised. Such reasoning is incompatible with the clear statements of Paul:

"This righteousness from God comes through faith in Jesus Christ to all who believe. There is no difference" (Romans 3:22).
"For there is no difference between Jew and Gentile – the same Lord is Lord of all and richly blesses all who call on him" (Romans 10:12).

The passage in Acts 15:9, 10, also omits reference to baptism. Are Gentiles not expected to be baptized because it is not mentioned in the list of those necessary items? Neither is the Lord's Supper, nor most of the Ten Commandments; neither are the commands to Love God with our all and our neighbors as ourselves! What freedom we Gentiles have!

Paul says those who have been baptized into Christ have put on Christ – has anybody put on Christ who refuses baptism? That, also, is declared a possibility by some! Let's also suggest that since "entering rest" is in the New Testament addressed only to the Hebrews [show it to be otherwise!] that it does not pertain to Gentiles as well! Such reasoning is not scripturally based.

However, God's rest, the sabbatismos that remains, the Promised Land rest, pertains to all men, because if we are Christ's, then we are Abraham's seed and heirs according to the promise God made to Abraham and his heirs (Galatians 3:29).

The book of Hebrews, to the Hebrews, and James' letter to "To the twelve tribes scattered among the nations" and the "rest" promised to the seed of Abraham, plus all the provisions and responsibilities of the seed of Abraham belong to all who are in Christ Jesus *"OUR* Lord!"

---

known for ages. "It is my judgment, therefore, that we should not make it difficult for the Gentiles who are turning to God. Instead we should write to them, telling them to abstain from food polluted by idols, from sexual immorality, from the meat of strangled animals and from blood. For Moses has been preached in every city from the earliest times and is read in the synagogues on every Sabbath."

The "rest" (noun) in Hebrews 3, 4 points to the promised rest which *is being entered* and *is yet to be entered!* It is speaking of the inheritance of the saints, fulfillment of the promise to Abraham and his seed that they would inherit the earth.

---o-O-o---

A *Sabbatismos* Remains

Keeping in mind context and audience considerations, how would Hebrew Christians understand the statement, "There *remains* therefore a Sabbath rest (a *sabbatismos*) for the people of God"?[82] What would it mean to them?

---

[82] This noun "sabbatismos," is a derivative of the verb σαββατιζω –*sabbatidzo* – found in the Septuagint, the Greek Old Testament, where the verb means "sabbath keeping" or "keeping sabbath." It is used there only to refer to observing the seventh-day Sabbath and land rest sabbath and never to "Promised Land rest." Below are the earlier usages in the Septuagint of the verb from which "sabbatismos" comes:

Exod. 16:30: καὶ *ἐσαββάτισεν* ὁ λαὸς τῇ ἡμέρᾳ τῇ ἑβδόμῃ.

Exod. 16:30: "So the people rested on the seventh-day" (NASB).

Exod. 16:30: "And the people kept sabbath on the seventh-day." (Brenton trans.)

Lev. 23:32: σάββατα σαββάτων ἔσται ὑμῖν, καὶ ταπεινώσετε τὰς ψυχὰς ὑμῶν· ἀπὸ ἐνάτης τοῦ μηνὸς ἀπὸ ἑσπέρας εως ἑσπέρας *σαββατιεῖτε τὰ σάββατα* ὑμῶν (literally, from even to even you shall sabbatize your sabbath, or "keep sabbath your sabbath."

Lev. 26:34: τότε εὐδοκήσει ἡ γῆ τὰ σάββατα αὐτῆς καὶ πάσας τὰς ἡμέρας τῆς ἐρημώσεως αὐτῆς, καὶ ὑμεῖς ἔσεσθε ἐν τῇ γῇ τῶν ἐχθρῶν ὑμῶν· τότε σαββατιεῖ ἡ γῆ καὶ εὐδοκήσει τὰ σάββατα αὐτῆς.

Lev. 26:34: "Then the land shall enjoy its sabbaths all the days of its desolations."

Lev. 26:35: "And ye shall be in the land of your enemies; then the land shall keep its sabbaths, and the land shall enjoy its sabbaths all the days of its desolation; and **it shall keep sabbaths** which it kept not among your sabbaths, when ye dwelt in it" (Brenton Trans.)

Lev. 26:35: πάσας τὰς ἡμέρας τῆς ἐρημώσεως *αὐτῆς σαββατιεῖ* α οὐκ *ἐσαββάτισεν* ἐν τοῖς σαββάτοις ὑμῶν, ἡνίκα κατῳκεῖτε αὐτήν.

Lev. 26:35: ςAs long as it lieth **desolate it shall rest (it shall sabbatize)**; because it did not **rest (sabbatize) in your sabbaths, when ye dwelt** upon it."

2 Chr. 36:21: τοῦ πληρωθῆναι λόγον κυρίου διὰ στόματος Ιερεμιου εως τοῦ προσδέξασθαι τὴν γῆν τὰ *σάββατα αὐτῆς·* πάσας τὰς ἡμέρας τῆς ἐρημώσεως αὐτῆς *ἐσαββάτισεν* εἰς συμπλήρωσιν ἐτῶν ἑβδομήκοντα.

1) That Sabbath observance continues as a command of God?

2) That the Promised Land would someday be theirs?

3) That a spiritual rest in Christ replaces Sabbath observance?

4) That spiritual rest in Christ replaces Promised Land rest?

5) That spiritual rest in Christ replaces Sabbath observance and the promise of rest in their own land?

Some assert that Hebrews 4:9 is the first time this word "sabbatismos" is used – impossible to prove since we don't even have all of Paul's writings,[83] much less all the writings of the scribes. But, let's assume it is the first time. To what, then, would this Hebrew-Christian, sabbath-observing audience suppose *sabbatismos* refers?

If Hebrews 4:9 *were* the first time *sabbatismos* was used, and a different meaning is not explained here or elsewhere to its readers, they would not likely understand *sabbatismos* to mean a different and entirely new meaning such as "rest in Christ," which to that point was not a familiar phrase in Christian or Jewish literature.

Neither would they likely at first have understood "sabbatismos" to mean "Promised Land" rest because "sabbatize," the verb from which "sabbatismos" comes, is used in the Greek Septuagint[84] to refer to seventh-day sabbath observance and land-sabbath observance, but not to Promised Land rest.

They would more readily have understood "sabbatismos" to have the same etymological meaning that the word had connoted to the Hebrews for the 300 years existence of the Septuagint Old Testament.

---

2 Chr. 36:21: "That the word of the Lord by the mouth of Jeremias might be fulfilled, until the land should enjoy *its sabbaths* in resting and *sabbath keeping* all the days of its desolation, till the accomplishment of seventy years" (Brenton Trans.)
1 Esd. 1:55: Ἕως τοῦ εὐδοκῆσαι τὴν γῆν τὰ σάββατα αὐτῆς, πάντα τὸν χρόνον τῆς ἐρημώσεως αὐτῆς, *σαββατιεῖ* εἰς συμπλήρωσιν ἐτῶν *ἑβδομήκοντα*.
(Cf. 1 Esd. 1:58: "...saying, "Until the land has enjoyed its sabbaths, *it shall keep sabbath* all the time of its desolation until the completion of seventy years." (NRSV).

[83] Col. 4:16: "After this letter has been read to you, see that it is also read in the church of the Laodiceans and that you in turn read the letter from Laodicea." This appears to indicate Paul had written a letter to Laodicea.

[84] The Old Testament in Greek, available and used in NT times.

There, in the Septuagint, the verb from which *sabbatismos* comes is used several times, referring only to seventh-day Sabbath rest and land sabbath rest. So, the Hebrews would likely have understood it to mean one or the other, whichever is mentioned.

Since land sabbaths are not mentioned in the book to the Hebrews, "sabbatismos" logically would have been understood to refer to the seventh-day sabbath, which *is mentioned – in the very same chapter.*

However, "rest" – both Promised Land *rest* and seventh-day Sabbath *rest* – are referred to in Hebrews 3, 4 using "κατάπαυσις," in both the verb and noun forms.

The Hebrews were already acquainted with the use of the verb σαββατιζω (sabbatidzo) which is the basic verb from which *sabbatismos* is derived, in reference to both the seventh-day Sabbath and land rest sabbath.

Hence, if there were contextual reason to do so, they may well have readily transferred the meaning of "sabbatismos" (sabbath-keeping) to Promised Land rest, if the context plainly indicated that was the meaning.

But what would cause them to transfer the meaning of either "κατάπαυσις" or "σαββατισμος" to "rest in Christ," when rest in Christ is not mentioned in these chapters or elsewhere in the Bible?

Why would they have understood that *without* contextual evidence? Their understanding such a meaning seems doubtful, *since the context had also been referring to the seventh-day Sabbath.*

More importantly, why would a 21st century Christian understand such a meaning just because some other Christian says it means that? Some person other than an author of the Bible saying *sabbatismos* means "rest in Christ" is all the evidence one can find!

Showing such dual usages of words for rest, 2 Maccabees 15:1 uses the expression "τῆς καταπαύσεως ἡμέρα," *the day of rest,* referring to the seventh-day weekly Sabbath. The Greek word "κατάπαυσις" is more commonly used for inheritance "rest," kingdom of God rest, and appears in Hebrews chapters 3-4 eleven times in both its noun and verb forms. A verb form of the same word ("κατέπαυσε") is used in the Septuagint version of Genesis 2:1, referring to what God did on the seventh-day.   ---o-O-o---

A Change of Focus

Two places in Hebrews four there are quite unexpected injections of material about the seventh-day Sabbath. The first is in verse 4, the second is in verse 10. In verse four the reason for mentioning the Sabbath seems fairly well explained in that it is offered as proof that the place of rest for the people of God has been ready for them ever since the end of the sixth day of creation.

Another injection of thought about the seventh-day Sabbath comes in verse 10: "... *anyone who enters God's rest also rests from his own work, just as God did from his."*

What is the meaning of "anyone who enters God's rest *also rests* from his own work, just as God did from his"? How shall we understand the implications of *"also* rests"?

If *entering God's rest is entering the promised inheritance,* as referred to in "there remains a *sabbatismos* for the people of God," then what is meant by *"also"* rests as God rested?

"Entering God's rest" (the promised kingdom rest) is not resting as God rested – God did not do that for rest. The "Sabbath-rest" or *sabbatismos* rest that remains for the people of God refers to the promise God made to His people that is yet to be fulfilled.

The promised kingdom rest anyone may enter is one rest. It is the *sabbatismos* (sabbath-rest) that remains because it was not fulfilled. It is not presented as the same rest next mentioned, an "... also rests as God rested." Resting as God rested is a rest in addition to the Promised Land rest. "Also rests" is identified as resting from our own works just as God rested from His works.

What is meant by resting "just as God did"? Finding out how God rested should illustrate what is meant. Resting *"just as God did"* is a sameness of resting in some manner. It is seen in

1) Doing what God did, working six days; and

2) Resting a similar duration of time (the seventh day).

Entering God's rest, the promised inheritance, is the first rest mentioned in verse 10, the main rest discussed in both chapters 3 and 4.

"God's rest" is a rest provided for man, not for God. *"Also* resting as God rested," is man resting in the same way God rested.

"God's rest" means the rest God provided for man in the promised land inheritance. "God resting" refers to what He did at the end of six days' work creating, He ceased working, He rested, the seventh day.

So two types of rest are mentioned in chapter four. The first type is the rest promised Israel, a Promised Land rest. The second type of rest is seventh-day Sabbath rest.

But some students of the passage interpret resting from ones own work just as God rested from His work as referring to a rest not even mentioned in chapters 3-4 – rest in Christ.

The *focus* in verse 9, as in both chapters three and four, is on the rest it is our goal to enter – kingdom of God Promised Land rest.

Then the focus changes in verse 10 *to resting as God rested:* "Anyone who enters God's rest *also...* " – *also* introduces an additional action done by anyone who enters God's rest. 1) He enters God's rest; 2) He *also does what?* He "also rests from his own work, just as God did from his" (v. 10).

Just a simple statement. No preamble announcing anything shocking or of seeming great significance – just a simple, straight-forward statement, that *anyone* who enters God's rest does something else. He rests. But he doesn't *just* rest. One would take it for granted that if you enter rest *you rest!* That's why you enter rest, *to rest!*

The statement is not made just to state the obvious, that if you enter rest you rest! The passage isn't just spinning its wheels, it's headed somewhere! The statement is made to focus on something else, *that anybody, anyone, who enters God's rest does something else.* It's almost like identification papers, or a ticket, or at the very least, *if you do THIS, you also do THIS!*

This much we seem to agree on with those who make other propositions, that there is an additional qualification in verse ten. Some think it is the qualification that you quit trying to save yourself – as previously discussed and shown to be erroneous.

Let's identify the parts. As has been shown, if you "enter God's rest" you enter God's kingdom as part fulfillment of God's promised inheritance. But *what do you also do?* If you enter God's rest, *you also rest from your work.* In other words, if you enter rest, *you quit doing your own work.* We seem to agree even on that point!

But the kind of work we rest from doing is in dispute. Whereas the Sabbath command is to rest from the normal work of providing the necessities of life – one's employment or livelihood, some suggest the work we rest from in Hebrews 4 is work related to entering the kingdom of God.

One might even see logic in the concept of having achieved the goal of work to enter, once you have entered you do not continue to work to enter; but the passage doesn't support that either, for those who have entered are admonished to continue working to enter: *"Let us, therefore, make every effort to enter that rest, so that no one will fall by following their example of disobedience"* (Hebrews 4:11).

We explained this in the discussion of different phases of the kingdom of God. We have entered the spiritual phase of the kingdom of God, but we must endeavor, labor, make every effort to remain obediently faithful to the end, to enter the next phase, being resurrected to eternal life and our earthly eternal Promised Land – "the meek will inherit the earth."

So ceasing work to enter is not the work we quit doing. It is not a work God ever did! The passage makes a simple statement that anyone who enters God's rest *rests just as God rested.* He rests from his own work just as God rested from His work.

The writer doesn't leave us without information. He does not leave us to hunt through the Bible to find out how God rested – the writer tells us in verse four how God rested: *"... somewhere he has spoken about the seventh-day in these words: 'And on the seventh-day God rested from all his work.'"*

No big, long dissertation needed. It is evident that if one rests from his own works "just as God did from His," he rests on the seventh-day after six days of work. That's how God rested, and that's how we who enter God's rest *also* rest.

Resting as God rested is stated in the Ten Commandments: *"For in six days the LORD made the heavens and the earth, the sea, and all that is in them, but he rested on the seventh-day* (Greek, καὶ κατέπαυσεν τῇ ἡμέρᾳ τῇ ἑβδόμῃ – and he rested the day the seventh). *Therefore the LORD blessed the Sabbath day and made it holy"* (Exod. 20:11).

God explains resting from our work *as He rested from His:*

"Remember the Sabbath day by keeping it holy. Six days you shall labor and do all your work, but the seventh-day is a Sabbath to the LORD your God. On it you shall not do any work, neither you, nor your son or daughter, nor your manservant or maidservant, nor your animals, nor the alien within your gates.

"For in six days the LORD made the heavens and the earth, the sea, and all that is in them, but he rested on the seventh-day. Therefore the LORD blessed the Sabbath day and made it holy" (Exodus 20:8-11).

The passage above is God's explanation of what He means by *resting from our works as He rested from His works.* What of other explanations?

Other meanings people propose:

1. Entering God's rest means to observe the Sabbath – not supported in this thesis.

2. Entering God's rest means to cease trying to enter God's rest by obedience and rely completely on faith[85] – not supported in this thesis.

---

[85] One could compare what God expects of us with such "He will do it all" expectations. A "Stand still and see the salvation of the Lord" attitude doesn't always sit well with God: Eph. 2:10: "For we are his workmanship, created in Christ Jesus unto good works, which God hath before ordained that we should walk in them." For example: Ex. 14:14-16: "The LORD will fight for you; you need only to be still." Then

3. Related to number 2, some propose that the one who enters God's rest has quit working forever, supposing God quit working forever. He has entered a perpetual rest as God supposedly completed His work and entered a perpetual rest[86] – not supported in this thesis.

4. Entering God's rest now, in this life, means entering the spiritual phase of the kingdom of God – supported in this thesis.

5. "*Also* resting as God rested" is a rest in *addition* to Promised Land rest; a rest in addition to entering the rest that God promised Abraham and His seed. The first rest is kingdom of God rest; "also rests" is resting for one hallowed day after working six days – supported in this thesis.

Number three proposes that God's time period of rest was not and is not a 24 hour day. Rather, all time from the end of the sixth day even until now and beyond is God's rest, God's sabbath. It began at the end of creating six days, and continues throughout time afterward. As stated, that explanation is not supported in this thesis.

The claim that all time is holy is a major doctrine of some denominations who teach that neither the seventh nor the first day of the week is sanctified time in the Christian era.

In other words, beginning with the New Covenant, it is God's intent that we enter a rest in Christ that is continuing and unending, it is our "sabbatismos," and there is no such thing as a sanctified weekly sabbath.

But the very meaning of a day being "holy" or "sanctified" means to make it distinct from other like time periods, the other six days. That is what God did in regard to the day. He rested; He set it apart from the first six days by 1) not continuing to work; 2) resting the seventh-day;

---

the LORD said to Moses, "Why are you crying out to me? Tell the Israelites to move on. Raise your staff and stretch out your hand over the sea to divide the water so that the Israelites can go through the sea on dry ground."

[86] Referred to in number 3 is the concept that God's sabbath, God's seventh-day had no evening and morning and therefore God's sabbath, God's own cessation from work, continues even to this day, and is an eternal rest. God's sabbath, according to this concept, is not a 24 hour day, but a continuum without end.

3) blessing the seventh-day; and 4) making the seventh-day holy, sanctified, to be spent in a different manner than the other days.

"By the seventh-day God had finished the work he had been doing; so on the seventh-day he rested from all his work. And God blessed the seventh-day and made it holy, because on it he rested from all the work of creating that he had done" (Genesis 2:2, 3).

So if God entered a perpetual rest, then what God blessed was all time from the end of the sixth day on past our time into eternity.

If all time, every day, is equally holy, equally sanctified, then no time has *special* significance. The proposal removes the very distinction that God made and commanded us to make, sanctifying and resting the seventh-day after six days of labor.

The intent of the doctrine that all time is equally holy seems to be an "end run" around Hebrews 4:9, 10 by asserting that now, entering the kingdom of God is Sabbath observance, since "there remains, then, a Sabbath-rest for the people of God; for anyone who enters God's rest also rests from his own work, just as God did from his."

That would mean that in some manner, by entering God's rest we do not work anymore! But, the statement that everyone who enters God's rest "rests from his own work as God rested from His" has two elements. 1) the work done for six days; and 2) pausing from work on the seventh. The meaning of resting as God rested is one of the most clearly stated matters in the Bible:

Proposition: The resting we do when we enter the promised rest referred to in Hebrews 3, 4 is "resting just as God rested."

Response: The "rest" referred to in Hebrews 3, 4 is the "rest" promised to Abraham and his heirs. God is not one of Abraham's heirs, and God did not and does not find rest in the inheritance He promised to Abraham and his heirs. No such proposition is expounded in the Bible. Therefore "resting from our works as God did from His" cannot mean entering the promised kingdom rest.

Proposition: The resting we do when we enter rest as referred to in Hebrews 3, 4 is the same as accepting the invitation of Jesus to come to Him and He will give us rest, and that is "resting just as God rested."

Response: God did not come to His Son, Jesus Christ, for rest in response to the invitation *"Come to me, all you who are weary and burdened, and I will give you rest"* (Matthew 11:28). Therefore, our coming to Christ and "entering" Christ for rest cannot be "resting from our works just as God did from His," because God has never done that.

Proposition: The rest we enter as in Hebrews three and four is resting just as God rested, and means a permanent cessation of trying to be saved by our own good works.

Response: God did not cease from His own works as a means of being saved, because He was never lost; He has never sinned and therefore has never needed salvation. Therefore, when we enter rest as spoken of in Hebrews 4, shunning works for salvation cannot be resting from our works as God did from His, because God has never rested from works performed trying to be saved; further, there is no evidence God has remained at rest permanently.

Proposition: God entered a perpetual Sabbath extending to and past our own day when He ceased work after six days:

Response: God resting on the seventh-day is not explained in the Bible to mean an unending rest, a yet continuing *sabbatismos*. The Bible does not make an issue of the fact the creation story says nothing like "and the evening and the morning was the seventh-day."

It is an unproved theory developed from that omission, that God began an unending sabbath after six days of creation. No other passage in the Bible builds on or explains that omission.

Resting just as God rested cannot mean we enter a perpetual Sabbath, since no such explanation of God resting is given in the Bible, and nothing in the account even suggests the theory.

This theory must be recognized to be of no value in explaining Bible doctrine. It cannot be proof of the other unproved theory, that our entering rest as God entered rest means we forever take a rest from trying to save ourselves by good works. Unproved theory built upon unproved theory is like a skyscraper without a foundation.

Those concepts exist only in the mind and writings of men, not in the Bible. Therefore, that which is not explained to be a fact in the Bible cannot be a sound explanation of our ceasing to work as God ceased to work, especially when the Bible tells a different way God ceased to work!

The very passage says just the opposite: "Let us, therefore, *make every effort to enter that rest, so that no one will fall by following their example of disobedience"* (Hebrews 4:11).

---o-O-o---

Why Make Such a Point?

In these chapters, the Hebrew Christians are being warned not to fall by the *same example of disobedience* that caused ancient Israel's failure to find rest. What was that "same example"? Primarily, it was Israel's refusal to enter the Promised Land because they believed faithless leaders rather than God!

That can happen to us also, by listening to the modern theme that Christians keep right on sinning, and simply cannot stop sinning, even with the help of the Holy Spirit, even when they have already entered rest in Christ, even when God has made a way to escape every temptation!

The leaders of Israel again refused to enter God's rest when the same Rock that accompanied them in the wilderness, Jesus Christ, appeared on earth as the Son of God to renew the offer of rest in the Kingdom of God: *"Woe to you, teachers of the law and Pharisees, you hypocrites!*

You shut the kingdom of heaven in men's faces. You yourselves do not enter, nor will you let those enter who are trying to" (Matthew 23:13).

We are not commanded to cease working *in order to enter* the "rest" which is the goal of the two chapters. Just the opposite, being diligent to enter or laboring to enter rest is commanded! The command is not "Stop trying to save yourselves!" That is the theme of "saved by grace and not by works." The theme of these chapters is just the opposite – stop doing what prevents entering God's promised rest, and obey what God commands you to do.

The Hebrews who have already entered rest (the kingdom of God) are the very ones admonished to "labor" to enter. Why is the admonition given? It highlights the fact that entering the kingdom of God in this life is a tenuous matter, depending on remaining faithful and obedient, enduring unto the end.

One must endure faithfully unto the end of this life to receive eternal life at the resurrection. Compare: The saved already have eternal life: *"I write these things to you who believe in the name of the Son of God so that you may know that you have eternal life"* (1 John 5:13).

We have eternal life as a promised inheritance,[87] just as we have God's kingdom rest as a promised inheritance,[88] but we are neither immortal at this time, nor are we now kings and priests as we will be in the promised kingdom inheritance.[89] We enter rest now, but we still must enter rest. We are saved now, but it is not the final salvation:

---

[87] Matthew 19:29: "And everyone who has left houses or brothers or sisters or father or mother or children or fields for my sake will receive a hundred times as much and will inherit eternal life."

[88] 1 Cor. 6:9: "Do you not know that the wicked will not inherit the kingdom of God? Do not be deceived: Neither the sexually immoral nor idolaters nor adulterers nor male prostitutes nor homosexual offenders...."

1 Cor. 6:10: "... nor thieves nor the greedy nor drunkards nor slanderers nor swindlers will inherit the kingdom of God."

Galatians 5:21: "... and envy; drunkenness, orgies, and the like. I warn you, as I did before, that those who live like this will not inherit the kingdom of God."

[89] Rev. 5:9, 10, KJV: "And they sung a new song, saying, Thou art worthy to take the book, and to open the seals thereof: for thou wast slain, and hast redeemed us to God by thy blood out of every kindred, and tongue, and people, and nation; And hast made us unto our God kings and priests: and we shall reign on the earth."

"... So Christ was sacrificed once to take away the sins of many people; and he will appear a second time, not to bear sin, but to bring salvation to those who are waiting for him" (Hebrews 9:28).

"...Who through faith are shielded by God's power until the coming of the salvation that is ready to be revealed in the last time" (1 Peter 1:5).

That our present salvation is not the final salvation is evidenced by the fact some who have *entered rest* will fall after the same example of unbelief by which Israel fell before they die! This is reflected in Hebrews 5:9: *"... and, once made perfect, he* [Jesus] *became the source of eternal salvation for all who obey him."*

In the common discussion whether one can be saved by works or only by faith, *obedience* to the laws of God is equated with *works*. The "works vs. grace" discussion does not really focus on whether one ought to be charitable and give to the poor. That is not the kind of "works" the antinomian (anti-law) Bible students find objectionable.

The kind of works focused on is obedience to the law of God, and if another student of the Bible insists that God expects us to obey His laws, that student is labeled a "legalistic judaizer."

We must affirm that one cannot gain entrance into the kingdom of God by obedience – but we also must affirm that one will be barred from entering God's rest, the kingdom of God, by unrepentant disobedience. Such disobedience and lack of, loss of, faith are the very heart of the issues in Hebrews 3, 4.

Does our resting from our own works as God rested from His works *provide* us the rest God promised Israel? No, for a man to rest as God rested is to observe the Sabbath, and to say "Yes" would affirm that Sabbath observance saves us! It cannot, neither can observing the Lord's Supper save us! But we are commanded to do both. Disobedience is sin!

Ceasing from our own works, whether ceasing Sabbath observance or ceasing obedience to other provisions of God's law does not provide the promised rest – a rest that remains to be entered! That is not the kind of "ceasing from our own works" Hebrews 4:10 is talking about.

The interpretation that the entering rest of Hebrews 4 refers to "a blessing of spiritual rest in Christ resulting from belief," fails to pass the test.

That is not the promised rest, and resting in Christ is not part of the discussion! Further, *that is not resting as God did, for God did not cease His work and enter rest through faith in His Son!*

Moreover, neither Paul nor any other Bible writer advocates or allows ceasing obedience to the law of God, nor do they advocate ceasing any other kind of good works.[90]

We rest just as God rested by doing what God did   work six days, then rest and hallow the seventh! It is obvious that if we work six days and cease work, then refrain from work the seventh-day and hallow the seventh-day, we have rested from our work just as God rested from His work.   ---o-O-o---

Resting on the Sabbath *Is Resting Just as God Rested*
A Review

Having established that God's promised *rest* is God's *Kingdom* that we enter by faith, and that we fail to enter if we are disobedient, we needed to integrate with the theme of the chapter the statement "anyone who enters God's rest also rests from his own work*, just as God did from his."* Resting "just as" God rested simply cannot mean *something God did not even do!*

It is affirmed here that God rested, however:

1) God did not rest from His own works by ceasing to do good works.

---

[90] Eph. 2:10 (KJV): "For we are his workmanship, created in Christ Jesus unto good works, which God hath before ordained that we should walk in them." 2 Cor. 9:8: "And God is able to make all grace abound toward you; that ye, always having all sufficiency in all things, may abound to every good work."

2) God did not rest from or cease "obedience" because He has never obeyed anyone.

3) God did not rest or cease work in order to enter His own Kingdom, the promised rest.

4) God did not enter rest by believing in His Son.

5) God did rest, for one day, the seventh-day, because the work he was doing was complete.

It is affirmed here that we rest just as God rested, however:

1) Entering God's rest does not mean "being saved."

2) Resting from our own work does not mean ceasing the effort to enter God's kingdom.

3) Resting from our own work as God rested does not mean stop working to be saved.[91]

4) Resting from our own work as God rested does not mean obey, but cease doing it for the wrong reason.

5) Resting from our own work as God rested does not mean to cease obeying *for any reason.*

6) Believing in God's Son does not allow resting from obedience or good works.

7) Resting from our own work *just as God rested from His work* means resting in the same manner that God rested.

8) Entering God's rest necessitates "being in Christ" – which is tenuous, depending on our remaining faithful and obedient.[92]

---

[91] Eph. 2:10: "For we are God's workmanship, created in Christ Jesus to do good works, which God prepared in advance for us to do." It is not revealed in God's plan that man is ever to cease good works.

[92] Heb. 10:26-30: "If we deliberately keep on sinning after we have received the knowledge of the truth, no sacrifice for sins is left, but only a fearful expectation of judgment and of raging fire that will consume the enemies of God. Anyone who rejected the law of Moses died without mercy on the testimony of two or three witnesses. How much more severely do you think a man deserves to be punished who has trampled the Son of God under foot, who has treated as an unholy thing the blood of the covenant that sanctified him, and who has insulted the Spirit of grace? For we know him who said, "It is mine to avenge; I will repay," and again, "The Lord will judge his people."

9) "Entering God's rest" does not equate with "being in Christ"; however, one cannot enter God's rest without being in Christ.

10) Entering "God's rest" means entering the kingdom of God, which coincides with being "baptized into Christ,"[93] but this entrance is only by faith and does not provide rest in this life.

11) Kingdom rest follows entering the eternal inheritance coincident with the resurrection.

12) Because of all the above facts, our resting from our works as God rested from His works cannot mean stop laboring to enter rest, stop laboring to enter the kingdom of God, or stop laboring to remain heirs to the promised inheritance.

We cannot "rest" *to enter,* because our effort to enter is incomplete, and will remain incomplete until we die or until the Lord returns! The Bible calls it "endure to the end."

The statement of Hebrews 4:10 is that we rest from our own work "just as God rested." "Just as" – what is the similarity implied by "just as"? *"Just as" means what?*

What is this elusive rest? Nothing complicated! The similarity, the "just as" is the act of ceasing work after having worked for six days, and resting the following day of rest *because that is what God did.* The example cited in the same chapter, Hebrews 4, is God working six days, ceasing work and remaining at rest the seventh day.

God's ceasing from His works encompassed both the act of ceasing to create then remaining at rest from creating during the period of hallowed time. Our working six days, ceasing work, then remaining at rest the seventh *is resting just as God rested.*

Having eliminated every other proposed meaning, we must presume the text is saying literally what it sounds like it is saying! We who enter the kingdom of God rest on the seventh day after six days of work as God rested on the seventh day after six days of work. In short, the children of God, those who enter God's rest, observe the Sabbath.

---

[93] Galatians 3:27: "...for all of you who were baptized into Christ have clothed yourselves with Christ."

But why make a point of that one commandment?

Let's run through verses 10 and 11 again: *"... for anyone who enters God's rest also rests from his own work, just as God did from his. Let us, therefore, make every effort to enter that rest, so that no one will fall by following their example of disobedience."*

Our resting just as God rested, our keeping the Sabbath, is a part of our making every effort to enter kingdom rest. Can we inherit the kingdom of God and not rest just as God rested? It is a command of God that we rest just as He rested.

Resting as God rested is a part of the obedience we are admonished to be careful to perform, and refusal to obey God bars entering! *Make "every effort"* means *do not leave out any commanded effort!* It means obey all God commands us to do.

We Can Almost Hear the Gasps!

How *dare* we say that sinning bars people from entering the kingdom of God!

Especially, *how dare we say* that not resting on the seventh-day Sabbath is sinning, and therefore makes us ineligible to enter the real inheritance, the kingdom of God and eternal life?[94]

Does resting from our own work have anything to do with having worked a while before resting? Of that much we are sure! That work is real, and it consists of something understandable. The work is real, the rest is real, and God gave instructions how to do them both!

The effort one continues making *to enter, after having entered,* is real, identifiable effort. It is the exact opposite of disobedience! It refers to obeying God. Obeying God involves known instructions, known commandments, identifiable conduct which God expects of His children, without which they cannot enter His kingdom!

---

[94] One minister, after a recent conference discussing the Old and New Covenants, remarked, "The real question being dealt with is, 'Is it a sin not to observe the Sabbath?' and that question was not answered!" He was right!

Resting from one's own work cannot mean we stop obeying the righteous requirements of God's law! That would defy God's purpose for sending His Son (Romans 8:3, 4). One thing is absolutely certain, *man does not cease obeying God if he wishes to enter the promised rest! He continues to obey. That is what the Book of Hebrews is all about – "trust and obey"!*

"God is not unjust; he will not forget your work and the love you have shown him as you have helped his people and continue to help them. We want each of you to show this same diligence to the very end, in order to make your hope sure. **(What a novel idea!)**

"We do not want you to become lazy, but to **imitate those who through faith and patience inherit what has been promised.** *When God made his promise to Abraham, since there was no one greater for him to swear by, he swore by himself, saying, 'I will surely bless you and give you many descendants'"* (Hebrews 6:10-14).

The work is real, the rest is real. The command for man to work as God worked is real, the command to cease work and rest a day as God did is real. It refers to working six days to provide the necessities of life, then resting one day physically and congregating to worship God. This is part of the obedience man properly complies with so as not to be disqualified from entering God's rest.

Does man resting from his own work signify he works until he enters, then works no more? Not in this life, for he is admonished to labor to enter *even after he enters.* This is an unfathomable enigma unless one understands the concept of entering the spiritual phase of God's rest now, by faith, then entering rest literally after the resurrection. It is also not fathomable if one denies that the promised rest in Hebrews 3 and 4 is the kingdom of God.

So again, what kind of work *was man doing,* what kind of work *is man doing,* that he must cease from in order to work *then rest as God did?* Is obeying the laws of God the "work" one ceases? No, for if one ceases to obey, he will fall after the same example of disobedience ex-emplified by the fall of Israel.

The work one does, that he must cease doing in order to rest from his own work just as God rested from His own work, is six days of normal work to provide the necessities of life. Resting just as God rested is observing the seventh-day Sabbath.

---o-O-o---

A Ceasing from Work, then a Period of Rest

"For anyone who enters God's rest also rests from his own work, just as God did from his" (Hebrews 4:10).

It is to be observed there are two aspects to resting as God rested from His work:

1) A cessation, "κατέπαυσὶς" [ka-te'pausis], from of the act of creation. God rested after six days of the work of creation; and

2) A hallowed time period of no labor in honor of what He had cre-ated – a "σαββατισμος" [sabbatismos] a "sabbath-keeping" – thus he calls the hallowed time period, *"My holy day, a delight, the holy day of the LORD honorable"* (Isaiah 58:13).

Likewise, there were and are two parallel aspects of rest for the Christian Israel of God:

1) A *cessation of work* at the end of six days of labor; and

2) A *hallowing of the seventh-day* of the week in honor of God's creative work after six days of labor, as God did Himself, and as God commanded His people to do: *"Neither carry forth a burden out of your houses on the sabbath day, neither do ye any work, but **hallow ye** the sabbath day, as I commanded your fathers"* (Jeremiah 17:22, KJV).

Both of these aspects qualify as complying with Hebrews 4:10: *"For anyone who enters God's rest also rests from his own work, just as God did from his."*

God ceased to work at the end of six days, and He commanded His people to cease working at the end of six days, as God did.

God hallowed the seventh-day, made it holy and did not work that day, and commanded man to do the same after each six days of work:

> *"Remember the sabbath day, to keep it holy. Six days you shall labor and do all your work, but the seventh-day is a sabbath of the LORD your God; in it you shall not do any work, you or your son or your daughter, your male or your female servant or your cattle or your sojourner who stays with you.*
>
> *"For in six days the LORD made the heavens and the earth, the sea and all that is in them, and rested on the seventh-day; therefore the LORD blessed the sabbath day **and made it holy"** (Exodus 20:8-11).*[95]

Both of these are ways a Christian *"has himself also rested from his works, as God did from His"* (Hebrews 4:10).

Is there some other way God rested, than ceasing from work and hallowing the day? This question becomes important when considering the validity of such a statement as the following:

> *"The treatment of the word sabbatismos in the article is a concern to me. The word is introduced in v. 9 of chapter 4. This is the only place in Scripture it is found and points to the unique meaning intended by the author of Hebrews. The meaning of the word is a keeping of Sabbath and is often translated Sabbath rest. This Sabbath rest is not related to either possession of the land or the sev-*

---

[95] See also Jeremiah 17:22, 24 (KJV): "Neither carry forth a burden out of your houses on the sabbath day, neither do ye any work, but hallow ye the sabbath day, as I commanded your fathers" "And it shall come to pass, if ye diligently hearken unto me, saith the LORD, to bring in no burden through the gates of this city on the sabbath day, but hallow the sabbath day, to do no work therein."

enth-day Sabbath. This rest refers to a blessing of spiritual rest in Christ resulting from belief (Hebrews 4:3)."[96]

However, it has been amply illustrated in this study that the promise of rest that "stands" and "remains"[97] is the promise to Abraham and his seed of a land of their own. Entering that rest, God's kingdom by faith, has been in process of fulfillment ever since the promise was first made to Abraham. It is being and *is yet to be fulfilled* when faith is rewarded with reality.

The promise relates to the kingdom of God in all four phases:

1) Abraham to Christ, the kingdom of God under the priests and Levites.

2) The spiritual phase which began with preaching the new covenant gospel of the Kingdom and continues till the return of Christ.[98]

3) The millennial phase, the 1,000 reign of Christ and His saints; and

4) The eternal phase, when the New Jerusalem comes out of heaven from God to the new earth at the close of the 1,000 year reign.[99]

---

[96] A comment received referring to an article on Heb. 4 in the December, 1997 issue of the *Bible Advocate*.

[97] Heb. 4:6: "It still remains that some will enter that rest, and those who formerly had the gospel preached to them did not go in, because of their disobedience."

[98] Luke 17:20, 21: "Once, having been asked by the Pharisees when the kingdom of God would come, Jesus replied, "The kingdom of God does not come with your careful observation, nor will people say, 'Here it is,' or 'There it is,' because the kingdom of God is within you."

Luke 11:20: "But if I drive out demons by the finger of God, then the kingdom of God has come to you."

Luke 9:27: "I tell you the truth, some who are standing here will not taste death before they see the kingdom of God."

[99] Rev. 21:1-3: "Then I saw a new heaven and a new earth, for the first heaven and the first earth had passed away, and there was no longer any sea. I saw the Holy City, the new Jerusalem, coming down out of heaven from God, prepared as a bride beautifully dressed for her husband. And I heard a loud voice from the throne saying, "Now the dwelling of God is with men, and he will live with them. They will be his people, and God himself will be with them and be their God."

The main concern of Hebrews three and four is that the Israel of God should believe and not make the same mistake of disobedience and unbelief that ancient Israel made – *in order that what? In order to enter what ancient Israel did not enter,* the promised rest in the Promised Land!

Their disobedience resulted in their not achieving the Promised Land rest; and that kind of disobedience and unbelief will result in the same disaster for us. These chapters explain that since the promise of rest had not been fulfilled, it remains to be fulfilled. The promise of rest had to do with, and will always have to do with, the saints' inheritance as children of Abraham.

It is wrong to conclude that

1) *This Sabbath-rest is not related either to possession of the land or the seventh-day Sabbath,* and wrong to conclude

2) *This rest refers to a blessing of spiritual rest in Christ resulting from belief.*

Both conclusions are wrong, and make complete illogic of the reasoning of those two chapters, although *it borders on comprehending the spiritual phase of the Kingdom of God* – a phase of the kingdom that does not bring rest, just as the era under priests and Levites did not bring rest, as shown in this study.

The promise of rest in the Promised Land was the promise not fulfilled under Joshua's leadership (see 4:8). *Spiritual rest in Christ is not what was promised Abraham, Isaac, Jacob, Israel, and is not what Joshua failed to give Israel. Also, it is not what those of us who belong to Christ inherit as seed of Abraham.*

Kingdom rest *through Christ* to the Seed of Abraham is what was promised! Heirs according to the promise are to inherit rest in their own homeland. That is the rest, that is the promise, that remains to be fulfilled.

Therefore, it not only is related to possession of the land, but that is the promise: *"And if you belong to Christ, then you are Abraham's offspring, and **heirs according to the promise"** (Galatians 3:29).

The "promise" of Galatians 3:29 is the same promise referred to in Hebrews 3 and 4, and whatever God promised Abraham is the promise under discussion.

Nothing in Chapter three speaks of entering any kind of rest other than the rest promised Israel, which Israel failed to obtain because they lost faith and disobeyed. The main message of chapter three is not to miss ones opportunity to enter God's rest, the "today" theme of the chapter.

The same theme continues in chapter four, and in fact remains the most important part of the message. "Do not be hardened by the deceitfulness of sin," "Retain your confidence firm until the end" are reflected in chapter four's statement, "be careful not to fall short," and in verse 11: *"Let us, therefore, make every effort to enter that rest, so that no one will fall by following their example of disobedience."*

If "trust and obey" are the continuing themes, how could a different "rest" enter the picture, one which embraces *ceasing* efforts to enter the Kingdom of God?   ---o-O-o---

Is the Rest that Remains a "Better" Rest?

Some say rest in Christ, a better rest, replaces seventh-day Sabbath rest. The idea is that seventh-day Sabbath rest was just a shadow of rest in Christ, intended to terminate when the reality came.

For the sake of discussion, assume the chapters do refer to a new and better rest. Is rest in Christ – not discussed – a better rest than the rest *that is discussed?*

The less desirable rest to be replaced by a better rest in Christ would have to be either kingdom of God rest, or Sabbath rest, both of which are mentioned in the chapters. The whole concept is a figment of theological imagination, since *rest in Christ* is not a biblical theme!

A careful reading of Hebrews three and four does not provide information to assume a "better rest" is being discussed. No rest better than seventh-day Sabbath rest, or better rest than any other rest, is discussed or even hinted at.

Through other passages, and even later in the book of Hebrews, a sound thesis can be developed that we do look for a better rest, a "better kingdom of God" than the previous theocracy set up in Canaan: *"But the ministry Jesus has received is as superior to theirs as the covenant of which he is mediator is superior to the old one, and it is founded on better promises"* (Hebrews 8:6).

"Better promises" includes a better promised inheritance, the Promised Land of the redeemed, the meek inheriting the earth, is one of the better promises! However, that the rest yet to be entered is a "better rest" does not constitute the main topic, nor even a sub-topic of chapters three and four.

The topic is that we can fail to enter the Kingdom of God through disobedience and unbelief just as Israel did, and that the time for us to act is limited to our "today" – basically, our life-span. You can wait too late and be denied entrance by provoking the same God Israel provoked, with *the same sins* Israel committed, whereby they provoked God.

It is proper to reason that the Promised Land for the saints of the New Covenant is a better Promised Land than that for the saints of the Old Covenant, drawing a contrast between the Kingdom of God on earth under Jesus and the Kingdom of God on earth under Joshua. However, establishing the truth of that reasoning from other scriptures does not make that truth the subject of Hebrews 3, 4!

It is also right to reason that the promised rest is not just a better promise, but also a better rest, especially in view of the fact that rest was not found in the B.C. era of the kingdom of God, nor in the current spiritual phase of the kingdom of God. Of the four kingdom phases, neither of the first two give rest.

The subject is not a "better promise of rest," because ***it is not a different promise of rest,*** but the *very same promise* of rest that is discussed in Hebrews three and four; and as affirmed in the Greek word translated "remains," it is a *left-over* promise of rest, a *hold-over of the same promise of rest.*

The affirmation is that Israel's former *failure to enter* cannot prevent God's faithful from entering *because the same promise remains valid:*

"If you belong to Christ, then you are Abraham's seed, and heirs according to the promise" (Galatians 3:29). Not heirs according to a new promise, but heirs of the same promise! This point must be factored into our understanding of these chapters.

Why focus on replacing *Sabbath rest* instead of replacing *Promised Land rest, when all the discussions of missing out on rest in chapters three and four were about kingdom rest?* A more logical proposition would have been a better kingdom providing a better kingdom rest than a better rest replacing seventh-day Sabbath rest.

The promised rest that remained was a kingdom over which God was the intended ruler: *"But you have now rejected your God, who saves you out of all your calamities and distresses. And you have said, 'No, set a king over us'"* (1 Sam. 10:19 and context).

The factors providing rest were "saving you out of all your calamities and distresses" by giving Israel a homeland. This homeland is ultimately the whole earth – *"Blessed are the meek, for they will inherit the earth"* (Matthew 5:5).

But, does rest in Christ replace the promise to the seed of Abraham that they would inherit the earth? No. In fact, these chapters say nothing of replacing either seventh-day Sabbath rest or kingdom rest, now or in the earth made new.

They say nothing of discontinuing one kind of rest in favor of another kind of rest. Annulment or replacement of *any* kind of rest is not discussed in either chapter, or elsewhere in the book of Hebrews.

Kingdom rest and seventh-day Sabbath rest are not mutually exclusive, as though you cannot or should not enjoy them both, as well as being "in Christ." They are not antithetical, they are not alternates. One may and should enjoy each of these blessings.

Being "in Christ" is a guarantee of participating in the rest promised to the seed of Abraham: *"If you belong to Christ, then you are Abraham's seed, and heirs according to the promise"* (Galatians 3:29). Heirs of what? Heirs of the kingdom of God, heirs of salvation and heirs of eternal life.[100]

---

[100] Matthew 5:5: "Blessed are the meek, for they will inherit the earth."

"Heirs according to the promise" refers to God's promise to Abraham that he and his heirs would inherit the Promised Land, which by extension refers to the Kingdom of God, which is not a place-less promise. The *place* is seen in the statement of Christ in the beatitudes that the meek will inherit the earth.

Christians are still entering the Kingdom of God, which is parallel to entering the Promised Land. Entering the spiritual Kingdom of God during this life is the means by which the seed of Abraham become heirs of the earth after the resurrection.

A phrase such as "resting in Christ" (not a biblical phrase) would of necessity embrace being saved and therefore having entered the Kingdom of God. Resting in Christ therefore cannot replace or nullify "kingdom" rest, which is the "Promised Land" of Christianity.

---o-**O**-o---

Can We Rest Without Working?

For discussion only, let's assume that the premise is true that God's own Sabbath rest is an eternal Sabbath, begun at the end of creation week (as some claim). Let's assume that God is still resting from the end of Creation week to our own time. Let's assume that when we enter God's rest we also begin an eternal Sabbath – in that sense having ceased our own work just as God did.

Assume then that resting "just as God did" would mean that we have had our own period of work prior to beginning that rest; and that the work we cease is an effort to save ourselves, that at the point of

---

Matthew 19:29: "And everyone who has left houses or brothers or sisters or father or mother or children or fields for my sake will receive a hundred times as much and will inherit eternal life."

Galatians 5:21: "...and envy; drunkenness, orgies, and the like. I warn you, as I did before, that those who live like this will not inherit the kingdom of God."

Heb. 1:14: "Are not all angels ministering spirits sent to serve those who will inherit salvation?"

Heb. 6:12: "We do not want you to become lazy, but to imitate those who through faith and patience inherit what has been promised."

our entering God's rest, we cease whatever work we were doing to save ourselves.

The question arises then, is the work we cease doing in order to enter salvation rest a legitimate work? Obeying the commandments of God as embodied in God's law is as "legitimate" as work can be legitimate. But did God *ever* instruct mankind to save himself by good works? Or, even by making sacrifices?

When man offered sacrifices for sin under the Old Covenant, he made the sacrifices in faith that he would be forgiven his sins, and that God would remember his sins no more. That was the plan. God's forgiveness was the salvation, not the sacrifice.

The book of Hebrews speaks extensively about terminating the making of sacrifices, the ineffective blood of bulls and goats being replaced by the effective blood of Christ.

But our terminating the works of making sacrifices is not ceasing from our works as God ceased from His works! God did His work of sacrifice (His Son on the cross) to effectively remove our guilt *during the very time during which He supposedly is not working!*

So when the fourth chapter of Hebrews speaks of us ceasing our works, are we speaking of terminating a means of salvation by works in favor of a means of salvation by faith? Or are we speaking of trying to be saved by being good enough? God did not command such "works" in either the Old or the New Covenant.

What about people *who have never worked to save themselves,* either by "good works," such as charitable donations and building houses for the poor; or by obeying the Ten Commandments, trying to be good enough to enter, or any other kind of works in order to enter Christ?

Can people enter Christ, can they enter God's rest if they have never "worked" (*whatever* "work" means)? Does one *have to work* in order to *cease work,* in order to enter God's rest?

In other words, can a common, every-day sinner who has never entered a church in his life, who has never heard of the Ten Commandments (at least couldn't tell what they are), who has never before tried to become a child of God, who has never done any kind of charitable work, who has never before been concerned about pleasing God – can such a person go straight from that status into God's rest *just by believing?* Most evangelicals affirm that he could, by singing the songs "Only Believe!" and the other invitation song we love, "Just as I Am."

But, what kind of works *does he cease doing* in order to be saved by "only believe"? Can he enter God's rest without having tried to save himself by good works first? Or, does the passage refer only to persons afflicted with having tried to save themselves by good works?

Since "entering" God's rest takes place in this life, what work do we cease doing when we enter God's rest? We should note that no criticism is made of any kind of work in Hebrews 3, 4. Each kind of work mentioned is either com*men*ded or com*man*ded!

The futility of trying to be saved by "works" is seen in Romans 9 and Ephesians 2. That was never a legitimate effort! The concept is not referred to in Hebrews 3, 4, and rather than speaking of ceasing work to enter the promised rest, making every effort to enter is commanded!

---o-O-o---

Work We Could Cease but Must not Cease

Making every effort not to fall into faithless disobedience:
"Therefore, my dear friends, as you have always obeyed – not only in my presence, but now much more in my absence – continue to work out your salvation with fear and trembling" (Phil. 2:12 NIV).

This verse puzzles Christians. Assuming we are already saved, it simply advises us to remain obedient.

The assignment to take care our Lord's business:
"As long as it is day, we must do the work of him who sent me. Night is coming, when no one can work" (John 9:4).

"For the Son of man is as a man taking a far journey, who left his house, and gave authority to his servants, and to every man his work, and commanded the porter to watch" (Mark 13:34).

How long were these works to continue?

"And he called his ten servants, and delivered them ten pounds, and said unto them, Occupy till I come" (Luke 19:13).

"Jesus saith unto them, My meat is to do the will of him that sent me, and to finish his work" (John 4:34). *"But Jesus answered them, My Father worketh hitherto, and I work"* (John 5:17).

"Verily, verily, I say unto you, He that believeth on me, the works that I do shall he do also; and greater works than these shall he do; because I go unto my Father" (John 14:12). (The series is from KJV).

This cannot be the work we cease to do as we enter the kingdom of God (spiritual phase). Our work is not finished until Jesus comes! We cannot rest from this work until it is finished.

The works of compassion and charity:

"For we are God's workmanship, created in Christ Jesus to do good works, which God prepared in advance for us to do" (Eph. 2:10). That cannot be the work we cease from, because it is part of the purpose of our being "in Christ."

It is apparent that there is much work that needs to be done, legitimate work, work we are commanded to do, good work, none of which is a kind of work we cease when we enter the kingdom of God.

No command in the Bible calls for ceasing any of the above works to enter God's rest, the kingdom of God; and none of the works listed above are even proscribed activity for the Sabbath.

Confronted with the question, "Is healing legitimate on the Sabbath?" and having indicated it was legitimate to save a sheep from a pit on the sabbath, Jesus said, *"How much more valuable is a man than a sheep! Therefore it is lawful to do good on the Sabbath"* (Matthew 12:12).

But the Bible does command us to cease our works and rest. The work which precedes resting as God rested is not only legitimate, it is commanded!

Two elements in verse eleven deny the explanation that we permanently cease working when we enter God's rest:

1) "Let us make every effort to enter," and

2) "... so that no one will fall by following their example of disobedience."

"Disobedience" is disobeying the commands and instructions of God. The very objective of the "cease working to be saved" explanation is to infer there is no relationship between obedience or disobedience and ones salvation.   ---o-O-o---

The Relevance of Sabbath Obedience

Entering the Kingdom of God is the topic of Hebrews 3-4. The text guarantees fulfillment of the promised rest in the literal, physical kingdom of God. Entering the promised rest does not nullify or replace, entering the kingdom of God. Rather, entering the promised rest is another term for entering the kingdom of God.

These chapters affirm kingdom of God rest. They also affirm seventh-day Sabbath rest. No contrast is made between physical and spiritual rest as though one excludes the other. No contrast is drawn between one type of rest and another.

If *anything at all* is clear in the book of Hebrews, particularly from chapters 3, 4, 6 and 10, it is that faithless disobedience is the cause of God's children being separated from God and being denied entrance into kingdom rest.

God is preparing an obedient people for Himself – a people who cease from their own work as God ceased from His. This would be a people that takes a seventh-day "pause" as God did, a "kata'-pau-sin" rest.

The word "kata'pau-sin" ($\kappa\alpha\tau\acute{\alpha}\pi\alpha\upsilon\grave{\sigma}\iota\nu$) is the Greek word for rest in Hebrews 3, 4. It plays a dual role in the Septuagint Greek Old Testament. It is used most commonly to refer to Promised Land rest, and less frequently to God and His people ceasing work in seventh-day Sabbath rest.

Jeremiah prophesied that one reason for Israel's captivity would be continued Sabbath profanation. His prophecy was fulfilled, and ancient Israel neither achieved their Promised Land "kata'pau-sin," their Promised Land "sabbatis'mos"[101]; nor did they faithfully observe their seventh-day "kata'pau-sin," their seventh-day "sabbatis'mos"; therefore they had *no* rest. In both cases, faithless disobedience was the cause.

And in our own day, both kingdom rest and weekly Sabbath rest remain unfulfilled by disobedient believers, because they deny the very purpose of Hebrews three and four and ignore the warning against failing to enter rest by continuing faithless disobedience!

As prophesied by Jeremiah, failure to observe the Sabbath led to Israel's destruction.[102] That prophecy came to pass, Israel went into captivity, and on their return, Sabbath desecration began all over again!

---

[101] Although used first in Genesis of God resting the seventh-day, in the Septuagint Old Testament, "Katapausin" (κατάπαυσὶν) is used mainly in reference to rest in the Promised Land. Thus, it is the only word for rest in Hebrews 3 and 4 except for the one instance of "sabbatismos."

When Jesus invited the weary and heavy laden to come to Him, he promised to give them "ἀναπαύσω [anapau'so]." This is the word most commonly used in the Septuagint Old Testament referring to rest on the seventh-day or other sabbaths. Many of our English words have Greek stems. Both "κατάπαυσὶν" and ""ἀναπαύσω" have the stem "-παύσ- [paus]" upon which our word "pause" is also built. One "pauses" when one rests.

[102] Jeremiah 17:21-27: "Thus says the LORD, 'Take heed for yourselves, and do not carry any load on the sabbath day or bring anything in through the gates of Jerusalem. 'And you shall not bring a load out of your houses on the sabbath day nor do any work, but keep the sabbath day holy, as I commanded your forefathers. 'Yet they did not listen or incline their ears, but stiffened their necks in order not to listen or take correction.'

"'But it will come about, if you listen attentively to Me,' declares the LORD, 'to bring no load in through the gates of this city on the sabbath day, but to keep the sabbath day holy by doing no work on it, then there will come in through the gates of this city kings and princes sitting on the throne of David, riding in chariots and on horses, they and their princes, the men of Judah, and the inhabitants of Jerusalem; and this city will be inhabited forever. 'They will come in from the cities of Judah and from the environs of Jerusalem, from the land of Benjamin, from the lowland, from the hill country, and from the Negev, bringing burnt offerings, sacrifices, grain offerings and incense, and bringing sacrifices of thanksgiving to the house of the LORD.

"'But if you do not listen to Me to keep the sabbath day holy by not carrying a load and coming in through the gates of Jerusalem on the sabbath day, then I shall kindle a fire in its gates, and it will devour the palaces of Jerusalem and not be quenched.'"

Not observing the Sabbath was part of the disobedience Nehemiah recognized to have caused the Babylonian Captivity and destruction of Jerusalem (Nehemiah 13:15-22). Therefore, failure to observe the Sabbath is part of the example of disobedience warned against in Hebrews 3 and 4.

How can that be true, since Jeremiah lived and prophesied hundreds of years after the disobedience of the elders of Israel in the wilderness that caused their failure to enter God's rest?

It can be true and is true because by lack of faith and disobedience those who did enter the Promised Land also broke their covenant with God, and therefore also were denied rest in the Promised Land.

This is the very reason for Jeremiah's prophecy of a new covenant. He recognized that Israel had not achieved the promised rest in the Promised Land before his own time, and it was revealed to him that disobedience would continue, necessitating the New Covenant.

This same lack of faith and disobedience continued until the cross: *"He was in the world, and though the world was made through him, the world did not recognize him. He came to that which was his own, but his own did not receive him"* (John 1:10, 11).

And even then, when He came to His own and they did not receive Him, the promise remained valid to Abraham and those of his seed who were faithful! "Yet to all who received him, *to those who believed in his name, he gave the right to become children of God – children born not of natural descent* [i.e., not Abraham's offspring], *nor of human decision or a husband's will, but born of God"* (John 1:12, 13).

The warning to the Hebrew Christians is still against breaking their covenant with God:

> *"Anyone who rejected the law of Moses died without mercy on the testimony of two or three witnesses. How much more severely do you think a man deserves to be punished who has trampled the Son of God under foot, who has treated as an unholy thing the blood of the covenant that sanctified him, and who has insulted the Spirit of grace?"* (Hebrews 10:28, 29).

Faithless disobedience continues today among believers who claim to be children of God. Warning against *believers* disobeying *is the very purpose of the book of Hebrews!* Regardless, that promise of rest to the descendants of Abraham (including all who belong to Christ) will forever remain valid.

That promised rest will not even be voided by "Christian sinners" who do not wish to obey God's law. "Christian" disobedience of the law God promises to write on our hearts will not nullify the promise any more than "Hebrew" disobedience of God's law He wrote on tables of stone.   ---o-O-o---

Are Not Other Commands
More Important than Sabbath Observance?

Yes! One must recognize that some commands of God are more important than others, shown in the response of Christ to the question, "Which is the greatest commandment?" Jesus affirmed the greatest is to love God, and next in line is loving our neighbor as ourselves.

> Why would anyone make the point that Hebrews 3 and 4 neither affirm seventh-day Sabbath rest nor Promised Land (kingdom of God) rest? Is it reluctance to *make every effort* to enter God's rest? If kingdom rest and Sabbath rest are affirmed elsewhere, these chapters need not affirm them to make them valid! But in fact, both are affirmed here!

Jesus also speaks of the "least of these commandments." However, in doing so, He states emphatically that breaking and teaching to break even the least of the commandments affects one's standing with the Lord.[103] The point? One command being greater than another does not nullify or exclude the other unless the text and context declare it so!

---

[103] Matthew 5:20: "For I tell you that unless your righteousness surpasses that of the Pharisees and the teachers of the law, you will certainly not enter the kingdom of heaven."

Stating Hebrews 3, 4 do not affirm Promised Land rest is patently false, for **that is the very rest constituting the promise under discussion, a promise of rest that remains valid!** Likewise, stating that seventh-day Sabbath observance is not affirmed is also false, for it is affirmed two ways.

1) Indirectly in the admonition of Hebrews 4:11: *"Let us, therefore, make every effort to enter that rest, so that no one will fall by following their example of disobedience";* and

2) Directly, in stating *"... anyone who enters God's rest also rests from his own work, just as God did from his"* (Hebrews 4:10).

The text had been speaking of the rest God swore disobedient Israel could not enter in chapter three, and chapter four immediately affirms that *that very promise of rest* still stands*: "Therefore, since the promise of entering his rest still stands..."* (Hebrews 4:1). If it *"still stands"* fulfillment of the previous promise that was made at an earlier time is guaranteed.

What "still stands" refers to the rest spoken of in chapter three, when 4:3 says, "Now we who have believed enter *that rest"* – not some other rest, not "rest in Christ," but *THAT REST!*

Have we become completely unaware of the concept of antecedents in grammar? *THAT REST* does not and cannot refer to a rest that is not previously mentioned or inferred!

Neither can the rest spoken of replace some other rest such as Sabbath keeping, *unless the text speaks of replacing one with the other – and it does not do that!*

---o-O-o---

Jesus Also Will Inherit the Promised Rest

As pointed out earlier, in the doctrine that Hebrews 3 and 4 teaches rest in Christ is a better rest than Sabbath rest, confusion arises between identifying the "Door," the "Way" – the means of entrance – and what is being entered. Jesus Christ, the Son of God, is the means by which we become a part of the people of God.

He is the means by which we become one of the sheep, He is the way by which we become heirs, and He is the door by which we enter the promised inheritance; but we inherit the promised rest, we do not inherit Christ. We are *heirs together with Christ* of the rest promised to the seed of Abraham. As Abraham's heir, Christ will Himself enter the promised rest:

"The Spirit himself testifies with our spirit that we are God's children. Now if we are children, then we are heirs – heirs of God and co-heirs with Christ, if indeed we share in his sufferings in order that we may also share in his glory" (Romans 8:16, 17).

We Gentiles *were* of another fold: *"I have other sheep that are not of this sheep pen. I must bring them also. They too will listen to my voice, and there shall be one flock and one shepherd"* (John 10:16).[104]

Having become a part of the flock of which Jesus is the Shepherd, His new sheep need a place of rest, the "sheep-pen," or as the KJV says, "sheepfold": *"This mystery is that through the gospel the Gentiles are heirs together with Israel, members together of one body, and sharers together in the promise in Christ Jesus"* (Eph. 3:6).

This "sheep pen" or "sheepfold," corresponds to the "rest" Jesus promises to those who come to Him, both Jew and Gentile. In this age, it is called the kingdom of God, the Church, the body of Christ. But, in this age, the promised rest is only hoped for, and entered by faith.

---

[104] This is fulfillment of the prophecy of Isa. 56:8: "The Sovereign LORD declares – he who gathers the exiles of Israel: 'I will gather still others to them besides those already gathered.'" Isaiah prophesied before the exile, and considering the stress in previous verses on welcoming strangers (i.e., Gentiles) to take hold of God's covenant and keep the Sabbath without polluting it, this gathering of others in addition to those gathered after the exile, must of necessity be in a messianic setting, as indicated by the first verse: "This is what the LORD says: 'Maintain justice and do what is right, for my salvation is close at hand and my righteousness will soon be revealed'" (Isa. 56:1). The effort to exclude Gentiles from Sabbath keeping in both the old and new covenants fails at every turn.

In the ages to come, it will be the earth, the inheritance of the off-spring of Abraham, the Promised Land of the meek. In this age, there is only a hoped for rest. In the ages to come, the reality will begin. As Paul says:

> *"The Spirit himself testifies with our spirit that we are God's children. Now if we are children, then we are heirs – heirs of God and co-heirs with Christ, if indeed we share in his sufferings in or-der that we may also share in his glory.*
>
> *"**I consider that our present sufferings are not worth comparing with the glory that will be revealed in us.** The creation waits in ea-ger expectation for the sons of God to be revealed.*
>
> *"For the creation was subjected to frustration, not by its own choice, but by the will of the one who subjected it, in hope that the creation itself will be liberated from its bondage to decay and brought into the glorious freedom of the children of God. We know that **the whole creation has been groaning as in the pains of childbirth right up to the present time.***
>
> *"Not only so, but **we ourselves, who have the firstfruits of the Spirit, groan inwardly** as we wait eagerly for our adoption as sons, the redemption of our bodies. For in this hope we were saved. **But hope that is seen is no hope at all. Who hopes for what he al-ready has? But if we hope for what we do** not yet **have, we wait for it patiently"** (Romans 8:16-25).*

The above passage, especially the last verse, bears out the explana-tion that the promised rest is not achieved in this life except as a hope, that its reality comes with the "redemption of our bodies" – that is, resurrection from the dead.

It is biblical to teach that the promised eternal inheritance[105] is a bet-ter rest than Israel's Promised Land rest, because it is eternal, and actu-ally affords rest from our enemies.

---

[105] Heb. 9:15: "For this reason Christ is the mediator of a new covenant, that those who are called may receive the promised eternal inheritance – now that he has died as a ransom to set them free from the sins committed under the first covenant."

But, the theme that "resting in Christ is a better rest than seventh-day Sabbath rest" is neither stated by the Bible nor developed in the Bible. The literal kingdom of God after the resurrection will in fact be the very fulfillment of the promised rest for the saints! Kingdom rest is the theme of Hebrews 3, 4.

In no place does the Bible present rest in Jesus as a replacement for the kingdom of God, nor as a replacement for the Sabbath. The Sabbath is presented as a concurrent blessing with the Presence of God, to be enjoyed simultaneously as one enjoys fellowship with God. It was given to Israel as a time for Holy Convocation:

> *"'There are six days when you may work, but the seventh-day is a Sabbath of rest, a day of sacred assembly. You are not to do any work; wherever you live, it is a Sabbath to the LORD"* (Lev. 23:3).

> *"And foreigners who bind themselves to the LORD to serve him, to love the name of the LORD, **and to worship him, all who keep the Sabbath without desecrating it** and who hold fast to my covenant – **these I will bring to my holy mountain and give them joy in my house of prayer"*** (Isaiah 56:6, 7).

God's action, *"I will bring to my holy mountain and give them joy in my house of prayer"* is God making a concerted effort to include the Gentiles. It is a policy change from the Old Covenant approach which was, "The Gentiles will be accepted if they make the first move" to join the chosen people.

> *"'If you keep your feet from breaking the Sabbath and from doing as you please on my holy day, if you call the Sabbath a delight and the LORD's holy day honorable, and if you honor it by not going your own way and not doing as you please or speaking idle words, then you will find your joy in the LORD, and I will cause you to ride on the heights of the land and to feast on the inheritance of your father Jacob.' The mouth of the LORD has spoken"* (Isaiah 58:13, 14).

"Then he said to them, 'The Sabbath was made for man, not man for the Sabbath. So the Son of Man is Lord even of the Sabbath'" (Mark 2:27:28).   ---o-O-o---

He Will Give Rest to Those Who Come to Him – When?

If "kingdom" rest is under discussion, why does the text say that we "enter" (present tense) that rest, rather than we "will enter" (future tense)? This is comprehended in the concept of a spiritual era of the kingdom of God prior to the Second Coming, then at His coming, a literal kingdom wherein we find the promised rest.

The Kingdom of God is being entered, and it will be entered, just as we have been saved and will be saved: *"And do this, understanding the present time. The hour has come for you to wake up from your slumber, because our salvation is nearer now than when we first believed"* (Romans 13:11).

We now enter the spiritual kingdom, *we will enter* the literal kingdom when resurrected to immortality. If we do not enter the spiritual kingdom now, we will not enter the physical kingdom then.

Seventh-day Sabbath rest, kingdom of God rest, and the concept of rest in Christ have no reason to conflict with each other. They are perfectly compatible and concurrent one with the another. While Israel was preparing to enter the Promised Land they were commanded to observe the seventh-day Sabbath. After entering the Promised Land they were commanded to observe the Seventh-day Sabbath.

Likewise, when the Lord Jesus was physically on earth He taught how to observe the Sabbath, Who was Lord of it, and what it was made for. Neither being baptized into Christ nor entering the kingdom of God gave cause to discontinue Sabbath observance during His earthly ministry. Why would it after His resurrection? At the very same time people were entering the kingdom of God, they continued observing the Sabbath.

When the earth is made new, and the saints have possessed the promised inheritance (the earth), the Sabbath will still exist and the people of God will still observe it![106]

Have not most Evangelicals in fact stood the matter completely on its head? Jesus promised to give rest to those who come to Him. Where? When? Now, in this life, or after the resurrection in the literal Kingdom of God?

It is not specified in Hebrews 3 and 4 when the rest comes – we enter it now, just as we have entered eternal life now, just as believers have been entering the kingdom of God for nearly 2,000 years, just as we have been saved and are yet to be saved.

We have confidence in Christ, and that brings a type of peace; but we do not now, in this life, receive the rest promised to those who come to Christ!

The "now" phase is not a restful phase, it is not the promised rest of Hebrews four! In fact, the promise of rest in "come unto me and I will give you rest" much more logically refers to Abraham's Promised Land, the Kingdom of God:

"By faith he (Abraham) *made his home in the Promised Land like a stranger in a foreign country; he lived in tents, as did **Isaac and Jacob, who were heirs with him of the same promise.** For he was looking forward to the city with foundations,[107] whose architect and builder is God"* (Hebrews 11:9, 10).

---

[106] Isa. 66:22, 23: "'As the new heavens and the new earth that I make will endure before me,' declares the LORD, 'so will your name and descendants endure. From one New Moon to another and from one Sabbath to another, all mankind will come and bow down before me,' says the LORD."

[107] As Nomads, Abraham, Isaac and Jacob dwelled in tents, "dwelling places" which had no foundations, no permanency. "By faith he made his home in the promised land like a stranger in a foreign country; he lived in tents, as did Isaac and Jacob, who were heirs with him of the same promise" (Heb. 11:9). Thus, Abraham looked for a city with "foundations" rather than living as Nomads in tents, symbols of a temporary status.

We also are heirs with Abraham "of the same promise," but neither Abraham nor we have entered the promised rest in this life, except by faith.

Why? Rest in their own land is the promised "rest," as in Deuteronomy 3:20 and Exodus 33:14:

"...until the LORD gives rest to your brothers as he has to you, and they too have taken over the land that the LORD your God is giving them, across the Jordan. After that, each of you may go back to the possession I have given you";, "And He said, 'My presence shall go with you, and I will give you rest'"; and of 2 Samuel 7:11, *"... even from the day that I commanded judges to be over My people Israel; and I will give you rest from all your enemies."*

This is the promised rest to which the third and fourth chapters of Hebrews refer; a rest that was not permanently achieved, and therefore the promise still stands, because the promise to Abraham and his seed is not conditioned on every offspring of Abraham being perfect.

The fact that the promise of rest still stands is evident in these statements of Jesus:

"I say to you that many will come from the east and the west, and will take their places at the feast with Abraham, Isaac and Jacob in the kingdom of heaven" (Matthew 8:11).
"There will be weeping there, and gnashing of teeth, when you see Abraham, Isaac and Jacob and all the prophets in the kingdom of God, but you yourselves thrown out" (Luke 13:28).

The fact that Abraham Isaac and Jacob are not now enjoying the promised kingdom and the rest to be enjoyed there is evidence that we also do not enjoy the promised rest during this life.

This must be understood in the light of Hebrews 11:39-40: *"These were all commended for their faith, yet none of them received what had been promised. God had planned something better for us so that only together with us would they be made perfect."*

There is a very close relationship between these statements: ***"My presence shall go with you,** and I will give you rest"* (Exodus 33:14), and the statement of Jesus in Matthew 28:20: ***"And surely I am with you always, to the very end of the age."***

The close relationship is also seen in Matthew 11:28: *"Come to Me, all who are weary and heavy-laden, and I will give you rest."* If we "come to Christ" we come into His Presence, a relationship that will continue to the end of the age.

The relationship between Exodus 33:14 and Matthew 28:20 is much closer than one may think at first. Paul wrote: *"They all ate the same spiritual food and drank the same spiritual drink; for they drank from the spiritual rock that accompanied them, and that rock was Christ. Nevertheless, God was not pleased with most of them; their bodies were scattered over the desert"* (1 Corinthians 10:3-5).

It was Christ that constituted the Presence of God in the desert, and it was also Christ who promised rest in Exodus 33:14 and Matthew 11:28. Christ provides the rest in both promises, for He was the Rock that followed Israel in the desert (1 Corinthians 10:4); and it is Christ who will be with us always, to the very end of the age; and it is Christ who promises rest in Matthew 11:28 to those who come to Him.

Israel and the Presence of God were traveling companions in the desert, as we are traveling companions with Christ when we by faith enter rest in this life and when we obey His command to go into all the world to evangelize.

The viewpoint that the "rest" spoken of in Hebrews 4 is salvation rest in Christ, and refers neither to seventh-day Sabbath rest nor Promised Land rest is imposed on the text.

The viewpoint advocated and shown here is that the rest which Christ promises to those who come to Him is the promised rest Israel did not achieve under Joshua's leadership, even though Christ was *with them;* likewise, we do not achieve rest in this life even though we have come "to" Him and are "with" Him.

Israel had "come to Him" – but the rest was not to be achieved simply because of that. They must of necessity have kept company until they entered the promised rest.

That is typical of our coming to Christ and keeping company with Him until we receive the promised rest in the kingdom of God after the resurrection. The resurrection is our "crossing Jordan," and as the song says, "I won't have to cross Jordan alone."

---o-O-o---

If in This Life Only We Have Hope[108]

We have discussed two viewpoints regarding Matthew 11:28-29. One, that the rest Christian Hebrews and Gentiles enter is coming to Christ to enter salvation rest, and salvation rest replaces seventh-day Sabbath rest (not agreed to here); and two, that the rest Jesus promises to those who come to Him is rest in the Kingdom of God, and does not replace any kind of rest (affirmed here). Both viewpoints connect Matthew 11:28-29 with the rest of Hebrews 3, 4, but for different reasons.

It is affirmed here that fulfilling the promise of rest made by Jesus awaits the resurrection. Why? Even though we "enter" Jesus now in this life, and thereby enter the kingdom of God, the "rest" of Jesus' invitation (Matthew 11:28-29) cannot be equated with being "in Jesus" now in this life.

Our present salvation with all its vicissitudes – martyrdom, sickness, tears, toils, heartaches, broken families, church schisms, disrespectful youth and blasphemous adults in rebellion – in and out of the

---

[108] 1 Cor. 15:19: "If in this life only we have hope in Christ, we are of all men most miserable" (KJV).

church – is not "rest."[109] Salvation does not now fulfill the promise of rest God gave to Israel, which was not fulfilled, and it is not the rest Jesus promised to those who come to Him.

Why do we say the sufferings of this present time are not mitigated for those who come to Christ? We must consider the words of the One Who gave the invitation:

> *"'Do not suppose that I have come to bring peace to the earth. I did not come to bring peace, but a sword. For I have come to turn a man against his father, a daughter against her mother, a daughter-in-law against her mother-in-law – a man's enemies will be the members of his own household'"* (Matthew 10:34-36).

What is the cause of these crossed-sword relationships? It is one party believing in Christ and entering the kingdom of God, but the other rejecting the invitation of Christ to "Come unto me."

Notice in particular *a man's enemies will be the members of his own household*. This must be compared with the original promise of rest: "But you will cross the Jordan and settle in the land the LORD your God is giving you as an inheritance, **and he will give you rest from all your enemies around you so that you will live in safety"** (Deuteronomy 12:10).

One's enemies being members of one's own household is not the promised rest from our enemies! The turmoil described in Matthew 10:34-36 results from someone in a household coming to and becoming a follower of Christ! It is apparent that the reason for this division is that some of the relatives have accepted Jesus as Lord, have "come to Him," and others have rejected Him, distancing themselves from Him.

These words of Jesus are the reality of this life. He will give us rest, *but not now!* This is not to deny that in general the life of obedient Christians is much more peaceful than that of households plagued with incest, murder, abuse, and children participating in gangs.

---

[109] Paul bears witness to this lack of "rest" in this life. See the litany of his trials in 2 Corinthians 11:23-28.

So how can we reconcile Jesus' promise of rest to those who come to Him with this very clear statement of Jesus that He did not come to bring peace but a sword?

We can reconcile it by recognizing when and where that rest will be given. This present life, described in Matthew 10:34-36, cannot fulfil Jesus' promise to give rest to those who come to Him. We *enter* that promised rest now – by faith that what God has promised He is *able to* and *will* deliver!

It is advocated here that the promise of Matthew 11:28 is the promised "rest" of Exodus 33:14; Deuteronomy 12:10; 2 Samuel 7:11 and Hebrews 3 and 4, *and that we are not now experiencing God's promise of rest,* even though we enter it now by faith.

This also is parallel to the experience of Israel, that after they entered the Promised Land, a great struggle ensued to overcome the enemy; but they, like Abraham were aliens in their own country,[110] as we ourselves are!

They had physically entered their place of rest, but the struggle to attain rest continued. We spiritually enter rest now, but the struggle to attain rest continues until the end: *"All men will hate you because of me, but he who stands firm to the end will be saved"* (Mark 13:13).

Is this life the promised rest? Paul said, *"If only for this life we have hope **in Christ**, we are to be pitied more than all men"* (1 Corinthians 15:19). This life, *even in Christ,* is not God's promised rest!

We must side with Paul in the matter: *"For I consider that **the sufferings of this present time** are not worthy to be compared with the glory that is to be revealed to us"* (Romans 8:18).

The glory that is yet to be revealed to us is the rest that remains to be entered, spoken of in Hebrews three and four, which we must labor to enter, even though we have already entered!

It should be painfully clear that the rest we now enter – the "spiritual phase" of the kingdom of God – does not provide the promised rest of Hebrews four, it does not fulfill the promise to the seed of

---

[110] "By faith he made his home in the promised land like a stranger in a foreign country; he lived in tents, as did Isaac and Jacob, who were heirs with him of the same promise" (Heb. 11:9).

Abraham, ***but being in Christ is the Door to that promised rest!*** We are in the Door, the Entryway! Let us be diligent to be ready to go on in before the door is closed! (Matthew 25:10).

Fulfillment of the promise will bring life incomparably more satisfying, incomparably more restful than what this life brings to God's children. One does not enter the promised rest in this life except by faith as a sure promise, just as we now have eternal life as a sure promise,[111] but we continue to get sick and die, the faithful continue to be martyred, harassed, imprisoned, persecuted – and in fact it is appointed that we do so:

"But before all this, they will lay hands on you and persecute you. They will deliver you to synagogues and prisons, and you will be brought before kings and governors, and all on account of my name" (Luke 21:12). *"And as it is appointed unto men once to die, but after this the judgment"* (Hebrews 9:27; 2 Tim. 3:12).

Although Israel was said to have entered rest, there was little or no rest for the people of God after Joshua, neither under the judges of Israel, under the kings of Israel, nor under Assyrian and Babylonian captivities; there was little to none under Ezra and Nehemiah, little under the Greeks or Maccabees, little under the Romans, and little even now!

When the book of Hebrews was written, Palestine was still under Roman rule and had been for over a hundred years. Titus and the destruction of Jerusalem were on the horizon, while the faithful were entering rest! The people of God were advised by Jesus regarding the destruction by Titus, *"But pray that your flight may not be in the winter, or on a Sabbath"* (Matthew 24:20).

Then followed persecution of Christians and their being fed to the lions, the suppression of dissenting Christians by the officially sanctioned church of Rome, the Reformation, and over five hundred years of squabbling and bickering among different Protestant groups since the

---

[111] 1 John 5:13: "I write these things to you who believe in the name of the Son of God so that you may know that you have eternal life."

Reformation – even bickering as to whether one *is Protestant* or some other brand of dissenting believer!

This is not the promised rest!

For over three thousand years the people of God have not really had rest, so the admonition of Hebrews 4:1, *"Therefore, let us fear lest, while a promise remains of entering His rest, any one of you should seem to have come short of it,"* is both present and future, and is just as full of meaning today as it was the day it was first written.

We must acknowledge that *we have not entered the "ultimate rest," the promised rest, except by faith.* This is reflected in the book of Hebrews' summation of where we stand in relation to the promised rest:

> *"All these died in faith, without receiving the promises, but having seen them and having welcomed them from a distance, and having confessed that they were strangers and exiles on the earth. For **those who say such things make it clear that they are seeking a country of their own.***
>
> *"And indeed if they had been thinking of that country from which they went out, they would have had opportunity to return. But as it is, they desire a better country, that is a heavenly one. Therefore God is not ashamed to be called their God; for He has prepared a city for them"* (Hebrews 11:13-16).
>
> *"And all these, having gained approval through their faith, did not receive what was promised, because God had provided something better for us, so that apart from us they should not be made perfect"* (Hebrews 11:39-40).

We, too, have gained approval through our faith; and we too have not received what was promised, so that those who have gone before, so that we, and so that those who come after, may be made perfect together in the resurrection!

We see the promises and welcome them from a distance just as those who had already died in faith during the Old Covenant and the first century of the New Covenant. We must also be clear that we are seeking a country of our own, for that is what the "promised rest" is about!

The book of Hebrews (2:5) identifies the promised rest spoken of in chapters three and four. It is *the world to come:* "For unto the angels hath he not put in subjection the **world to come, whereof we speak.**"

The subject under consideration, the subject of the promised rest is "the world to come," the time when all things would be in subjection under the feet of Christ:

"Thou hast put all things in subjection under his feet. For in that he put all in subjection under him, he left nothing that is not put under him. **But now we see not yet all things put under him"** (Hebrews 2:8).

The same duality of having entered and must yet enter is seen even in that *All things have been put in subjection under Christ, but not yet!*

The time had not yet come *"that at the name of Jesus every knee should bow, of things in heaven, and things in earth, and things under the earth; And that every tongue should confess that Jesus Christ is Lord, to the glory of God the Father"* (Philippians 2:10, 11).

---o-O-o---

Jesus Is the Shepherd, He Is the Door
He Is Not the Sheepfold

"The promise of entering his rest still stands" (Hebrews 4:1) and *"there remains **therefore"** (Hebrews 4:9) means a Promised Land *sabbath-keeping* remains **because Joshua did not provide Promised Land sabbath-keeping-rest.**

Failing to achieve *Promised Land* rest does not result in a different kind of rest being substituted to fulfill the promised rest. It is the same promise of rest that remains valid; therefore the same promised inheritance remains valid. It is not a different kind of "rest" than what was promised. That which *was not* the promise cannot *remain* the promise!

The promise remains, and is fulfilled in the kingdom of God. Some who are to enter have not entered, and therefore some must still enter that promised rest. We *enter* rest *through Christ* – He is the Door (John 10:1-4), He is the Way, He is the Truth, and in Him we have life; but He is not the sheepfold, He is the Shepherd *through whom we enter rest.*

He is not the saints' inheritance. He and we are joint heirs of the same inheritance: *"Now if we are children, then we are heirs – heirs of God and co-heirs with Christ, if indeed we share in his sufferings in order that we may also share in his glory"* (Romans 8:17). Sharing in His sufferings is not rest! Sharing in His glory will be!

Our being "co-heirs" with Christ echoes the statement that Christ is the Seed of Abraham: *"The promises were spoken to Abraham and to his seed. The Scripture does not say 'and to seeds,' meaning many people, but 'and to your seed,' meaning one person, who is Christ"* (Galatians 3:16).

Being "in Christ," a part of the "body of Christ," we participate in the promises to Christ: *"If you belong to Christ, then you are Abraham's seed, and heirs according to the promise"* (Galatians 3:29).

Don't Confuse the Heirs With the Inheritance

Being "in Christ" and entering Christ through baptism, becoming a part of the body of Christ through baptism, is distinct from entering the inheritance, the promised rest, which is the *place of inheritance.* One becomes a part of the people of God when he enters the body of Christ (the Church); we, with them, are the heirs, the inheritors; we are not the inheritance. The "rest" of Hebrews 3 and 4 is the inheritance, not the body of believers.

"Now if we are children, then we are heirs – heirs of God and co-heirs with Christ, if indeed we share in his sufferings in order that we may also share in his glory" (Romans 8:17).

A sabbath-keeping remains *because Joshua did not provide Promised Land rest.* How is it possible for anyone to say, then, that Promised Land rest is not related to the rest that remains, *because of* Joshua's failure to provide rest in the Promised Land?

How can it be reasoned that rest in Christ replaces the very thing promised the seed of Abraham, when belonging to Christ is the very assurance of *being* seed of Abraham and *heirs **according to the promise?*** Hebrews four verifies the continuing validity of the promise to Abraham that he and his Seed (Christ and all "in Christ") would inherit the earth.

The Psalmist rejoiced to say, *"But the meek shall inherit the earth; and shall delight themselves in the abundance of peace"* (Psalm 37:11). It is in that inheritance that the peace, the rest, comes. Rest in Christ is not a rest substituted either for the seventh-day Sabbath or the Promised Land. There is no evidence that a *substituted* sabbath-keeping is talked about in these passages or elsewhere!

Verse ten, in fact, says just the opposite: *"For the one who has entered His rest has himself also rested from his works, **as God did from His.***" One must work as God worked to rest as God rested, because that is the basis of what God commanded.[112] Our working as God worked is six days of working;. Our resting as God rested is resting the seventh-day after working six.

---o-**O**-o---

---

[112] Exodus 20:9-11: "Six days you shall labor and do all your work, but the seventh-day is a Sabbath to the LORD your God. On it you shall not do any work, neither you, nor your son or daughter, nor your manservant or maidservant, nor your animals, nor the alien within your gates. For in six days the LORD made the heavens and the earth, the sea, and all that is in them, but he rested on the seventh-day."

Can Disobedience Prevent Entering Christ?

The wealth of doctrinal information in the book of Hebrews is phenomenal! The doctrine of eternal security is denied, in that those who have entered must still labor to enter.

The doctrine that Christians remain practicing sinners is denied, in that continued disobedience prevents our entering Christ, and through Christ the Door, into the promised rest.

Disobedience prevents our entering Him; and if those who have entered the promised rest (by faith) fall after the same example of faithless disobedience, they will never experience the promised rest![113]

The question being raised is whether an unrepentant sinner can enter Christ. Jesus preached, *"Repent, for the kingdom of heaven is near."* Do we suppose a person who disobeys the command to repent would be allowed to enter that kingdom? The answer clarifies whether a believing but unrepentant sinner ought to be baptized:

"From that time on Jesus began to preach, 'Repent, for the kingdom of heaven is near'" (Matthew 4:17). *"... unless you repent, you too will all perish"* (Luke 13:5). *"Therefore go and make disciples of all nations, baptizing them in the name of the Father and of the Son and of the Holy Spirit"* (Matthew 28:19).

An unrepentant individual is not a disciple! Baptizing an unrepentant individual does not make him a disciple!

"Peter replied, 'Repent and be baptized, every one of you, in the name of Jesus Christ for the forgiveness of your sins. And you will receive the gift of the Holy Spirit'" (Acts 2:38). *"...for all of you who were baptized into Christ have clothed yourselves with Christ"* (Galatians 3:27).

---

[113] Isa. 57:20: *"... the wicked are like the tossing sea, which cannot rest, whose waves cast up mire and mud."*

However, obedience does not obtain entrance into rest – that is an operation of faith; but disobedience can prevent entrance, and continued disobedience results in those who have entered rest being cast out!

Jesus taught repentance. Why? Because unless you repent, you will perish! Notice that we are admonished by Peter to repent before baptism. Note that baptism is "for the forgiveness of sins." Notice the relationship between baptism and "entering" Christ.

Are we discussing idealism, or reality? Who wants to take a chance on trying to enter Christ, on inheriting eternal life, on inheriting the earth, without obeying the command to *repent and to be baptized?* Are we willing to try entering Christ while refusing to allow His ministers to baptize us? "Not I!" should ring out loud and clear!

Or, consider Paul's admonition to *believing Christians who have already been baptized into Christ,* reminding both the Corinthian and the Galatian churches that those who practice sin cannot inherit the kingdom of God.[114] Why give such a warning to believing Christians, when they have already entered Christ and the spiritual kingdom of God?

Because sin not repented of disqualifies God's heirs from receiving their inheritance. That is the very message of Hebrews 3, 4!

Again, the fact is demonstrated that those who have already entered the kingdom of God must yet enter their inheritance, which is also the kingdom of God – the meek shall inherit the earth. One is the spiritual, the other is the physical reality.

The sequence of making every effort to enter, then resting, is important: *"For anyone who enters God's rest also rests from his own work, just as God did from his. Let us, therefore, make every effort to enter that rest, so that no one will fall by following their example of disobedience"* (Verses 10, 11). The effort is directed at avoiding disobedience which prevents entering either the spiritual phase of the kingdom or inheriting the kingdom after the resurrection.

---

[114] 1 Cor. 6:9, 10: "Do you not know that the wicked will not inherit the kingdom of God? Do not be deceived: Neither the sexually immoral nor idolaters nor adulterers nor male prostitutes nor homosexual offenders   10 nor thieves nor the greedy nor drunkards nor slanderers nor swindlers will inherit the kingdom of God." Also Galatians 5:19-21.

The text teaches us to make every effort to enter – making every effort is complying with God's instructions, His commands and the law He writes in our hearts.

Then having entered, continue making the effort to enter. This reinforces the truth that the rest we enter now is not the final rest, as explained in the multiple phases model of the kingdom of God.

How does this correspond to ceasing from our own works *in order to enter?* (That is, in order to be saved.) How does it correspond with the oft repeated comment that we do not "maintain our salvation with good works"?

It does not correspond! We do not cease from our works in order to enter kingdom of God rest; we continue our works as admonished! If we are accepted of God, we never cease obedience!

But so far as seventh-day Sabbath observance is concerned, we cease from normal work to sustain physical life and provide its necessities *because the time comes each week to enter that kind of rest when* the six days of work ends, when the Sabbath begins.

The time will also come to cease from our effort *to enter* the kingdom of God, when Jesus returns and we are resurrected to immortality! We will cease from *making every effort to enter* the inherited kingdom rest when we are immortal, reigning as kings and priests with our Savior and King, Jesus Christ our Lord.

We *believe* in order to enter; and we *obey* [in part] in order to avoid being barred from entering. Some who expect to enter will be barred from entering:

"But while they were on their way to buy the oil, the bridegroom arrived. The virgins who were ready went in with him to the wedding banquet. And the door was shut. Later the others also came. 'Sir! Sir!' they said. 'Open the door for us!' But he replied, 'I tell you the truth, I don't know you.' Therefore keep watch, because you do not know the day or the hour" (Matthew 25:10-13).

Obedience is the basis of man's acquaintance with God: *"The man who says, 'I know him,' but does not do what he commands is a liar, and the truth is not in him"* (1 John 2:4).

What is the basis of an all-knowing all-seeing God not knowing anyone? *"But he will reply, 'I don't know you or where you come from. Away from me, all you evildoers!'"* (Luke 13:27).

It makes sense that our entering rest results in resting from work, including the labor, the effort, *to enter.* The work was *to enter;* what was being entered was a place of rest, and having achieved that goal, one does what the effort was to achieve – he rests!

But all through this life we are laboring to enter. In the Hebrews 4 scenario, one who has entered continues the endeavor to enter. This would make no sense at all without understanding the concept of our entering the spiritual Kingdom of God now in this life, and entering the inheritance after the resurrection.

"Resting" from work means either taking time out, or considering ones work complete. Our Sabbath observance is the "taking time out" type of rest. It's *the court will take a ten minute recess* type of rest. Being raised from the grave to receive immortal life and our inheritance in the millennial phase of the kingdom is like a lawyer saying "The Prosecution rests, your Honor!" He has finished the work of preparation and presentation. On being raised from the dead, we will no longer "labor to enter" rest – our inheritance – we will be there!

---o-O-o---

Hebrews Four Is not About Works vs. Grace

Let's contemplate verses 9-11 again:

"There remains, then, a Sabbath-rest for the people of God; for anyone who enters God's rest also rests from his own work, just as God did from his. Let us, therefore, make every effort to enter that rest, so that no one will fall by following their example of disobedience."

Some see *"rests from his own work"* as admonition not to depend on good works for the privilege of entering God's rest – rest in Christ, equated with salvation.

As ardently as Paul preached that we cannot be saved by works, works versus grace is not a theme of the book of Hebrews, and certainly not a theme of Hebrews 4:11: *"Let us, therefore, **make every effort** to enter that rest, so that no one will fall by following their example of **disobedience**."* Making effort involves man's will and initiative.

One means of supporting the contention that the passage is a declaration of salvation by faith and not by works is the claim that "as God rested from His work" intends to say that God's Sabbath began and never stopped;[115] then as God stopped working at the end of six days *and has never begun work again,* we forever cease to work as an effort to enter God's rest.

To test the validity of that proposition, one must examine the similarity between God's entering rest and our entering rest. The similarity is offered in either of two ways:

1) We cease forever trying to be saved by our own good works; we do not try to enter rest on the basis of **belief *and* obedience,** we cease relying on obedience for the purpose of entering rest, and rely solely on belief to enter rest – that is, *"spiritual rest in Christ resulting from belief."*

2) Once we enter rest, it is an eternal rest, which requires no more work or effort.

Very peculiar reasoning, since Hebrews 4:11 says **to believers:** "Let us, therefore, *make **every effort** to enter that rest,* so that no one will fall *by following **their example of disobedience.**"* This is not exactly an "only believe" message!

One problem with understanding it to be a works vs. grace message is that the passage is addressing people already saved, people already believers; and it is this group of already saved, already believing Christians who were admonished to continue making the effort *to enter.*

---

[115] This is based on the observation that God's seventh-day rest is not said to have had an "evening and morning" as did the six days of creation; therefore, God's rest continues to this day (See Gen. 1-2:3).

This again highlights and reinforces the position taken here that we have only entered God's rest by faith, and that the rest itself is yet to come.

Militating against the position that it is a works vs. grace statement (which would basically be the eternal security doctrine) is this fact: Nothing is mentioned in the context about working to be saved, and like it or not, "make every effort to," or "labor to" equates with "works," a step beyond faith demonstrating the validity of that faith.

The portion which admonishes "labor" or endeavor to enter God's rest does not convey the idea of ceasing *whatever* kind of work was involved, for *whatever purpose!* Obedience is not down-played, it is highlighted as expected of those who enter God's rest![116]

1) "Let us, therefore, *make every effort* to enter that rest, *so that no one will fall* by following their example of disobedience." Make every effort *"so that"* relates directly to obedience to keep from falling – effort which avoids falling by Israel's example of disobedience!

2) Make *every effort* does not fit the explanation of ceasing to work or rely on obedience for whatever reason!

In this context, let's consider two verses from the other epistle addressed directly to the Hebrew Christians:[117] *"But someone will say, 'You have faith; I have deeds.' Show me your faith without deeds, and I will show you my faith by what I do. You believe that there is one God. Good! Even the demons believe that – and shudder"* (James 2:18).

It is important to understand the purpose of this theoretical dialogue. It illustrates that we men cannot look on another person's heart to determine whether the other person believes or does not.

How, then, does one believer know the other person believes? By what he does! The challenge is, "Show me your faith without deeds!" According to James, it cannot be done!

---

[116] Heb. 4:6: "It still remains that some will enter that rest, and those who formerly had the gospel preached to them did not go in, because of their disobedience."

Heb. 4:11: "Let us, therefore, make every effort to enter that rest, so that no one will fall by following their example of disobedience."

[117] James 1:1: "James, a servant of God and of the Lord Jesus Christ, To the twelve tribes scattered among the nations: Greetings."

Both in James and in Hebrews *obey* is the clear message! If you believe, *act like it!* Why Obey? So that no one will fall **because of disobedience!** *Notice what is being said!* The subject is avoiding *failure,* avoiding *falling* caused by disobedience.

The subject is not how to be saved. It assumes one is saved and therefore *could fall*, but to keep from falling, obey God! We must agree that good works do not save us, but the effects of disobedience on entering that promised rest remains the same under both covenants. The continued practice of disobedience bars entrance, either by faith now or by participating in the resurrection.

The book of Hebrews was written to saved Hebrew Christians. They were not admonished to make every effort *to save themselves – that would be works-based salvation,* and that is not God's plan.

"Make every effort to enter," "endeavor to enter," "labor to enter," speaks of devoting ones energies to obey God *in order not to be disqualified* from participating in the final salvation, the resurrection.

If the admonition of Hebrews 3, 4 were to mean "make every effort to enter Christ" rather than *having entered Christ,* make every effort not to become disqualified to enter God's kingdom rest, then Hebrews 3, 4 would teach salvation by works, which of course they do not!

"It still remains that some will enter **that rest**, and those who formerly had the gospel preached to them[118] **did not go in, because of their disobedience..."** (v. 6). "Did not go in" means did not go into the Promised Land, and our "going in" or "entering" refers to the Kingdom of God, encompassing the present "spiritual phase" of the kingdom, the "millennial" phase, and the "eternal phase."

> *"There remains, then, a Sabbath-rest for the people of God; for anyone who enters God's rest also rests from his own work, **just as God** did from his. Let us, therefore, make every effort to enter **that rest**, so that no one will fall by following their example of disobedience"* (4:9-11).

---

[118] "Formerly had the gospel preached to them" – did they have the gospel of salvation through faith in Christ preached to them? No. What they had preached to them was the gospel – good news – of the Kingdom.

We too can fall, or fail to achieve rest in the kingdom of God by the same means – disobedience.   ---o-O-o---

Good Works Prepared in Advance For Us to Do

Please do not pass over the matter lightly. Obviously one must have been working in order to cease working; and just as obvious, God has never encouraged man to cease obeying or doing good works: *"For we are God's workmanship, created in Christ Jesus to do good works, which God prepared in advance for us to do"* (Ephesians 2:10).

What are the good works God prepared *in advance* for us to do? Can we know what they are? Ought we to know what they are? Will we know what they are as we are "doing" them?

Ought we know God's "job assignment" for us? God prepared these good works "in advance" – God prepared them *in advance of what?* How do we determine what these works consist of which God prepared in advance for us to do?

Does "prepared in advance" have anything to do with God giving instructions in the past? Does this "in advance" have anything to do with Paul's statement to the Romans: *"For everything that was written in the past was written to teach us, so that through endurance and the encouragement of the Scriptures we might have hope"?* (Romans 15:4). Of necessity it does!

Does it have any reference to God's statement through Paul:

"For what the law was powerless to do in that it was weakened by the sinful nature, God did by sending his own Son in the likeness of sinful man to be a sin offering. And so he condemned sin in sinful man, in order that the righteous requirements of the law might be fully met in us, who do not live according to the sinful nature but according to the Spirit"? (Romans 8:3, 4).

It would be unreasonable not to affirm "yes" in each case. Remember God's stated intent as part of the new Covenant, stated twice in the Book of Hebrews:

"This is the covenant I will make with the house of Israel after that time, declares the Lord. I will put my laws in their minds and write them on their hearts. I will be their God, and they will be my people" (Hebrews 8:10). *"This is the covenant I will make with them after that time, says the Lord. I will put my laws in their hearts, and I will write them on their minds"* (Hebrews 10:16).

Does God's plan to write his laws in the hearts of his people have anything to do with the "good works prepared in advance"? If *prepared in advance,* they are not different good works than the works God always had spelled out as guidelines for His children's behavior and benevolence!

God writes His laws in our hearts to correct past deficiencies! Written on our hearts, they are a constant reminder of the good works God has prepared in advance for us to do!

---o-**O**-o---

The Balance of Faith and Obedience

The verses below in *italic* show that retaining one's **faith** (belief, confidence) is requisite to entering God's rest. The verses in bold type face show that **obedience** is requisite to entering God's rest. The one both bold and italic shows both faith and obedience are required.

Six of the thirteen show that faith is required to enter God's rest; six of the thirteen show that obedience is required, and one (verse 8) is a commentary on both!

1) 3:6: *"But Christ is faithful as a son over God's house. And we are his house, if we hold on to our courage and the hope of which we boast."*

2) 3:12: *"See to it, brothers, that none of you has a sinful, unbelieving heart that turns away from the living God."*

3) 3:13: **"But encourage one another daily, as long as it is called Today, so that none of you may be hardened by sin's deceitfulness."**

4) 3:14: *"We have come to share in Christ if we hold firmly till the end the confidence we had at first."*

5) 3:17: **"And with whom was he angry for forty years? Was it not with those who sinned, whose bodies fell in the desert?"**

6) 3:18: **"And to whom did God swear that they would never enter his rest if not to those who disobeyed?"**

7) 3:19: *"So we see that they were not able to enter, because of their unbelief."*

8) 4:1: **"Therefore, since the promise of entering his rest still stands, let us be careful that none of you be found to have fallen short of it."**

9) 4:2b: *"... the message they heard was of no value to them, because those who heard did not combine it with faith."*

10) 4:3a: *"Now we who have believed enter that rest...."*

11) 4:6b: **"... those who formerly had the gospel preached to them did not go in, because of their disobedience."**

12) 4:11: **"Let us, therefore, make every effort to enter that rest, so that no one will fall by following their example of disobedience."**

13) 4:14b: *"... let us hold firmly to the faith we profess."*

As shown, both faith and obedience are required to enter the current rest, the spiritual phase of the kingdom of God, and both are required after entering the spiritual phase of God's kingdom in order to be in the first resurrection and reign with Christ on earth. The admonition is, "make every effort ... so that no one will fall by ... disobedience," and *"... let us hold firmly to the faith we profess."*

Obedience is not how to be saved, but disobedience is how to fall! Disobedience and disbelief are how to be barred from inheriting the kingdom of God. Paul warned the Corinthians, *"Do you not know that the wicked will not inherit the kingdom of God? Do not be deceived: Neither the sexually immoral nor idolaters nor adulterers nor male prostitutes nor homosexual offenders nor thieves nor the greedy nor drunkards nor slanderers nor swindlers will inherit the kingdom of God"* (1 Corinthians 6:9).   ---o-O-o---

The "Same Example" of Disobedience
A Review

That disobedience which we are warned against (*"same example of disobedience,"* Hebrews 4:11, KJV), included "profaning" the seventh-day Sabbath, which God through the prophet Jeremiah prophesied would lead to disaster:

"This is what the LORD says: Be careful not to carry a load on the Sabbath day or bring it through the gates of Jerusalem. Do not bring a load out of your houses or do any work on the Sabbath, but keep the Sabbath day holy, as I commanded your forefathers" (Jeremiah 17:21, 22).

How well did they listen to God's warning? *"Yet they did not listen or pay attention; they were stiff-necked and would not listen or respond to discipline"* (verse 23). So God warned again:

"But if you do not listen to Me to keep the sabbath day holy by not carrying a load and coming in through the gates of Jerusalem on the sabbath day, then I shall kindle a fire in its gates, and it will devour the palaces of Jerusalem and not be quenched" (Jeremiah 17:27).

Was God just bluffing? Israel continued Sabbath desecration. What were the results? The Babylonians came, destroyed the temple, took away the temple treasuries, and carried Israel away captive. *Did it have anything to do with Israel not observing the Sabbath as God warned them?*

After God's warning through Jeremiah had become reality, after both Israel and Judah had gone into Assyrian and Babylonian captivity for a predicted seventy years, God arranged for their return to their home-land. Nehemiah, a leader after their return, declared that Sabbath breaking had been a main cause for Israel going into captivity:

"In those days I saw in Judah some who were treading wine presses on the sabbath, and bringing in sacks of grain and loading them on donkeys, as well as wine, grapes, figs, and all kinds of loads, and they brought them into Jerusalem on the sabbath day. So I admonished them on the day they sold food.

"Also men of Tyre were living there who imported fish and all kinds of merchandise, and sold them to the sons of Judah on the sabbath, even in Jerusalem.

"Then I reprimanded the nobles of Judah and said to them, 'What is this evil thing you are doing, by profaning the sabbath day? 'Did not your fathers do the same so that our God brought on us, and on this city, all this trouble? Yet you are adding to the wrath on Israel by profaning the sabbath.'" (Nehemiah 13:15-18).

If in Hebrews 3 and 4 we are warned not to fall after *the same example of unbelief and disobedience,* we ought to give earnest heed to the fact Sabbath desecration is one of the prime examples related by the prophets directly to Israel's dispersion. It is one of the two main examples of disobedience resulting in their Babylonian captivity. The other was idolatry.

But, how can that be? Both Jeremiah and Nehemiah lived hundreds of years after Israel entered the Promised Land. Is Israel's later disobedience *while in the Promised Land* related to the subject? Wasn't the example of disobedience from the 40 years wandering in the wilderness *before Israel entered the Promised Land?*

In fact, the disobedience which prevented Israelites over 20 years of age from entering God's rest (the Promised Land) **was at the very beginning of the 40 years, their "day" for entering,** and largely involved refusal to enter because they did not believe God could deliver the land into their hands – both lack of faith to enter, and disobedience in refusing to enter. This is the message of Hebrews 3, that we not miss out on our "today" by faithless disobedience.

Have you ever marveled...

that God would place such emphasis on observing the Sabbath, to the point of threatening Israel's dispersion and destruction of Jerusalem if they didn't observe it properly?

Have you ever marveled that God cared very deeply about His people observing the Sabbath 500 years before the birth of His only begotten son Jesus, then shortly after His Son died to redeem Isracl from their sins, suddenly His Son reveals in Romans 14 that God could care less whether anybody observes one day, any day, or no day?

Have you ever tried to clear up this inconsistency with God saying through Malachi, *"For I am the LORD, I change not; therefore ye sons of Jacob are not consumed"* (Malachi 3:6 KJV)?

Or have you marveled again that immediately after Jesus came and took time to explain proper and lawful use of the Sabbath, that suddenly *without announcement to anybody* He would terminate Sabbath observance by His people?

Or that Christians would have to discover after the Bible had been completed that Sunday replaced Sabbath?

What happened to the prophet Amos' belief that *"Surely the Lord GOD will do nothing, but he revealeth his secret unto his servants the prophets"* (Amos 3:7)? Why did neither prophet, priest nor apostle – not even Jesus Himself – ever talk about instituting first day observance?

Was that policy *"surely the Lord GOD will do nothing, but he revealeth his secret unto his servants the prophets"* also changed, so that without telling His Apostles or His prophets that with the coming of the New Covenant God would quit making an issue about Sabbath observance by His people? Was Amos' assurance misguided?

But, let's not forget that the warning of Hebrews 4 is that we not fall *after we have entered God's rest! We must not gloss over this point!* Those being warned in the letter to the Hebrews had already "entered" rest by faith. They were already Christians.

Israel's disobedience *after entering* Canaan has as much to do with Hebrews 3, 4 as their disobedience before entering Canaan. Hebrews 3, 4 speak of disobedience after entering God's rest, and just as Israel lost the rest they had entered, so we who enter God's rest through faith in Christ can be and will be removed from that rest if we lose faith, and practice disobedience as Israel did *after entering Canaan!* Jesus said:

"Remain in me, and I will remain in you. No branch can bear fruit by itself; it must remain in the vine. Neither can you bear fruit unless you remain in me. I am the vine; you are the branches. If a man remains in me and I in him, he will bear much fruit; apart from me you can do nothing.

"If anyone does not remain in me, he is like a branch that is thrown away and withers; such branches are picked up, thrown into the fire and burned. If you remain in me and my words remain in you, ask whatever you wish, and it will be given you" (John 15:4-7).

Why this admonition to "remain" in Christ? This is not an "eternal security" message! This is the same message as delivered to the Hebrews in chapters 3, 4, 6, 10.

It was the sins of generations of Israel living in Canaan that prompted God to remove the Israelites from the Promised Land, terminating the "rest" that Joshua and David cited as having been achieved.

If we resume sinning after entering God's rest, we will also be removed from God's rest, after Israel's example of losing faith and resuming disobedience.

The passage below is quite long, but please read it carefully to see the continued theme in the book of Hebrews of retaining faith and avoiding disobedience:

*"It is impossible for those who have once been enlightened, who have tasted the heavenly gift, who have shared in the Holy Spirit, who have tasted the goodness of the word of God and the powers of the coming age, **if they fall away,** to be brought back to repentance, because to their loss they are crucifying the Son of God all over again and subjecting him to public disgrace" (Hebrews 6:4-6).*

***"If we deliberately keep on sinning** after we have received the knowledge of the truth, no sacrifice for sins is left, but only a fearful expectation of judgment and of raging fire that will consume the enemies of God.*

"Anyone who rejected the law of Moses died without mercy on the testimony of two or three witnesses. How much more severely do you think a man deserves to be punished who has trampled the Son of God under foot, who has treated as an unholy thing the blood of the covenant that sanctified him, and who has insulted the Spirit of grace?

"For we know him who said, 'It is mine to avenge; I will repay,' and again, 'The Lord will judge his people.' It is a dreadful thing to fall into the hands of the living God.

"Remember those earlier days after you had received the light, when you stood your ground in a great contest in the face of suffering. Sometimes you were publicly exposed to insult and persecution; at other times you stood side by side with those who were so treated.

"You sympathized with those in prison and joyfully accepted the confiscation of your property, because you knew that you yourselves had better and lasting possessions.

*"So do not throw away your confidence; it will be richly rewarded. You need to persevere so that **when you have done the will of God, you will receive what he has promised"** (Hebrews 10:26-36). ---o-O-o---*

How Hard Must We Try?

Hebrews 12:4 says: *"In your struggle against sin, you have not yet resisted to the point of shedding your blood."* Does God really expect such commitment? He does! Compare this verse to the three last quoted paragraphs above.

If God expects such commitment to righteousness, can we say it is works of righteousness that we cease doing when we enter God's rest? *If we continue them, we do not cease doing them!*

In speaking of ceasing from our own work as God ceased from His, the Book of Hebrews does not speak of ceasing work for the wrong reason, as one could reason if he were to admit we are expected to do good works, that we are expected to obey God; yet, *we just aren't supposed to do them for the wrong reason!*

In that scenario, the wrong reason for obeying God and doing good works would be to have an effect on whether we are saved or disinherited after being saved. That scenario proclaims we obey and do good works *only motivated by love.*

The message to the Hebrews is that our continued obedience, our "persevering" in "doing the will of God" has a direct relationship to whether we will receive what God has promised!

That being true, the entering rest spoken of in chapter four most clearly cannot suggest that "only believe" will tide us safely "over Jordan" into the kingdom of God. The entire book of Hebrews denies that! One must believe *and step into the water!*

There is no criticism in Hebrews 3 and 4 of the works we cease when we enter God's rest, as though they were improper works or works performed for the wrong purpose – there is no criticism of the motivation for having done the works, as though we had been working to save ourselves by good works.

Why is that? *Because the very works supposedly ceased are works God commands His people to perform!* They include the works of Exodus 20:9: *"Six days you shall labor and do all your work."* When we enter God's rest (His kingdom, through faith in Jesus Christ) we also cease working after our six days' work like God ceased working after His six days work – in other words, we obey His commands if we are heirs to the kingdom.

Hebrews 4:10 does indicate we cease something in order to rest. It is not obedience that we cease! It is the commanded six days of work we cease! As before pointed out, we were created in Christ Jesus unto good works; and as we see in Hebrews 12:4, God expects of us that if need arise, we willingly become martyrs in striving against sin. What we conclude about Hebrews 4 must agree with the rest of the book!

Modern Christians generally do not believe God holds man responsible to obey the command to keep the seventh-day holy to the Lord. Thus modern Christians in general still refuse to rest from their own work as God did from His! They still want to enter His rest without obedience – or at the best, selective obedience!

---o-O-o---

Is the Sabbath Still a Sign?

Earlier the question was posed, why the seemingly unrelated injection of seventh-day Sabbath rest into the discussion of the promised rest? It was observed that if we conclude Hebrews 4 upholds seventh-day Sabbath observance, we need a sound rationale for mentioning Sabbath rest in the midst of a different discussion, a discussion of not failing to enter the promised rest, a rest which "remains" and is not fulfilled.

When the subject had been fulfilling the promise of rest in the Promised Land, why would there be such a sudden injection of a different "rest" subject matter?

That rationale may be seen in the importance God had always placed on Sabbath observance. Many Sabbath-observing believers conclude that Sabbath observance is still a sign of the people of God in the New Covenant, as it was in the Old Covenant:

"It will be a sign between me and the Israelites forever, for in six days the LORD made the heavens and the earth, and on the seventh-day he abstained from work and rested" (Exod. 31:17).

Some mildly to vehemently deny the Sabbath is still a sign, even among those who think observing the Sabbath is still commanded.

One must *at least consider* whether in the New Covenant observing Sabbath continues to be a sign as it was in the old. Is that the implication of saying *"... anyone who enters God's rest also rests from his own work, just as God did from his"?* (Hebrews 4:10b).

Look again at Exodus 31:17 above, then again at Hebrews 4:10b. What do you see? In light of the *evolution vs. creationism* controversy, is there any reason the Sabbath would not be an appropriate sign between God and His people, He being their creator, and having chosen us in him before the foundation of the world?[119] Not recognizing God as our Creator is one of the major sins and a great folly of our day.[120]

One may even find *some* correlation between those who use the Sabbath for a day of sacred assembly but believe God no longer requires it, and those who believe God created the universe but took eons of time to do it.

There is also *some* correlation between those who voluntarily observe the Sabbath, believe God created life, but also believe God used evolution as the method. To them creation week, God resting the seventh-day, God making man of the dust of the earth are only symbolic of God's actual method.

In that mode of thought, *"... anyone who enters God's rest also rests from his own work, just as God did from his"* can also mean nothing more definite than the creation method!

---

[119] "According as he hath chosen us in him before the foundation of the world, that we should be holy and with-out blame before him in love" (Eph. 1:4).

[120] Romans 1:18.20: "The wrath of God is being revealed from heaven against all the godlessness and wickedness of men who suppress the truth by their wickedness, since what may be known about God is plain to them, because God has made it plain to them. For since the creation of the world God's invisible qualities – his eternal power and divine nature – have been clearly seen, being understood from what has been made, so that men are without excuse."

Do you believe God when He inspired the statement *"... anyone who enters God's rest also rests from his own work, just as God did from his"*? Probably not! *Hardly anyone does!* Not even those who staunchly affirm their belief that God inspired the whole Bible and that it is still a valid command to observe the seventh-day Sabbath!

If it is literally true that *"anyone who enters God's rest also rests from his own work, just as God did from his"* can a person identify those who enter God's promised rest by whether they observe the Sabbath?

Is there any reason the statement would not be literal? If you have entered God's rest (the spiritual kingdom of God), do you rest from your own work just as God rested from His work?

If you do not, then *have you entered God's rest?* The verse says *anyone* who enters God's rest also rests just as God rested.

Do you? If not, can you declare you have entered even though you do not rest as God rested?

One can almost hear an echo, "The way *I* like to think of it is...."! "The way *I* like to think of it...."! "The way *I* like to think...."!

Let's be frank about our convictions. Do we believe the fourth commandment is still a commandment? If it is, is it a sin, is it disobedience, not to observe the Sabbath? Consider:

"And, behold, one came and said unto him, Good Master, what good thing shall I do, that I may have eternal life? And he said unto him, Why callest thou me good? there is none good but one, that is, God: but if thou wilt <u>enter into life,</u> keep the commandments.

"He saith unto him, Which? Jesus said, Thou shalt do no murder, Thou shalt not commit adultery, Thou shalt not steal, Thou shalt not bear false witness, Honour thy father and thy mother: and, Thou shalt love thy neighbour as thyself" (Matthew 19:16-19).

Keep the commandments? How many of them?

"For whosoever shall keep the whole law, and yet offend in one point, he is guilty of all. For he that said, Do not commit adultery, said also, Do not kill. Now if thou commit no adultery, yet if thou

kill, thou art become a transgressor of the law. So speak ye, and so do, as they that shall be judged by the law of liberty" (James 2:10-12).

"He that hath my commandments, and keepeth them, he it is that loveth me: and he that loveth me shall be loved of my Father, and I will love him, and will manifest myself to him" (John 14:21).

"If ye keep my commandments, ye shall abide in my love; even as I have kept my Father's commandments, and abide in his love" (John 15:10).

"And hereby we do know that we know him, if we keep his commandments. He that saith, I know him, and keepeth not his commandments, is a liar, and the truth is not in him" (1 John 2:3).

"And whatsoever we ask, we receive of him, because we keep his commandments, and do those things that are pleasing in his sight" (1 John 3:22).

"And he that keepeth his commandments dwelleth in him, and he in him. And hereby we know that he abideth in us, by the Spirit which he hath given us" (1 John 3:24).

"By this we know that we love the children of God, when we love God, and keep his commandments. For this is the love of God, that we keep his commandments: and his commandments are not grievous" (1 John 5:2, 3).

"And this is love, that we walk after his commandments. This is the commandment, That, as ye have heard from the beginning, ye should walk in it" (2 John 6).

"And the dragon was wroth with the woman, and went to make war with the remnant of her seed, which keep the commandments of God, and have the testimony of Jesus Christ" (Revelations 12:17).

"Here is the patience of the saints: here are they that keep the commandments of God, and the faith of Jesus" (Revelations 14:12).

"Blessed are they that do his commandments, that they may have right to the tree of life, and may enter in through the gates into the city" (Revelations 22:14). (Series above are KJV.)

"To the Jews who had believed him, Jesus said, "If you hold to my teaching, you are really my disciples" (John 8:31, NIV).

"By this all men will know that you are my disciples, if you love one another" (John 13:35, NIV).

The pertinent question is, did you find yourself among those declarations? They are all "signs" or means of knowing whether you and I are disciples of Christ!

Can you be identified as a commandment keeper?

It may seem unreasonable to many that observing the Sabbath would remain a sign between God and His people; however, if it was not unreasonable to God in the Old Covenant, there is nothing unreasonable about it in the new!

If Sabbath keeping remains a sign, is it the only sign? No, but Sabbath observance was never the only sign! Circumcision was a sign, faith and obedience also were signs – they still are!

But *is it true that anyone who enters God's rest also rests from his own work, just as God did from his? Yes, because that's what the Bible says!*

Do we believe it? Probably not! We should hesitate before we try to make the text say something different than *anyone who enters God's rest also rests from his own work, just as God did from his!*

Consider a moment the implications of Isaiah 56:1-8. This is a Messianic prophecy, and notice the prominence given to Sabbath keeping in relation to aliens "laying hold" on God's covenant:

"This is what the LORD says: "Maintain justice and do what is right, for my salvation is close at hand and my righteousness will soon be revealed. Blessed is the man who does this, the man who holds it fast, who keeps the Sabbath without desecrating it, and keeps his hand from doing any evil." Let no foreigner who has bound himself to the LORD say, 'The LORD will surely exclude me from his people." And let not any eunuch complain, "I am only a dry tree.'

"For this is what the LORD says: 'To the eunuchs who keep my Sabbaths, who choose what pleases me and hold fast to my covenant – to them I will give within my temple and its walls a memorial

and a name better than sons and daughters; I will give them an ev-
erlasting name that will not be cut off.

"And foreigners who bind themselves to the LORD to serve him,
to love the name of the LORD, and to worship him, all who keep the
Sabbath without desecrating it and who hold fast to my covenant –
these I will bring to my holy mountain and give them joy in my
house of prayer.

"Their burnt offerings and sacrifices will be accepted on my al-
tar; for my house will be called a house of prayer for all nations.'
The Sovereign LORD declares – he who gathers the exiles of Israel:
'I will gather still others to them besides those already gathered'"
(Isaiah 56:1-8).

That this passage concerns Gentiles "joining themselves to the
Lord" under both the old and new covenants is evident:

A. New Covenant:

1. *"...my salvation is close at hand and my righteousness will soon*
be revealed" (v. 1). This refers to the coming and ministry of Christ.

2. *"To the eunuchs who keep my Sabbaths, who choose what pleases*
me and hold fast to my covenant – to them I will give within my temple
and its walls a memorial and a name better than sons and daughters; I
will give them an everlasting name that will not be cut off" (vv. 4b. 5).

This did not happen before the cross, no such name is found outside
the name of Christ. Under the Old Covenant, Eunuchs could not enter
the temple. This further testifies to the New Covenant nature of Isaiah
56.[121]

---

[121] This no doubt refers to OT rules against certain men serving in the temple, a ruling that excludes eunuchs:

Lev. 21:17-28: "Say to Aaron: 'For the generations to come none of your descendants who has a defect may come near to offer the food of his God. 18 No man who
has any defect may come near: no man who is blind or lame, disfigured or deformed;
19 no man with a crippled foot or hand, 20 or who is hunchbacked or dwarfed, or who
has any eye defect, or who has festering or running sores or damaged testicles. 21 No
descendant of Aaron the priest who has any defect is to come near to present the offerings made to the LORD by fire. He has a defect; he must not come near to offer the

3. *"And foreigners who bind themselves to the LORD to serve him, to love the name of the LORD, and to worship him, all who keep the Sabbath without desecrating it and who hold fast to my covenant – these I will bring to my holy mountain and give them joy in my house of prayer ... my house will be called a house of prayer for all nations"* (vv. 6-7). Jesus quotes this passage, and it is quoted no other place in the Bible.

4. *"The Sovereign LORD declares – he who gathers the exiles of Israel: 'I will gather still others to them besides those already gathered'"* (v. 8). This and verses 4, 5 refer to the Apostles turning to the Gentiles to preach the Gospel.

B. Old Covenant:

1. *"These I will bring to my holy mountain and give them joy in my house of prayer. Their burnt offerings and sacrifices will be accepted on my altar; for my house will be called a house of prayer for all nations"* (v. 7).

During the entirety of the Old Covenant, aliens were welcome to become a part of the people of God:

"Six days do your work, but on the seventh-day do not work, so that your ox and your donkey may rest and the slave born in your household, and the alien as well, may be refreshed" (Exod. 23:12).

"The same law applies to the native-born and to the alien living among you" (Exodus 12:49).

If Isaiah 56 is a Messianic prophecy as shown, why the prominence given to these aspects of joining themselves to the Lord, *all in one verse?*

1) "And foreigners who bind themselves to the LORD to serve him",

2) "... to love the name of the LORD",

3) "... and to worship him",

4) "... all who keep the Sabbath without desecrating it",

5) "... and who hold fast to my covenant."

---

food of his God. 22 He may eat the most holy food of his God, as well as the holy food; 23 yet because of his defect, he must not go near the curtain or approach the altar, and so desecrate my sanctuary. I am the LORD, who makes them holy. '"

All the other commandments are comprehended in the phrase, "and keeps his hand from doing any evil." In Hebrews 3, 4 other commandments are comprehended in the general admonition to be obedient, but the Sabbath is highlighted in both Isaiah 56 and Hebrews 4.

It is perfectly in keeping with the prophet Isaiah for the writer of Hebrews to state: *"...for anyone who enters God's rest also rests from his own work, just as God did from his." "Make every effort to enter"* is equal to *"holding fast to my covenant."*

---o-O-o---

A Striking Parallel Relating to the Other Rest
The Seventh-day Sabbath

In their pilgrimage to Canaan, even before God made the Old Covenant with Israel, God gave Israel the Sabbath for rest. The Sabbath was then included in the Old Covenant, and continued a commanded blessing during the 40 years of Israel's wilderness journey. Entering the Promised Land did not change the need, or God's command, to rest and worship.

Then comes preaching the Gospel and believers begin to enter the Kingdom of God under the ministry of Jesus and the twelve Apostles. Entering the kingdom of God under their ministry did not change the need for or expectation that the seed of Abraham observe the Sabbath.

Instead, Jesus preached a better understanding of God's command to rest and worship on the Sabbath. Its purpose and proper observance were explained more fully.

The type matches the anti-type. Entering Canaan did not signal the end of Sabbath observance. Canaan afforded a more meaningful place in which to observe the Sabbath. As with Israel entering Canaan, when we enter the spiritual Kingdom of God, Sabbath observance becomes more meaningful. Entering kingdom rest does not end Sabbath observance:

"... anyone who enters God's rest also rests from his own work, just as God did from his" (Hebrews 4:10).

This is a statement of fact. Basically the passage says *anyone* who enters God's kingdom either is or becomes a sabbath-observer. He enters rest, the sabbatismos that remains for the people of God, and *also rests from his own work, just as God did from his.*

We, too, are pilgrims in our own land, a part of the People of God, a part of God's chosen few. By faith, we enter the Promised Inheritance, but this present life is not the promised rest, it is not the promised inheritance. When the reality comes, when the new heavens and new earth are a reality, there will still be a literal sabbath-keeping for the Chosen of God:

"'As the new heavens and the new earth that I make will endure before me,' declares the LORD, 'so will your name and descendants endure. From one New Moon to another and from one Sabbath to another, all mankind will come and bow down before me,' says the LORD" (Isaiah 66:23, 24).

But hasn't that old prophecy been fulfilled already? Can you pinpoint any time in history when *all mankind even came before God and bowed down before Him?* You cannot! *Much less has it ever been a practice for it to happen on the Sabbath!*

A record of it happening is not in the Bible, and a record of such a singular event isn't recorded in any history of the Christian Church. In fact, the majority of Christendom is doing whatever they can to prevent it from ever happening!

So what will it be? God predicted, "From one New Moon to another and from one Sabbath to another, *all mankind will come and bow down before me"* – did He then change His mind?

If God's declaration *"From one New Moon to another and from one Sabbath to another, all mankind will come and bow down before me"* has been abandoned, will God also change His mind about the New Heavens and New Earth? Will He change His mind about the resurrection and eternal life?

Our God Is Dependable!

"God is not a man, that he should lie, nor a son of man, that he should change his mind. Does he speak and then not act? Does he promise and not fulfill?" (Numbers 23:19).

How do we answer these questions? How do we respond? Do we believe the declaration?

That all flesh has already at some time bowed before God is not evident; neither is it evident that God has changed His mind, for Paul wrote: *"It is written: 'As surely as I live,' says the Lord, 'every knee will bow before me; every tongue will confess to God.' So then, each of us will give an account of himself to God"* (Romans 14:11, 12).

Two Old Scripture passages affirm the point Paul makes:

Isaiah 45:23: *"By myself I have sworn, my mouth has uttered in all integrity a word that will not be revoked: Before me every knee will bow; by me every tongue will swear."*

Isaiah 66:24: *"'From one New Moon to another and from one Sabbath to another, all mankind will come and bow down before me,' says the LORD."*

How sure are we it is yet to happen? ***"By myself I have sworn, my mouth has uttered in all integrity a word that will not be revoked"!*** How much more sure can we be?

---o-**O**-o---

Hebrews 4 – A Review of Key Verses

Verse 1: *"Therefore, since the promise of entering his rest still stands, let us be careful that none of you be found to have fallen short of it."*

Verse 2: *"The message they heard was of no value to them, because those who heard did not combine it with faith."*

Verse 6: *"Those who formerly had the gospel preached to them did not go in, because of their disobedience."*

Verse 11: *"Let us, therefore, make every effort to enter that rest, so that no one will fall by following their example of disobedience."*

How does one "be careful" not to fall short of entering God's rest (His kingdom)? Being careful (verse 1), and making every effort (verse 11) require obeying to avoid disobedience, and believing to avoid disbelief – rather simple concept!

"Being careful" involves both faith and obedience, the lack of either resulted in those of Israel failing to enter: The admonition to be "careful that we not fall short" must of necessity involve the same thing as "let us make every effort to enter that rest." The effort is directed toward believing and obeying.

If the same author admonishes making every effort to enter "that rest," he cannot at the same time admonish ceasing one's works performed in order to be saved, or ceasing one's works even to "maintain" salvation. The passage admonishes believing and obeying so as not to fall from grace! It cannot at the same time admonish us to do just the opposite!

"Anyone who enters God's rest also rests from his own work, just as God did from his" cannot so much as admonish us to *cease doing good works* for the wrong purpose, while *continuing to do them for the right purpose!*

Why not? Because nothing in either Hebrews 3 or 4 explains the method of salvation. True as the doctrine of salvation through faith and not of works is, there is no hint whatever of the "saved by grace through faith and not of works" doctrine in either chapter.

---o-O-o---

God Expects Better of Us

In the sixth chapter of Hebrews we find a discussion of those who fail to heed the call of chapters three and four, not to fall after ancient Israel's example of disobedient unbelief.

A sad contrast is made between 1) those who enter God's rest and remain faithfully obedient, and 2) those who turn back into sin:

"It is impossible for those who have once been enlightened, who have tasted the heavenly gift, who have shared in the Holy Spirit, who have tasted the goodness of the word of God and the powers of the coming age, if they fall away, to be brought back to repentance, because to their loss they are crucifying the Son of God all over again and subjecting him to public disgrace. Land that drinks in the rain often falling on it and that produces a crop useful to those for whom it is farmed receives the blessing of God" (Hebrews 6:4-7).

The writer says he expects a better response from the Hebrews of his day who believed:

*"Even though we speak like this, dear friends, we are confident of better things in your case – things that accompany salvation. God is not unjust; he **will not forget your work** and the love you have shown him as you have helped his people and continue to help them. **We want each of you to show this same diligence to the very end**, in order to make your hope sure"* (Hebrews 6:9-11).

The Israel of God, the Church, is expected to give a better response than Ancient Israel gave, because *we have a better covenant established on better promises* (Hebrews 8:6).

A better response is expected because we are provided an immortal high priest (Jesus, the Son of God) rather than mortal high priests (the sons of Aaron).

A better response is expected because a better sacrifice has been offered.

A better response is expected because the indwelling Spirit of God through Jesus Christ, empowers us to make a better response:

"There is therefore now no condemnation for those who are in Christ Jesus. For the law of the Spirit of life in Christ Jesus has set you free from the law of sin and of death. For what the Law could not do, weak as it was through the flesh, God did: sending His own

Son in the likeness of sinful flesh and as an offering for sin, He condemned sin in the flesh, in order that the requirement of the Law might be fulfilled in us, who do not walk according to the flesh, but according to the Spirit" (Romans 8:1-4 NASB).[122] This passage deserves a great deal of meditation.

A better response is expected because of God's action on behalf of His chosen people:

"For I will take you out of the nations; I will gather you from all the countries and bring you back into your own land. I will sprinkle clean water on you, and you will be clean; I will cleanse you from all your impurities and from all your idols.[123] *I will give you a new heart and put a new spirit in you; I will remove from you your heart of stone and give you a heart of flesh. And I will put my Spirit in you and move you to follow my decrees and be careful to keep my laws"* (Ezekiel 36:24-27).

A better response is expected because God makes a way to escape every temptation to sin that comes our way:

"No temptation has seized you except what is common to man. And God is faithful; he will not let you be tempted beyond what you can bear. But when you are tempted, he will also provide a way out so that you can stand up under it" (1 Corinthians 10:13).

---

[122] Most references are from Zondervan macBible edition for Macintosh.

[123] Does the "regathering" context perturb you? Keep in mind that the book of Hebrews was written to the people who had been scattered and regathered; but most still had no new heart; the city of Jerusalem again was burned with fire by the Romans in 70 AD, the Hebrews were again scattered, and the prophets indicate their gathering again, now in process, but still no new heart among most of them. Great things are yet to happen in Israel: "I do not want you to be ignorant of this mystery, brothers, so that you may not be conceited: Israel has experienced a hardening in part until the full number of the Gentiles has come in. And so all Israel will be saved, as it is written: "The deliverer will come from Zion; he will turn godlessness away from Jacob" (Romans 11:25, 26:).

Keep Your Eyes on the Escape Route!

If God made the way to escape temptation to sin, He expects us to use that way of escape! When we enter a highly flammable situation we should look for the way out in case of fire.

When we enter a highly enticing situation, we should start looking for God's way of escape and be ready to take it immediately!

Paul Admonishes: "Flee also youthful lusts"– quickly take the way of escape!"... but follow righteousness, faith, charity, peace" (these are the escape routes), *"with them that call on the Lord out of a pure heart"* (follow the others taking the escape route!)

These changes in and for God's people are also the basis of "better promises." However, rather than teaching victory through Christ, or the possibility of escape *from sin* through Christ, many Evangelicals are teaching escape *in sin* through Christ.

Rather than teaching *obedience possibility* in Christ, some Evangelicals are teaching *obedience impossibility* – even in Christ – even though God has provided a way of escape for every temptation and will not allow us to be tempted beyond what we can bear!

"... consider him that endured such contradiction of sinners against himself, lest ye be wearied and faint in your minds"! (Hebrews 12:3 KJV).

"Therefore, since the promise of entering his rest still stands, let us be careful that none of you be found to have fallen short of it" (Hebrews 4:1).   **---o-O-o---**

Concluding Summary

The Book of Hebrews is addressed in particular to the twelve tribes of Israel as descendants of Abraham. They needed encouragement, having been told by the Lord Jesus Christ that *"... the kingdom of God will be taken away from you and given to a people who will produce its fruit"* (Matthew 21:43).

Hebrews, chapters 3 and 4, tells them that God's promise of rest in their own Land was still valid, but throughout the book of Hebrews and in particular chapters 3 and 4, they were reminded of the reason rest in their own land had not been achieved – lack of faith and disobedience were the problems.

Whereas Israel of old had missed their day to enter the promised rest, the Holy Spirit through David spoke of another day, called "Today." But for "Today" to be of value, one must not harden his heart as Israel did.

When Israel first approached the Promised Land from the south, they refused to proceed, not having faith God could deliver the land into their hands. They then spent the next forty years in the desert, stubbornly trying God's patience.

At one point God proposed to destroy Israel and start over with Moses and his descendants for a people. John the Baptist echoed that same sentiment when he warned Israel, *"And do not think you can say to yourselves, 'We have Abraham as our father.' I tell you that out of these stones God can raise up children for Abraham"* (Matt. 3:9).

John Baptist's warning is a continuing reminder that God can get along without any of us as individuals, and will do so if we remain disobedient or unbelieving.

Hebrews chapters three and four repeatedly warn the Hebrews (and all of us) that we can make the same mistakes, lack of faith and disobedience, and miss out on our "Today" opportunity to enter the promised rest. That promise is repeatedly affirmed to still be valid to the people of God.

In the fourth chapter, use is made of the creation story to prove that the place of rest had been prepared from the foundation of the world, it was finished at the end of the sixth day. That is, the earth, as the place of inheritance had been completed. Jesus affirmed that the meek will inherit the earth, as promised to Abraham and his seed, and as repeated by the prophets.

The promise to Abraham and his seed is guaranteed to all the children of God through Christ Jesus. He, Himself, is of direct lineage from Abraham. He purchased the chosen of God, Jew and Gentile believers, with His own blood. All who belong to Christ are Abraham's seed and "heirs" according to the promise. This is the same promise referred to in Hebrews chapter 4.

The warning not to be faithless and disobedient resounds throughout the book of Hebrews. The very same examples of unbelief and disobedience which caused Israel not to enter the Promised Land and remain at rest are a snare to misguided New Covenant believers who enter the promised rest, the Kingdom of God, and reject portions of God's instructions.

Those who enter and those who have entered are all warned not to fall into sin and unbelief. The consequences are the same, disinheritance and removal from the kingdom, being trimmed from the tame olive tree and tossed in the fire.

In the process of reviewing these chapters, one discovers that although this life does not bring rest to the believing, obedient children of God, His children enter the promised rest now, in this life, in our "Today" – our day of salvation. This entrance is by faith only, and can occur only in what we call the Spiritual phase or era of the Kingdom of God.

This era of faith in which we enter the Kingdom of God is the second of four. One is past, in which Israel was in charge of the kingdom, and two more eras are anticipated, the millennial (1000 year) reign of Christ with His redeemed, and after the end of the Millennium, the establishment of the New Heavens and New Earth, "wherein dwelleth righteousness." The wicked are destroyed by fire at the end of the Millennium.

Seemingly incidental to the general thesis of these chapters is the mention in chapter four of a "sabbatismos" or "sabbath-keeping" that remains to the people of God. Because of the usual use of the word "sabbath," some Christians see in this word affirmation of seventh-day Sabbath observance.

However, the context indicates that "sabbatismos" is here used to refer to fulfillment of the "promise" that remains, Promised Land rest, which Joshua did not achieve for Israel – although He and David thought rest had been achieved.

This dual use of words for "rest" is not unusual. In the Septuagint Old Testament, two other Greek words are used for "rest," both in relation to Sabbath observance and also rest in the Promised Land.

"Kata'-pausis," (meaning "to cease," "to pause") is more commonly used in relation to Promised Land rest than a related word, "ana'-pausis," the meaning of which is almost indistinguishable from the meaning of "kata'-pau-sis."

"Anapausis" is more commonly used in relation to Sabbath rest, than is "katapausis," but both are used in that context. The Greek word for "rest" in Hebrews three and four is "katapausis," the word used in Genesis (the Septuagint-Alexandrian version) where God is said to have rested the seventh-day at the end of six days of creation. It is used in Hebrews four for the same event.

However, in the thesis developed in Hebrews four is found the statement that *"anyone who enters God's rest also rests from his own work, just as God did from his."*

After careful analysis, it appears inescapable that this is simply stating that anyone who enters God's rest, rests the seventh-day as God rested the seventh-day, for the only way God "rested" was ceasing work and hallowing the seventh-day by remaining at rest through the seventh-day.

It appears, therefore, that the point in mentioning that anyone who enters God's rest *also rests* as God did, is to reinforce the warning not to fail to enter God's Promised Land rest through disobedience.

Sabbath desecration was stated by both Jeremiah and Nehemiah to be one of the major reasons Israel was deprived of rest in their homeland, and Christians are warned not to imitate their disobedient acts.

Both obedient and disobedient **Israelites** were *all* held responsible for observing the seventh-day Sabbath. Gentiles who became a part of Israel, taking hold of God's covenant, were also held responsible to obey the Sabbath (Exodus 12:49; Isaiah 56:1-8).

In the New Earth, God's final "rest" for His chosen people, all mankind will be held responsible to observe the Sabbath: *"And it shall be from new moon to new moon, and from sabbath to sabbath, all mankind will come to bow down before Me,' says the* LORD" (Isaiah 66:23 and context).

All Israel, obedient and disobedient, faithful and unfaithful, emancipated alien and native, were held responsible for observing the Sabbath. All mankind will observe the Sabbath in the New Earth.

Therefore, it is logical to find a simple statement in Hebrews 4:10 that "anyone who enters God's rest also rests from his own work, just as God did from his."

The fact a statement that anyone who enters God's rest also rests as God did – observes the Sabbath – would be inserted so matter-of-factly is easily understood in the context of the importance Sabbath observance always played among God's chosen people.

Resting from their own work as God did from His had been a sign between God and Israel from the days of Moses. According to Hebrews 4:10, it is still true that "anyone who enters God's rest also rests from his own work, just as God did from his."

Sabbath-keeping still has great significance as an indicator of one's willingness to be an obedient believer.

We still need physical rest and a time to congregate and worship the Lord in this, our "Today," our day for entering God's promised rest by faith.

While we are still pilgrims on earth waiting for the return of Christ we still rest from our works as God did from His. Having entered the promised kingdom rest by faith, God expects us to rest the seventh-day Sabbath as part of the benefit of spiritual obedience.

There is a parallel between our sojourn on earth and Abraham' living in the Promised land but not yet having charge of his inheritance. This is described in Hebrews 11:9, 10:

"By faith he (Abraham) lived as an alien in the land of promise, as in a foreign land, dwelling in tents with Isaac and Jacob, fellow heirs of the same promise; for he was looking for the city which has foundations, whose architect and builder is God."

Tents had no foundations. Abraham looked forward to a permanent dwelling.

This is our own condition. The place of our inheritance is the earth: *"Blessed are the meek, for they shall inherit the earth."* We're already here, but the "Philistines" are in control, and therefore we have no rest except by faith! We, too, are *aliens in the land of promise!*

The dwellings we have here are also temporary, subject to destruction by later generations tearing down and rebuilding. Termites, rust, fire, storms and war reduce them to nothingness.

This is our interim period, our "wandering in the wilderness period." This is our pilgrimage, wandering the earth looking for a city with foundations - permanency – "whose architect and builder is God."

Israel wandered the wilderness looking for the day of their entering the Promised Land. They were commanded to observe the Sabbath both as they wandered in the wilderness, and after entering the Promised Land. The commandment continued as they temporarily found rest in the land of promise. The obedient of Israel continued to keep the Sabbath at God's command.

Similarly, this is also our time of having entered God's rest, but we find no rest, as Israel entered Canaan but still had no rest, encountering opposition from the enemy – and on occasion, defeat, when they quit trusting in the Lord. Note the advantage we have:

"For though we live in the world, we do not wage war as the world does. The weapons we fight with are not the weapons of the

world. On the contrary, they have divine power to demolish strong-holds.

"We demolish arguments and every pretension that sets itself up against the knowledge of God, and we take captive every thought to make it obedient to Christ. And we will be ready to punish every act of disobedience, once your obedience is complete" (2 Corinthians 10:3-6).

We, as aliens in the land of Promise (the promise is to inherit the earth), also find no rest; and we, like Israel, if obedient to God, continue to rest from our own work, just as God did from his. We continue in this land of Promise to observe the seventh-day Sabbath.

Entering kingdom-rest does not now or ever terminate seventh-day Sabbath observance! Hebrews 4 declares, "anyone who enters God's rest *also* rests from his own work, just as God did from his." This statement has both current and post-resurrection implications.

Biblical types do not teach termination of the Sabbath; biblical doctrines of the anti-type do not teach termination of the Sabbath. Nothing suggests the seventh-day Sabbath had been a type of spiritual rest in Christ, which would terminate upon entering the kingdom of God by faith.

Just as Israel continued to observe the Sabbath upon entering the rest that did not actually bring rest, so we too continue to observe the Sabbath upon entering the rest that does not really bring rest, and will not bring rest in this life!

Israel in the wilderness was commanded to observe the Sabbath, some complying, some not. Those who were obedient entered the Promised Land, but found no rest because they, like we, were as aliens while in the land of promise.

We should not say we have no need of the weekly Sabbath during this time of persecution and trial. During this age we still struggle with thorns and thistles to provide the necessities of life![124]

---

[124] Gen. 3:19: "By the sweat of your brow you will eat your food until you return to the ground, since from it you were taken; for dust you are and to dust you will return."

We still need a regular time for a holy convocation, gathering together for worship and mutual encouragement: *"Let us not give up meeting together, as some are in the habit of doing, but let us encourage one another – and all the more as you see the Day approaching"* (Hebrews 10:25).

But more than that, there will never come a time when regular gatherings before the Lord to worship Him will be outdated. If the Sabbath will be observed by all mankind in the new heavens and new earth, it remains an appropriate part of a Christian's need in this life!

There is more to our entering rest as God did than some of us are ready to affirm. What Hebrews 4:9-10 in fact says about Sabbath observance is this: "For *anyone* who enters God's rest also rests from his own work, just as God did from his."

"There remains, then, a Sabbath-rest[125] for the people of God" has a dual implication:

1) The promise of rest still stands, a place of inherited rest, the earth; and

2) Anyone who enters God's rest also rests from his own work, just as God did from his.

Why does entering the promised rest involve sabbath-keeping? Because it is a part of obedience! *"Let us, therefore, make every effort to enter that rest, so that no one will fall by following their example of disobedience."*

Our continuing Sabbath instructions are, *"The seventh-day is a Sabbath to the LORD your God. On it you shall not do any work, neither you, nor your son or daughter, nor your manservant or maidservant, nor your animals, nor the alien within your gates.*

---

[125] It is interesting that popular versions interpret this "sabbath rest" instead of "sabbatizing" or "sabbath-keeping," which the word "sabbatismos" means. Why? To steer away from the idea of observing sabbath in favor of just resting in Jesus?

"For in six days the LORD made the heavens and the earth, the sea, and all that is in them, but he rested on the seventh-day. Therefore the LORD blessed the Sabbath day and made it holy" (Exodus 20:10, 11).

Why are these our continuing instructions? Paul explains:

"All who sin apart from the law will also perish apart from the law, and all who sin under the law will be judged by the law. For it is not those who hear the law who are righteous in God's sight, but it is those who obey the law who will be declared righteous" (Romans 2:12, 13).

That the Sabbath command is included in the very law Paul was talking about is shown in his questions in the same chapter:

"You, then, who teach others, do you not teach yourself? You who preach against stealing, do you steal? You who say that people should not commit adultery, do you commit adultery? You who abhor idols, do you rob temples?" (Romans 2:21, 22).

That same law that forbids stealing, adultery, and idol worship also says:

"Remember the Sabbath day by keeping it holy. Six days you shall labor and do all your work, but the seventh-day is a Sabbath to the LORD your God. On it you shall not do any work, neither you, nor your son or daughter, nor your manservant or maidservant, nor your animals, nor the alien within your gates. For in six days the LORD made the heavens and the earth, the sea, and all that is in them, but he rested on the seventh-day. Therefore the LORD blessed the Sabbath day and made it holy" (Exodus 20:8-11).

This commandment is first an expression of God's love and concern for us; second, it teaches us to love our families or servants by having them to rest as we ourselves rest; third, it teaches us to remember creation week and our Creator.

God promised a kingdom rest, a "κατάπαυσίς" [kata'pausis]. Although by faith we have entered our "κατάπαυσίς" (also called a "sabbatismos") our kingdom rest, we still labor to enter because we are still subject to temptation to disobey and lose faith. We still *labor to enter* because this life is not the rest promised to the seed of Abraham.

Christ has not yet returned: *"Let us, therefore, make every effort **to enter** that rest, so that no one will fall by following their example of disobedience"* (Hebrews 4:11).

"Make every effort to enter" implies remaining faithful and obedient to the end. The results of not doing so are spelled out clearly in Hebrews chapters 6 and 10.

Peter adds clarity of thought:

"But there were also false prophets among the people, just as there will be false teachers among you. They will secretly introduce destructive heresies, even denying the sovereign Lord who bought them – bringing swift destruction on themselves."

"While they promise them liberty, they themselves are the servants of corruption: for of whom a man is overcome, of the same is he brought in bondage. For if after they have escaped the pollutions of the world through the knowledge of the Lord and Saviour Jesus Christ, they are again entangled therein, and overcome, the latter end is worse with them than the beginning.

"For it had been better for them not to have known the way of righteousness, than, after they have known it, to turn from the holy commandment delivered unto them. But it is happened unto them according to the true proverb, The dog is turned to his own vomit again; and the sow that was washed to her wallowing in the mire" (2 Peter 2:1, 19-22).

How quickly we can forget the conclusions the Scriptures bring to us! We have settled it that good works are not the means of salvation.

But have we settled it that either *bad works* or *no works* are the means of separation from God?

Have we settled it that ceasing to believe, loss of confidence, loss of faith in God, can cause us to fall out of God's good graces?

Have we settled it that returning to sin rebuilds our old man of sin and that our latter state is worse than before we believed?[126] What is the consequence of such a fall? The consequence is not entering the promised rest:

"But if, while we seek to be justified by Christ, we ourselves also are found sinners, is therefore Christ the minister of sin? God forbid. For if I build again the things which I destroyed, I make myself a transgressor. For I through the law am dead to the law, that I might live unto God" (Galatians 2:17-19, KJV).

"Know ye not that the unrighteous shall not inherit the kingdom of God? Be not deceived: neither fornicators, nor idolaters, nor adulterers, nor effeminate, nor abusers of themselves with mankind" (1 Corinthians 6:9, KJV).

"But Christ as a son over his own house; *whose house are we, if we hold fast the confidence and the rejoicing of the hope firm unto the end." "Take heed, brethren, lest there be in any of you an evil heart*

---

[126] Hebrews 6:4-6: "For in the case of those who have once been enlightened and have tasted of the heavenly gift and have been made partakers of the Holy Spirit, and have tasted the good word of God and the powers of the age to come, and then have fallen away, it is impossible to renew them again to repentance, since they again crucify to themselves the Son of God, and put Him to open shame."

2 Peter 2:17: "These are springs without water, and mists driven by a storm, for whom the black darkness has been reserved. 18 For speaking out arrogant words of vanity they entice by fleshly desires, by sensuality, those who barely escape from the ones who live in error, 19 promising them freedom while they themselves are slaves of corruption; for by what a man is overcome, by this he is enslaved. 20 For if after they have escaped the defilements of the world by the knowledge of the Lord and Savior Jesus Christ, they are again entangled in them and are overcome, the last state has become worse for them than the first. 21 For it would be better for them not to have known the way of righteousness, than having known it, to turn away from the holy commandment delivered to them. 22 It has happened to them according to the true proverb, 'A DOG RETURNS TO ITS OWN VOMIT," and, "A sow, after washing, returns to wallowing in the mire.'"

of unbelief, **in departing from** *the living God"* (Hebrews 3:6, 12, KJV).

One cannot depart from the living God if he has never been with God! These verses (Hebrews 3:6, 12) have a close relationship to the admonition in chapter four, *"Let us, therefore, make every effort to enter that rest, so that no one will fall by following their example of disobedience." This is* **the very focus of both chapters!**

That is what these chapters are about, with Israel's consequent failure to enter their promised kingdom, their Promised Land, where they could have had rest. These chapters admonish us not the make the same mistakes and consequently be barred from the kingdom of God, our Promised Land, our promised "rest." The one serves as an example for the other.

Hebrews 3, 4 are clear statements of what happens if you quit believing, quit having confidence in God, and return to sin as Israel did. Loss of confidence, loss of belief, disobedience, and exclusion from the kingdom of God and loss of inheritance.

---o-O-o---

Echoes from the Desert – Ancient and Modern

"Moses, did you just bring us out here into the desert to die?"

"Aaron, we don't know what happened to Moses! Make us another God!"

"Since Moses has disappeared and we have a new god, 'Let's party!'"

Those sounds reverberate throughout the Christian community with our own echoes:

"We cannot relate to last Generation's worship styles."

"The old ways are not relevant to the new generations!"

"Let each man, in his own way, before his own god, or before no god as his choice may be, just live-and-let-live in our glorious diversity of cultures and beliefs!"

"Truth? What *is* truth? My truth may not be your truth! Each person has his own truth! Truth is what I want it to be!"

"The way I like to look at is, God doesn't really care what day we keep, just so long as it's one day in seven!"

"Rest? Yes, I rest! I rest in freedom from the old law and it's strict requirements!"

"A temple to worship in? The mountains, deserts and forests are my temple!"

"God? God is everywhere in everything! Get in touch with your own spirit! God loves you Baby!"

---o-O-o---

Scenes from Ancient Israel

"The LORD would speak to Moses face to face, as a man speaks with his friend. Then Moses would return to the camp, but his young aide Joshua son of Nun did not leave his tent.

"Moses said to the LORD, "You have been telling me, 'Lead these people,' but you have not let me know whom you will send with me. You have said, 'I know you by name and you have found favor with me.' If you are pleased with me, teach me your ways so I may know you and continue to find favor with you. Remember that this nation is your people."

"The LORD replied, "My Presence will go with you, and I will give you rest." Then Moses said to him, "If your Presence does not go with us, do not send us up from here. How will anyone know that you are pleased with me and with your people unless you go with us? What else will distinguish me and your people from all the other people on the face of the earth?"

"And the LORD said to Moses, "I will do the very thing you have asked, because I am pleased with you and I know you by name" (Exod. 33:11-17).

"There, in the presence of the LORD your God, you and your families shall eat and shall rejoice in everything you have put your hand to, because the LORD your God has blessed you. You are not to do as we do here today, everyone as he sees fit, since you have not yet reached *the resting place and the inheritance the LORD your God is giving you.*

"But you will cross the Jordan and settle in the land the LORD your God is giving you as an inheritance, and he will give you rest from all your enemies around you so that you will live in safety" (Deuteronomy 12:7-10).

"Now when Joshua was near Jericho, he looked up and saw a man standing in front of him with a drawn sword in his hand. Joshua went up to him and asked, "Are you for us or for our enemies?"

"Neither," he replied, "but as commander of the army of the LORD I have now come."

"Then Joshua fell facedown to the ground in reverence, and asked him, "What message does my Lord have for his servant?"

"The commander of the LORD's army replied, "Take off your sandals, for the place where you are standing is holy."

"And Joshua did so."

Have we entered God's rest? Then for a moment let's remove our shoes and reflect that "the place where we are standing is holy."

Is it worth our "every effort"? Ah, Yes! "He who testifies to these things says, 'Yes, I am coming soon.' Amen. Come, Lord Jesus!" (Revelations 22:20).

—o-O-o—

Unless otherwise noted, Scripture quotations in this book are from the New International Version, © 1973, 1978, 1984 used by permission of the *International Bible Society* and *Zondervan Bible Publishers.* Quotations from *New American Standard Bible* © 1960, '61, '63, '68, '71, '73, '75, '78, '87 are used by permission of *The Lockman Foundation* and *Zondervan Bible Publishers.*